GLOBAL
Benchmarks

GLOBAL
Benchmarks

comprehensive measures of development

OPHELIA M. YEUNG AND **JOHN A. MATHIESON**

BROOKINGS INSTITUTION PRESS / WASHINGTON, D.C.
SRI INTERNATIONAL / MENLO PARK, CALIFORNIA

This book may be ordered from:
Brookings Institution Press
1775 Massachusetts Avenue N.W.
Washington, D.C. 20036
Tel: 1-800-275-1447 or 202-797-6258
Fax: 202-797-6004

Library of Congress Cataloging-in-Publication Data
Yeung Ophelia M.
    Global benchmarks : comprehensive measures of development /
Ophelia M. Yeung and John A. Mathieson.
      p. cm.
    Includes bibliographical references.
    ISBN 0-8157-9681-1 (alk. paper)
    1. Economic development—Mathematical models. 2. Economic
indicators. 3. Social indicators. I. Mathieson, John A. II. Title.
    HD75.5 .Y34 1998
    338.9—ddc21

                                        98-9040
                                        CIP

This book has been funded by the United States Agency for
International Development PCE 0026-C-00-3030-00

987654321

Typeset in Adobe Garamond and Helvetica Condensed
Composition and book design by Linda C. Humphrey
Arlington, Virginia
Printed by R. R. Donnelley and Sons Co.
Harrisonburg, Virginia

Foreword

In 1993 the United States embraced a Strategy for Sustainable Development in the bilateral development assistance program managed by the U.S. Agency for International Development (USAID). This strategy includes promoting broad-based economic growth, strengthening democracies, stabilizing world population, protecting human health, building human capacity, and protecting the world's environment.

This book presents data and graphs that, for the first time, make clear the degree to which countries have moved forward on a variety of matters essential to meeting their people's needs. For 108 developing countries, data on forty-three variables have been carefully selected and categorized into six dimensions of development reflecting USAID's sustainable development strategy: economic performance, competitiveness, education, health and population, the environment, and democracy and freedom. In order to achieve parity with the countries in the Organization for Economic Cooperation and Development (OECD), the only sustainable pattern of development in the long run, in my belief, is one that is balanced, progressing along all these dimensions simultaneously.

The evidence presented in this book illustrates how countries are moving toward integrated development. The development web diagrams, composed of scores on each of the six dimensions of development, reveal some very interesting conclusions. For me, the essential message is that successful development is *balanced development*. Some countries, usually the poorer countries, do well on democracy and the environment but score extremely low on education, health, competitiveness, and economic performance. Other countries, such as the East Asian economies that have been impressively dynamic in recent decades, do well on economic performance, competitiveness, education, and health but have lower performances on the environment and democracy.

This is why USAID is making investments in economic growth, education, population and health, democratic governance, and the environment. We know that development abroad will not be sustainable unless it is balanced and that our investments are effective only when we take an integrated approach to development.

J. Brian Atwood
Administrator
U.S. Agency for International Development

Preface

With this study,, the U.S. Agency for International Development (USAID) presents, for the first time, data measuring the balance between economic, social, political, and environmental elements in developing countries. These data provide insight and evidence on the development process and illuminate effective approaches to development. The web concept both graphically illustrates how balanced is each country's evolution and provides a tool for actors in the development process to engage in dialogue about future development efforts based on this integrated perspective.

USAID has sponsored the benchmarking analysis in order that it will be made widely available to policymakers and researchers who are advancing the development effort. This not only reflects USAID's commitment to an integrated sustainable development strategy, but will contribute to more extensive international cooperation between all the bilateral donor agencies of the advanced industrial countries and many of multilateral development institutions, such as the World Bank and the United Nations Development Program.

The sustainable development strategy of USAID is mirrored in a vision statement by the heads of all industrial country development assistance programs, titled *Shaping the 21st Century: The Contribution of Development Cooperation.* The six goals embodied in this statement are reducing poverty; providing universal primary education; fostering gender equality; lessening infant and child mortality; providing access to reproductive health services; reversing environmental deterioration; and fostering democracy, human rights, and the rule of law. These targets were agreed to by all countries (both developed and developing) at recent United Nations summits in Rio de Janeiro, Cairo, Copenhagen, and Beijing. They provide a common framework for the international community as a whole to advance sustainable development. These targets can only be met by the kind of balanced development effort represented by the six-dimensional webs discussed below.

Colin I. Bradford Jr.
Chief Economist
U.S. Agency for International Development

Acknowledgments

This book is the culmination of a two-year research and analytical process, a team effort involving numerous individuals who made valuable contributions along the way. First and foremost, the authors would like to thank the Office of Emerging Markets in the Center for Economic Growth (G/EG/EM) of the United States Agency for International Development (USAID) for supporting the work. In particular, the vision, guidance, and continuing encouragement of Kenneth Lanza and Grant Morrill made this book possible. The bulk of the research was funded by the Private Enterprise Development Support Project of USAID, under which SRI International is a subcontractor to Coopers & Lybrand. This study has also benefited significantly from the cooperation and technical inputs of various centers at USAID's Global Bureau, including the Centers for Health and Population, Democracy and Governance, Education, and Environment, for which the authors express their appreciation.

The authors wish to acknowledge and thank Tonia Callender, former economist at SRI International, for her substantive input to the initial model design and research for the development web model. Santiago Sedaca provided valuable research support and contributions to country case studies, and made painstaking efforts to ensure the consistency and accuracy of the data used in the model. Peter Boone and Kathleen Vickland helped to establish the analytical foundation for the model and participated in the country research. We would also like to thank Adam McConagha for research assistance. Danielle Hinkley-Abba deserves special thanks for her graphics design, which has greatly enhanced the visual appeal of the model concept.

Finally, the authors would like to thank the acquisitions and editorial staff of the Brookings Institution for their support and contributions in bringing this work to a wide audience.

Contents

1. **A New Focus on Development** 1

2. **The Development Web** 9
   Conceptual Premise / 9
   Objectives and Characteristics / 10
   Limitations / 10

3. **Research Background** 13
   Economic Performance / 14
   Competitiveness Foundations / 15
   Health / 17
   Education / 18
   Environment / 19
   Democracy and Freedom / 21

4. **Methodology and Country Rating System** 25
   Selection of Variables / 25
   Scoring System for Variables / 37
   Weighting System for Variables / 37
   Summary / 39

5. **Summary Findings** 41
   Regional Scores and Distributions / 41
   Regional Webs / 54
   Typologies of Development
      Performance / 60

6. **Country Webs** 79

APPENDIXES
A. **Summary of Vector Scores** 283
B. **Weighted Vector Scores** 291
C. **Scoring System for Vectors** 333
D. **Weighting Systems for Vectors** 341

References 345

Chapter 1

A NEW FOCUS ON DEVELOPMENT

How does one measure development performance? As nations, their economies, and the lot of their people change over time, how can one gauge standards of living, whether according to an absolute standard or relative to other countries? Is development a level of affluence or a sustained rate of growth? Should one focus on per capita income or output? And what about purchasing-power parity (PPP)? Perhaps development performance should encompass direct measures of well-being, such as health and education. What about the importance of a clean environment or a participatory political system? How does one appraise successes, shortfalls, or needs in the realm of development?

These questions have vexed national leaders, international donor agencies, and development practitioners for decades. They aim at the core of the development process, for they seek to define its actual goal (or goals). One must be able to measure achievements in order to design and implement development strategies, policies, and programs effectively. But despite the critical importance of measuring performance, no definitive method has emerged. The issue has been subject to ongoing controversy and debate, both within the scholarly community and among practitioners "on the ground." In a sense, no generally accepted answer is possible,

due to the philosophical dimensions of the problem. It is like asking how to measure fulfillment or happiness.

The difficulty of explaining progress in development has not deterred efforts to do so. Most have defined development in economic terms. In fact, such efforts date back to the very origins of economic discourse. Adam Smith applied himself to explaining the "nature and causes of the wealth of nations." Joseph Schumpeter developed a "theory of economic development" in 1912. Colin Clark spoke of the "conditions of economic progress." In the early 1950s, these lines of thought culminated in development being interpreted at the national level as economic growth, or more specifically, increase in output—gross national product (GNP) or gross domestic product (GDP). For those interested in the welfare of the population, the appropriate measure of progress was increase in output per capita, which encompasses the average amount of goods and services that are theoretically available for each person to consume.

The microeconomic principle of "optimization" implicitly accepts that increasing income can raise welfare, as the relaxation of the budget constraint allows the "utility curve" to expand. Nonetheless, in theory development economists do not assert that economic growth is by definition good, or that growth makes people better off or happier. It is quite possible that people living fifty or a hundred years ago were, on average, happier than people in the 1990s. In practice, however, an almost universal consensus has been forged around the notion that the accumulation of material wealth is preferable to the lack thereof. Wealth and income provide for food, shelter, education, health care, and other goods and services that contribute to material well-being. Under the right distributional circumstances, higher levels of income allow for the reduction or even elimination of poverty.

It is not surprising that the overall theory of economic development has been framed in terms of output or income. Fundamentally, countries are defined as "developed" or "developing" by their relative per capita outputs or incomes. From this static underpinning, development progress is logically defined as growth in output or income. Due to difficulties in measuring income, the standard practice has to use output.

Once growth became the centerpiece of thinking on development, scholars began to define progress in various ways, but always related to growth. One result was the emergence of "economic growth theory." In the 1950s and 1960s, neoclassical economists, such as James Meade, Robert Solow, and Sir John Hicks, stressed the growth of output capacity, in particular, the accumulation of capital stock. Walt Rostow defined success as industrial "take-off." Theories and measures were not limited to economics. Princeton sociologist Marion Levy measured development as the increasing ratio of inanimate to animate energy. Simply stated, his theory holds that the greater the use of combustion and electrical machinery (inanimate energy) as opposed to human and animal labor (animate energy), the higher the level of development.

With all of these concepts and explanations, GDP growth remains the ultimate measure—and goal—of development. However, in recent years two separate but related lines of thought have been pursued to improve the concept of development progress. The first focuses on enhancing the concept of per capita GDP, and the second introduces social indicators into the debate.

Per capita GDP measures the average output per person of a given country. It is calculated by dividing total national output by the country's total population. While it represents a reasonable estimate of economic well-being, it has two drawbacks. First, it does not take into consideration distributional characteristics. A nation with a highly skewed pattern of income distribution—a small share of rich families controlling the majority of income and the majority of poor families left with little income—is not the same, in welfare terms, as a nation where income is distributed relatively evenly. This problem has led to efforts to supplement per capita GDP figures with distributional measures such as Gini coefficients.

Another concern stems from the fact that for the sake of comparability, national per capita GDP statistics are usually reported in U.S. dollars. The common reporting and presentation of exchange rates in economics and financial publications typically do not take into consideration differences in local costs for needed goods and services. For example, a country with low per capita GDP figures might

GLOBAL Benchmarks

have basic costs that are lower (in dollar terms) than other countries, so that effective purchasing power in that nation would be higher than the per capita GDP statistic indicates. To correct for this problem, the United Nation's (UN) International Comparison Programme has developed a purchasing power parity measure, based on national price surveys, to adjust per capita statistics. These PPP estimates better reflect the actual purchasing power of varying income levels.

The (second) drawback of output and income statistics is more fundamental. As economic measures, they do not take social indicators into consideration. A nation's or an individual's output or income is an input rather than an output. Except for those who prize high incomes or the accumulation of wealth as ends in themselves, income is a means to purchase consumption goods and provide security. Income is not necessarily a true measure of well-being. It is how that income is spent that determines well-being. One can take the extreme example of a nation at war, where military production and activities often raise output and the national income level, but its citizens do not necessarily enjoy higher levels of well-being.

The first major effort to put forward social indicators as yardsticks for development was the Physical Quality of Life Index (PQLI) developed by the Overseas Development Council.[1] This index reflects the shift in emphasis of development strategies toward addressing basic human needs, especially the needs of the poor, in the 1970s. The PQLI measures the level of

physical well-being at a given time on a scale of 0 (the most unfavorable performance in 1950) to 100 (the best performance expected in the year 2000). The index consists of three components—life expectancy at age one, infant mortality, and literacy—weighted equally to provide a single national score. A major advantage of the PQLI is that data on the three variables are widely available. In addition, the index measures results rather than inputs.

The three variables in the PQLI were selected because they reflect and embody important aspects of human progress. For example, life expectancy can be a good indicator for the sum effects of nutrition, income, public health, and the general environment. Similarly, infant mortality captures the availability of clean water, the health of mothers, and home environment. Literacy rates can denote the current or future ability of poor groups to share the benefits of economic growth, and can also provide a good indication of the position of women in society.

While the PQLI appraises levels of social well-being, rates of change and progress toward meeting basic human needs are calculated in a companion indicator, the Disparity Reduction Rate (DRR).[2] This is defined as the rate at which the disparity, or gap, between a country's level of performance on any social indicator and the best performance expected in any country in the year 2000 is being closed. The DRR can thus be used to compare progress over time.

The PQLI and DRR have provided a number of important inferences to development practitioners. The PQLI shows, for example,

[1]See Morris (1979); Grant (1978).

[2]See Morris (1979); Grant (1978).

that countries could demonstrate better (or worse) performance in social well-being than would normally be expected at given levels of per capita GNP: China, Sri Lanka, and Cuba scored much higher than other countries at similar income levels, whereas Iran and Kuwait scored lower than their cohorts. The DRR rate of progress shows that economic and social progress are not necessarily linked. Both Taiwan and Sri Lanka were unusually successful at improving social performance, but Taiwan's increases in social indicators were simultaneous with rapid economic progress, whereas Sri Lanka's improvements were attained with only modest increases in per capita GNP.

In the early 1990s the United Nations Development Programme (UNDP) sought to capture the most important dimensions of human development by combining social and economic indicators in its Human Development Index (HDI).[3] This index comprises three equally weighted indicators: life expectancy at birth, reflecting the goal of a long and healthy life; educational attainment, representing knowledge; and GDP (in purchasing power parity dollars), measuring the objective of a decent standard of living. The educational attainment indicator includes two variables; adult literacy (with a two-thirds weight) and combined primary, secondary, and tertiary enrollment rates (with a one-third weight).

The substantive basis for the HDI is to capture statistically the basic capabilities that people must have to participate in and contribute to society. It gives only a snapshot of the status of human development and is not deemed to be a comprehensive measure. However, it is possible to construct comparable HDIs over time to monitor progress, and also to disaggregate the HDI by geographical region, ethnic group, income level, and gender. Based on the HDI methodology, the UNDP went on to develop a Gender-related Development Index (GDI) to explore how equitably basic human capabilities are distributed between men and women.

The HDI reveals that the developing world has witnessed unprecedented improvement in human development over the past thirty years. For example, on average life expectancy in 1995 was seventeen years longer than in 1960, and infant mortality has been more than halved. Nevertheless, there remains substantial deprivation in both developing and industrial countries. At the national level, the HDI shows that despite lower incomes, many developing countries attain human development levels comparable to those in industrial countries. Most of the highest scoring developing countries are found in Latin America and the Caribbean region (for instance, Barbados, Costa Rica, Belize, and Argentina) and East Asia (for example, Hong Kong, South Korea, and Singapore).

In recent years several indexes have been constructed for the purpose of gauging nations' overall economic policy environments. With support from the U.S. Agency for International Development (USAID), SRI International has developed a Commercial Policy Model and Matrix to measure the extent to which nations' economic and commercial policies are "friendly" to market forces and private sector businesses.[4]

[3]United Nations Development Programme, *Human Development Report* (various issues).

[4]SRI International (1993).

The model consists of thirty-six policy variables grouped in nine categories: import policies, export policies, tax policies, investment incentives, foreign investment restrictions, business start-up procedures, price and interest rate policies, foreign exchange policies and labor policies.

Data on each of the policy variables were subjected to a scoring and weighting system to generate scores ranging between 0 and 100. The East Asian "tigers" and the industrial countries scored highest. The scores were then evaluated against a set of economic performance variables. The results demonstrate that countries with more "business-friendly" commercial policy environments achieve higher growth in output, per capita GDP, investment, and exports. The SRI model was applied as a policy dialogue tool in several countries receiving USAID assistance and proved useful in pointing out inconsistencies in commercial policy to government and private sector leaders.

The Heritage Foundation's Index of Economic Freedom scores countries on ten economic factors: trade policy, tax policy, government consumption of economic output, monetary policy, capital flows and foreign investment, banking policy, wage and price controls, property rights, regulation, and the black market.[5] This index is used to promulgate the view that economic freedom generates higher living standards.

The Economic Freedom Index has been developed by several scholars and a consortium of research institutes led by the Fraser Institute of Canada.[6] The U.S. institutional sponsor was the Cato Institute. This index, established as an indicator of economic freedom across countries, contains seventeen components grouped around four major substantive areas: money and inflation, government operations and regulations, takings and discriminatory taxation, and restrictions on international exchange.

Data on these components are assigned weights in order to calculate index scores ranging from 0 to 10. Countries are then graded. Hong Kong receives an "A+," and three countries (New Zealand, Singapore, and the United States) earned an "A." The ten countries that are assigned a "B" are industrial countries, with the exception of Malaysia. At the other end of the spectrum, twenty-seven countries are graded "F–," indicating that their policies and institutional arrangements are inconsistent with economic freedom in almost every area. Those scoring lowest were Somalia, Congo (formerly Zaire), Iran, and Algeria.

The three indexes described above are based on roughly equivalent methodologies and arrive at similar conclusions. With few exceptions, the same group of countries fall into the top and bottom ranks, even though the specific variables and weights differ. One of the principal benefits of these indexes is that they support, and in fact were designed for, comparative policy analysis. Previously, there were no quantitative methods for comparing a country's policy framework with those of its neighbors, its competitors, or international "best practices." National leaders and development practitioners now have tools to undertake policy benchmarking and prepare strategies for policy reform.

In fact, economic indexes have exerted major economic and political influence for

[5]Johnson and Sheehy (1996).
[6]Gwartney, Lawson, and Block (1996).

decades. It is important to acknowledge that so-called economic indicators are themselves indexes. Inflation figures are in reality indexes, built upon a weighted index covering a basket of goods and services. National income and product accounts include weights and product categories. These statistics are revised periodically to incorporate new knowledge on relationships or to correct for errors. Stock markets respond vigorously to new reports on inflation, unemployment, or growth in the money supply. Central banks construct policy instruments on these same indexes, often leading stock markets to move in anticipation of central bank responses to the same variables. Internationally, investors pay close attention to the "sovereign risk ratings" assigned to individual countries by specialized rating institutions, such as Moody and Standard and Poor. In addition, elections can be won or lost as a result of economic indicator performance.

There is no doubt that quantitative indexing, scoring, and ranking are in vogue in many quarters of society. Students, parents, and college administrators anxiously await *U.S. News and World Report's* annual "best colleges" issue. Urban leaders applaud or wince at their cities' rankings as "most livable" or "most expensive." On a more serious plane, political analysts and leaders use the "freedom rankings" issued by Freedom House to assess political rights and civil liberties in different countries. Those at the top of positive lists use this information to publicize their merits, and those at the bottom increasingly base their strategic plans around means to improve (or mask) their rankings.

The rapid growth of comparative indexes has been spurred not only by the rising interest in and use of benchmarking, but also by the increasing availability of statistical data. In the sphere of development, international organizations such as the United Nations, the World Bank, and the International Monetary Fund are taking seriously their role to collect, evaluate, and publish data on an increasing range of topics, including social and environmental as well as economic indicators.

No one can claim that performance indexes are completely objective. The selection and weighting of indicators, by definition, involve subjective decisions. In addition, some of the raw indicators are inherently more neutral than others. Anyone familiar with data collection procedures can point to numerous technical flaws or subjective inputs. The recent debate over the accuracy and policy implications of the hallowed U.S. Consumer Price Index provides a good example of the controversies that can arise. On balance, though, development performance indicators are important. They provide concrete information as to where a nation stands in both absolute and relative terms, as well as monitoring progress and achievement over time. In a world where scarce resources are allocated to activities designed to reach development goals, it is essential that decisionmakers and relevant constituencies have access to information regarding the results of those activities.

In this book we present a "development web" model and indicators that provide a comprehensive picture of development performance. The model had its origins in the discussions following presentations on SRI's Commercial Policy Model. As noted above, the earlier model was designed solely to measure commercial policy frameworks, not to explain all aspects of development. Meeting participants, especially those from the policy-making, development, and academic circles, would inevitably ask whether other factors could be incorporated into the model. Are not education and health standards important as both inputs to and outputs of development performance? What about the significance of environmental standards? Is not good governance a determinant of development success? These comments collectively articulated the need for more comprehensive measures of development performance. Economic yardsticks alone are not sufficient. Improved human well-being, the central goal of development, is not just a matter of material wealth. The achievement of enhanced human potential and well-being is also dependent on the attainment of better health conditions, *but not* enriched educational standards, a decent living *free-market* environment, civil liberties, and the ability of *overhaul...* citizens to have a voice in political decisions that affect them. Development is a an integrated process, involving numerous variables and producing comprehensive results. Accordingly, the development web model was created to provide reasonable measures of performance in these important areas.

Chapter 2

THE DEVELOPMENT WEB

Thomas Hobbes wrote that life is "poor, nasty, brutish, and short." It could therefore be said that the essential goal of development is to prove Hobbes wrong. But how can one demonstrate the achievement of that goal?

The development web (the "web model") and database have been created in response to the increasing interest expressed by the development community for a more comprehensive and balanced development measurement system. The model is designed to cover not only traditional indicators of economic development, but also variables capturing new factors that have emerged as important inputs to and outputs of the development process.

CONCEPTUAL PREMISE

A review of the state of the art of economic development methodology shows that many cities, regions, and states in industrialized countries increasingly base their economic development strategies on indicators such as competitive strengths and weaknesses, quality-of-life measurements, and economic foundations. In the private sector, corporations often rely on indicators such as customer satisfaction, on-time delivery or arrival, cost competitiveness, market share, and just-in-time inventory control to guide their strategic planning.

The combination of innovative information technologies and the need for comparative analysis has led more and more organizations, both public and private, to produce and utilize new indicators of performance. In the emerging information age, new forms of objective, quantitative indicators increasingly are being developed and applied, such as strategic inputs, best practice and competitiveness benchmarking, management tools, progress monitoring systems, and strategy modification decisionmaking.

Many of these planning and evaluation tools and management techniques can supplement and enrich conventional methodologies and approaches to economic development. Analytical tools can help to meet evolving needs among the broader development community to expand the scope and definition of economic development. In recent years an emphasis on comprehensive development strategies has emerged: economic growth should be broad based, sustainable, environmentally sound, and participatory. Appropriate indicators are needed to monitor progress in these areas.

OBJECTIVES AND CHARACTERISTICS

Traditional measures of progress, which emphasize income and growth, are now considered too narrow. The international community is becoming increasingly concerned with encouraging development that improves the living standards and quality of life of nations' entire populations. The web model has been created as a measurement system that allows multidimensional analysis of development status and progress by leaders of developing countries and development practitioners.

The five objectives of the web model are as follows:

- To measure development performance across a broad range of indicators that address different aspects of human welfare, using objective criteria and quantitative indicators.
- To evaluate national and regional performance and benchmark nations against best practices in the region, within income groupings or worldwide.
- To provide a management tool for identifying and assessing priorities for national and donor development programs.
- To monitor progress over time and adjust initiatives to meet changing circumstances.
- To establish a framework for examining relationships among important but different aspects of development.

To meet these objectives, the development web has several key characteristics. It is multidimensional in scope, providing systematic indicators across a wide range of socioeconomic and standard of living variables. The variables assessed can all be measured using objective data sources. The system generates scores or indexes, so that countries can be benchmarked against each other. The resulting analysis will facilitate the evaluation of development priorities based on competitor, regional, or worldwide benchmarking, as well as assessments of the balance achieved among the various aspects of development. And the system enables national policymakers and development practitioners to monitor the progress of key variables over time.

LIMITATIONS

Although different aspects of development (for example, economic growth, education, health) tend to track one another, correlations observed between development indicators should not be interpreted as simple causal relationships. As will be discussed in the next section, relationships among development variables are complex. There is little consensus among economists and development practitioners on absolute causal relationships or the extent to which one indicator may affect another.

The development web is a multidimensional measurement system and, as such, is most appropriate for purposes of measurement, comparison, and benchmarking. It is not designed as a regression model to explain causal relationships between different aspects of development. Nor is it intended to predict in which direction one indicator would go based on the achievement in another variable or vector. For example, one should not use the web model to predict infant mortality rates using economic growth indicators or to explain economic competitiveness with education achievement. In fact, as will be demonstrated in later sections, countries at similar levels of economic development can differ tremendously in other aspects of human welfare. Thus the web model will be most useful if it is applied as a measurement tool rather than a predictive model.

Chapter 3

RESEARCH BACKGROUND FOR MODEL DEVELOPMENT

Worldwide development experience clearly demonstrates that economic growth and per capita income alone do not capture all dimensions of human well-being. As can be seen in the United Nations Development Programme's "development diamond," countries with similar levels of income may differ vastly on other human development indicators. The chart below shows that Sri Lanka and Pakistan have essentially the same per capita GDP, about U.S. $500. However, Sri Lanka has achieved much better social performance, at least in the areas of literacy, infant mortality, and life expectancy.

To be sure, people in countries with high levels of income and rapid growth can afford

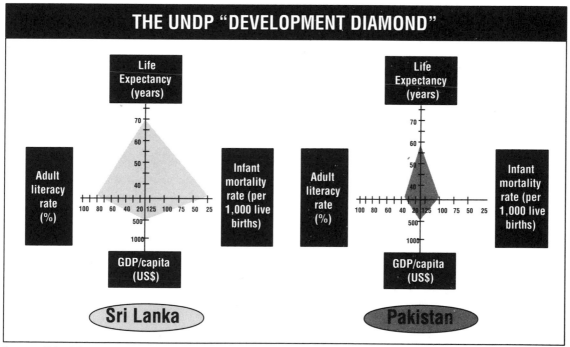

THE UNDP "DEVELOPMENT DIAMOND"

Source: United Nations Development Program

higher standards of education and health care. However, the extent to which some countries differ in various aspects of development despite similar levels of income underscores the importance of measuring those achievements in addition to standard economic indicators.

Six categories of indicators have been included in the web model:

- economic performance
- competitiveness foundations
- health
- education
- environment
- democracy and freedom

These development categories, or "vectors," were identified through extensive literature review and consultations with development practitioners. By definition, a vector has magnitude and direction and can therefore be represented by a line segment. These characteristics make the term preferable to the less specific "category" or "area" for use in the web model.

The web model vectors are generally accepted as key areas for achieving balanced development, from the perspective of overall human well-being. Bilateral and multilateral donors support active programs in each of these areas. While the web model is not designed to serve as an evaluation tool or a regression model, it nonetheless does support the fundamental composition of many donor programs and provides evidence of the progress achieved in each of these important categories.

Some correlations may be observed among the variables and variable categories. Nations with the political will and resources needed to invest in their future often make significant headway in many or all of the categories. Furthermore, success breeds success: economic growth leads to improvement in health, education, and competitiveness, which, in turn, stimulates further growth through a series of feedback loops. The key theoretical relationships between the different vectors in the web model are discussed below.

ECONOMIC PERFORMANCE

The attainment of economic outcomes has traditionally been the core objective of (economic) development initiatives, as discussed above. Only in recent years have social, political, or environmental goals have been introduced. Material well-being is certainly important, so economic performance is one of the six development vectors in the development web.

The summary score for this vector measures overall achievement in areas such as economic growth, per capita income, financial markets development, investment growth, and external trade and finance. These are the conventional indicators of economic performance used by national policymakers and development practitioners. While economic achievement alone is not representative of a country's development achievements, it is through economic expansion and rising incomes that a country can ultimately afford increasing standards of living and better public services for its citizens.

COMPETITIVENESS FOUNDATIONS

Economists and management consultants place competitiveness within, sometimes at the top of, the pantheon of desirable traits for firms and nations alike. Notwithstanding its critical importance, competitiveness is an input, rather than an ultimate output or goal, of the economic process. Competitiveness is a means to achieve growth, even though it is also the result of policy and market factors. This vector is thus different from the others in the development web, which constitute outputs or results. Its inclusion is based on the crucial impacts its components exert on both economic and social goals.

Competitiveness foundations, for the purposes of this analysis, are the set of macroeconomic, policy, and infrastructure variables that determine an economy's long-term dynamic competitiveness. Economists acknowledge the critical influence of government policies on economic efficiency and growth. Indeed, the modern discipline of economics was founded on the works of Adam Smith and David Ricardo, who argued for the elimination of protectionist trade policies because they create inefficiencies and welfare losses. The dominant policy focus worldwide in the post–World War II period has been on economic stabilization. In recent years a growing volume of economics literature has been devoted to the influence of economic and commercial policies on the growth prospects of developing countries.

Various aspects of competitiveness have been explored and measured by research think tanks, multilateral banks, and academic institutions. Economists argue that competitiveness foundations are correlated positively with economic growth. Economic theory states that firms will organize their operations to take advantage of cost savings to the extent that the cost-benefit analysis indicates it is profitable to do so. Thus large firms with operations around the world will select sites with the most hospitable economic environments for their businesses, where profitability can be maximized. Small purely domestic firms also make initial profitability calculations, so that the growth rate of small businesses and entrepreneurship is also affected by the competitiveness foundations. However, low costs in and of themselves are not sufficient to attract investment, either foreign or domestic; firms calculate both the costs and the benefits of doing business. For example, excessive regulations, even in low-cost locations, stymie business growth rates and hence economic growth rates.

Economic theory expects government choices to matter and to have real impacts on the economy. Alan Blinder writes, "For more than two centuries, economists have steadfastly promoted free trade among nations as the best trade policy."[1] Trade theorists argue that open economies will outperform closed economies, as they take advantage of gains from trading. Nations are endowed with widely varying levels of foundational attributes, such as quantity of labor, natural resources, and climate. However, as economist Robert Z. Lawrence observes, "The critical issue for each economy is whether it is making the best use of its resources."[2]

It is critical to note that such resources not

[1]Blinder (1993).
[2]Lawrence (1993).

only occur naturally but include the ability and will to build competitiveness foundations as well. This is often referred to as dynamic competitiveness. The newly industrializing nations of East Asia, in particular, have demonstrated that competitiveness can indeed be "created," as they have built up attributes such as limited regulation, incentives for investment, entrepreneurship, and innovation, active trade promotion, access to finance, and commitment to education.[3] They have paired their enhanced competitiveness foundations with abundant and competitively priced domestic labor to nurture development booms, whether in geographically limited areas such as export-processing zones or nationwide. In sum, it is apparent that "correct government policies can permanently raise growth rates."[4]

Based on both theory and extensive practical experience, economists and practitioners are forming an increasing consensus on the economic policies that stimulate growth, in developed and industrial economies alike. Among these are policies in the areas of finance, trade, investment, business regulation, exchange rates, trade, and fiscal discipline. To the extent feasible, policy variables that cover these areas are included in the development web.

Competitive economies require a stable and sound macroeconomic foundation that is conducive to productive and innovative economic activity. For example, excessive government spending historically has led to government budget deficits, which often result in

inflation, crowding out private investment and thus limiting capital formation and increases in productive capacity. Moreover, inflation can contribute to currency overvaluation, which also impairs the country's competitiveness. The web model seeks to gauge these competitive factors by including variables that indicate government budget discipline, monetary management, foreign exchange competitiveness, and the confidence of the private sector in a country's macroeconomic conditions (as evidenced by country bond ratings from objective sources, for example).

Competitiveness also depends on the degree to which an economy is integrated with global markets. International flows of capital, goods, and services encourage efficiency in the domestic economy by shifting resources to those sectors in which the country is most competitive. The relative size of the export sector and the amount of foreign direct investment are regarded as two of the better indicators of economic openness as well as of direct international competitiveness.

Another element of competitiveness is investment, both in the infrastructure necessary to support business and in research and development (R&D), which increases the productivity of national economies. The competitiveness foundations vector weighs these important considerations through several infrastructure indicators and the percentage of a country's population that is involved in R&D. The vector also includes the amount of national savings available to finance investment.

For brevity, the competitiveness foundations vector is referred to as Competitiveness in the web model.

[3]See World Bank (1993a).
[4]"Economic Growth: The Poor and the Rich," *Economist*, May 25, 1996, p. 25.

HEALTH

The health of their citizens is of premier importance to governments worldwide. Access to a minimum level of health care is regarded as a basic right in many countries, and many nations are striving for universal or near-universal coverage. However, health care is but one determinant of health. "Health depends on four groups of factors: Income, lifestyle, environmental pollution and occupational risks, and the quality of available health care. Of these, income and lifestyle are by far the most important."[5] Even government pricing policies are relevant; for example, food pricing policies affect access to food.

Beyond its inherent benefits, health also contributes to economic growth. Access to health care lowers maternal, infant, and child mortality rates, thus contributing to growth in the size of the labor force.[6] Lower morbidity rates in childhood could contribute to better school attendance and achievement. Reducing malnutrition "can increase labor productivity by improving mental and physical capacity. Weight for height (a measure of long-term nutritional status) and height alone (a proxy for childhood nutrition) are both closely associated with greater adult output per worker."[7] Better health standards in the work force translate into lower absenteeism and higher productivity.

Like many other social variables in this complex world, health can have multiple effects on economic growth rates; there are many links between a nation's health status, its level of poverty, and its rate of economic growth.[8] For example, there is a common perception within the development community that declines in birthrates tend to lag declines in death rates by approximately a decade, as family sizes adjust to take into account lower infant and child mortality rates and increased economic opportunities for women. Thus enhanced health care may actually lead to a period of declining per capita income as the population surges.

Research and experience also point to a feedback loop: higher living standards lead to increased expenditure on health care and more positive health outcomes.[9] In addition, the health care sector can become an important generator of demand and economic growth, creating jobs and revenues. In sum, high income levels and economic growth can be associated with lower mortality and morbidity rates and longer life expectancy.

While life expectancy at birth is the most widely used measure of national health, health policy experts also look at other factors with large effects on national health and economic welfare. These areas of concern include maternal mortality and health, child health and survival, the reduction of unintended pregnancies and population growth, and the containment of epidemics such as acquired immune deficiency syndrome (AIDS).

Experts agree that the provision of primary care to prevent maternal and child mortality can have the largest impact on overall national health, as these are particularly vulnerable

---

[5]Barr (1996, p. 26).
[6]Lavy and others (1995).
[7]World Bank (1995c, p. 36).

[8]Demery and others (1993); World Bank (1993b).
[9]Binswanger and Landell-Mills (1995).

groups in the population. The most widely used indicators of maternal health include the maternal mortality ratio and the percentage of births attended by trained health professionals. Child mortality can best be gauged by looking at mortality rates for infants and for children under five years old as well as at immunization rates among young children.

Reducing the number of unintended pregnancies has proved to be among the most effective ways of improving both maternal and child health. According to the World Bank, in some countries 25 to 40 percent of maternal deaths would be prevented if there were no unintended pregnancies.[10] The web model uses several indicators as proxies for success in reducing unintended pregnancies, including total fertility rates and the rate of contraceptive use among women.

The web model attempts to capture the prevalence of AIDS among adults by using the estimated rate of increase in infections by human immunodeficiency virus (HIV). This indicator is so important because the AIDS epidemic is raising mortality rates among adults and children in many parts of the world and dramatically increasing the burdens of health care.

EDUCATION

Both theory and practice suggest that investing in young children, in terms of education as well as health, "can help break the vicious intergenerational cycle of poverty in the developing world."[11] The value of education to the pursuit of human well-being is indisputable. Good access to high-quality basic education increases social mobility, equips people with the tools to acquire skills and means of livelihood, and fosters self-reliance. It also raises individuals' capacity to participate more effectively in civic and political affairs.

Researchers consistently find that education increases knowledge and critical thinking, contributing to greater productivity and greater earning power.[12] The benefits of education include greater productivity, higher rates of innovation, faster wage growth, and higher saving rates, all of which stimulate economic growth and development. The World Bank states that "educational attainment is the single most important predictor of individual labor incomes."[13] Surveys in the United States indicate that the most important determinant of income differentials between individuals is their respective levels of education.

Work force development is a critical issue in all economies today.[14] Since technological advances have made it possible to transmit large sums of money across the world in seconds electronically, transport inputs cost-effectively by land, air, and sea, and share product development and manufacturing designs among com-

[10]World Bank (1993b, p. 83).
[11]Young (1996, p. vii).
[12]World Bank (1995c).

[13]World Bank (1995c, p. 41).
[14]Reich (1992).

puters located around the world, increasingly the only truly immobile factor of production is labor. While labor does move as a result of migration and does shift as a result of demographics, change is much slower than for other factor inputs. This relative immobility of labor places a premium on education.

Proof of the critical importance of investment in human capital can be found in the fast-growing East Asian economies.[15] According to the World Bank, two-thirds of the growth in eight "high-performing Asian economies can be attributed to high rates of investment combined with high and rising endowments of human capital due to universal primary and secondary education."[16] The experience of these economies suggests that growth and productivity are most closely related to the level of primary education, followed by secondary and tertiary education.

Therefore these indicators are included in the education vector.

Education is intricately related to health outcomes as well. Higher levels of education lead to improved health, because of increased knowledge about the health impact of lifestyle decisions; greater earning power, which facilitates access to health care; and greater economic opportunity for women, which leads to lower levels of mortality and morbidity among infants and children.[17]

Among the most widely used measures of education are enrollment and completion rates at the primary, secondary, and tertiary levels, and repeater rates as a percentage of enrollment, where available. In addition, the adult literacy rate is commonly used as an "outcome" indicator of the overall education level of a country. These indicators are included in the education vector of the development web.

ENVIRONMENT

Worldwide concern has risen in recent years over the adverse effects of environmental degradation on sustainable economic development. In particular, the 1992 Earth Summit in Rio de Janeiro placed environmental issues at the forefront of the development agenda. It has become clear to economic theorists and practitioners, as well as to the public, that the unfettered pursuit of economic growth at the price of environmental despoliation does not serve the long-term interest of nations. Environmental contamination and the

depletion of resources reduce the quality of life, pose health risks, and may lower economic growth rates in the long term. They also reduce the intrinsic value of the environment.

Economists classify environmental problems in developing countries in one of two categories: (1) destruction of the natural land and marine resource base through deforestation, soil erosion, desertification, and other overexploitative activities; or (2) environmental degradation arising from industrialization and urbanization,

---

[15]"Economic Growth: The Poor and the Rich," *Economist*, May 25, 1996, p. 24.

[16]World Bank (1993a, p. 8).
[17]Pitt (1995).

including severe air pollution from uncontrolled industrial and vehicular emissions, inadequate industrial and municipal wastewater treatment facilities, and lack of appropriate disposal, treatment, and storage systems for solid and hazardous wastes. Destruction of the natural resources base reduces the endowment of assets that can support economic growth in the future and increases their cost, thus potentially lowering a nation's growth path. Environmental degradation reduces the quality of life, which can spur emigration and cause serious health problems. Those problems may, in turn, lower productivity and increase worker absenteeism, reducing economic growth. Environmental degradation will also likely have a negative impact on the tourism industry, a large growth-driving sector for many countries.

The World Bank states that "some [environmental] problems are associated with the lack of economic development: inadequate sanitation and clean water, indoor air pollution from biomass burning, and many types of land degradation in developing countries have poverty as their root cause. . . . But many other problems are exacerbated by the growth of economic activity."[18] Thus one can expect to see environmental problems associated with countries at both ends of the developmental scale. Some environmental problems improve with growth, others worsen, and still others first worsen and then improve. For example, access to safe water increases with economic growth, but municipal wastes per capita rise, and urban concentrations of sulfur dioxide tend initially to rise with growth before they fall.[19]

18 World Bank (1992, p. 7).
19 World Bank (1992, p. 11).

Some nations seek to boost economic growth through lax environmental regulation. Theory argues that this policy is shortsighted, as it will lead to long-term health problems, rising costs, and inappropriate allocation of resources. According to the World Bank, environmental priority areas include providing access to safe water, reducing air pollution and solid waste, protecting agricultural land, forests, and natural habitats, and safeguarding the earth's atmosphere.

The state of a country's water supply is crucial, not only because many diseases spread through contaminated water but also because of the impact of pollutants on fisheries and irrigated land. Air pollution and solid waste accumulation, which can also have serious impacts on the health and productivity of a population, depend on exogenous factors such as geography as well as on controllable practices such as production restrictions and treatment requirements. The degradation of land and habitats reduces the natural resource base of a country and can have serious negative impacts on its traditional economic sectors. Deforestation, for instance, can destroy timber resources, lead to soil degradation, affect rain cycles, and lead to the loss of plant and animal species. Through vertical linkages within the economy as a whole, the depletion of a nation's natural resource base may ultimately reduce its comparative advantage in both traditional and nontraditional sectors.

Research on the environmental aspects of development continually stresses the importance of appropriate policy responses from countries at all levels of development. Unfortunately, there is a dearth of reliable information on the adequacy and effectiveness of environmental law enforcement across nations. For example, very limited cross-country data are available, especially for the developing world, measuring the extent to which pollution abatement lessens the environmental impact of urbanization and industrialization. Despite data limitations, sound environmental management is such an integral part of development progress that an environmental vector is included in the development web. Proxy variables to gauge environmental conditions include both input indicators, such as the number of nongovernmental environmental organizations registered, and output indicators, such as access to safe water and rates of carbon dioxide emission per capita.

DEMOCRACY AND FREEDOM

Many development practitioners view democracy, governance, and social equity as important contributors to and outcomes of the developmental process. While the relationship between economic growth and democracy and freedom has been the subject of intense debate for decades, most would agree that basic human rights lie at the core of the ability to seek happiness and improve well-being. Therefore the guarantee and protection of those rights should be regarded as an important development objective in itself, and democracy and freedom are represented by a vector in the development web.

Development theory suggests that democracy has several causal effects on economic growth. Some researchers argue that well-developed participatory democratic pluralism is important to economic growth. They point to some of the world's greatest economic powers—the United States, western Europe, and Japan—to illustrate that economies flourish under democracy. It is also widely accepted that a legal structure that clearly defines property rights and enforces contracts provides the foundation for a market system conducive to growth.

A large volume of academic literature corroborates the premise that democracy supports economic development. Max Weber (1864–1920) argued that democracy is a necessary condition for economic advance. In a 1988 quantitative study of the determinants of development, Milton Friedman found that increases in civil liberties are associated with higher per capita GNP and lower infant mortality.[20] He emphasized that "correlation is no causation" and postulated that high income both leads to and is the result of a higher level of civil rights. And in a study covering 104 countries, Venieris and Gupta note that the sociopolitical environment is a crucial determinant of development. They conclude that "development requires sustained economic growth, changes in the sociopolitical environment, as well as flexibility in the institutional structure."[21] Their findings suggest that development donors should focus

[20]Friedman (1988).
[21]Venieris and Gupta (1982–83, p. 727).

on promoting economic growth and also on providing assistance to ensure that the institutional and political environments necessary for growth are in place.

Perhaps not surprisingly, other scholars take a contrary position. Pointing primarily to the East Asian economic development experience, as well as to some examples in Latin America, they suggest that a strong centralized, even authoritarian, government is better able to guide a country to rapid economic growth. For example, Vaman Rao argues that democracies do not respond quickly enough to the immediate demands placed on the political system by citizens impatient to raise their standards of living.[22] Indeed, political scientists have long asserted that economic growth can be politically destabilizing. For example, certain measures required to place an economy on a growth path are painful to groups that were formerly favored—recipients of subsidized products, monopolistic producers of goods protected by import barriers, or government managers and labor forces in inefficient state-owned enterprises. These groups might block reforms, initiate civil unrest, or collaborate with the military to overthrow the government. Under these circumstances, it is argued, participatory democracies are unable to implement and maintain necessary policy reforms. One school of political scientists also speculates that rapid economic growth may allow undemocratic governments to postpone democratic reforms, as they can placate their citizens with rising living standards.

A third potential linkage between democracy and economic growth involves a positive

feedback loop. As their economies grow, nations enter global markets and their citizens experience economic freedoms, creating pressures for greater democracy. Countries that embark on the path toward a larger role for the private sector often experience rising demands for concomitant societal and political openness. The recent democratization of Taiwan and South Korea demonstrate that rising living standards and prosperity can empower an expanding middle class to demand increased political participation. Since both these countries have been guided toward a high growth path by largely authoritarian regimes, they are viewed by theorists and researchers as case studies of the sequencing of the development process.

In general, contemporary political scientists see economic development and political systems as interacting variables. But many relationships, both positive and negative, exist between economic and political factors. Different schools of thought pose cogent arguments and showcase countries that support their own interpretations. It may be the case that each model of governance functions best in its own cultural and historical context. On the one hand, progressive governments can maintain popular support as a result of the economic gains they orchestrate through policy reform. On the other hand, corrupt governments can stifle reform in order to placate their political constituencies. All too many government leaders have pointed to unpopular (even if necessary) economic policies as the cause of their downfall.

Fundamentally, however, what is most important in terms of human development is the improvement of political as well as eco-

---

[22]Rao (1984–85, p. 67).

Research Background for Model Development

GLOBAL **Benchmarks**

nomic conditions. Individuals living in material wealth but also in politically repressed societies are not achieving true fulfillment. The same holds for the politically free but economically deprived.

Quantifying freedom and democracy is extremely difficult, if not impossible. Among the Western liberal democracies, the exercise of political rights and civil liberties is often regarded as central to a free and democratic society. Political rights and civil liberties worldwide have been surveyed and "scored" annually by Freedom House in its Comparative Survey of Freedom. The Freedom House scores are used as the key indicators in the democracy and freedom vector within the development web.

Chapter 4

METHODOLOGY AND COUNTRY RATING SYSTEM

The name of the development web is based on the premise that the development progress of a country or region can be plotted on a hexagonal web. Each of the six axes on the web represents a different cluster, or vector, of development indicators; there is a separate vector for each of economic performance, competitiveness, education, health, environment, and democracy and freedom (see page 26). Progress in each development cluster is indicated on the corresponding vector on a scale from 1 to 100, with a score of 100 representing perfect performance. Thus the development progress of each country is depicted in its own web on a multidimensional scale. (See appendix A for a summary of the vector scores.)

Web scores for individual countries can be benchmarked against regional averages, the world average, or the scores of competitor countries to assess performance in each development category (see pages 27 and 28). Inferences can then be drawn as to whether a country is achieving "balanced" development or, alternatively, as to which development areas require more attention from policymakers and the development community. In addition, observations can be made about the development paths taken by different countries or groups of countries as they make progress on each vector.

As an objective measurement tool, the development web can be utilized by policymakers or donor organizations to assess a nation's progress vis-à-vis its neighbors or competitors. The web can also be used to track a country's development progress over time, as indicated by the expansion or contraction of the web.

SELECTION OF VARIABLES

A key element in the model design was the determination of the variables that constitute the six vectors. To the extent possible, the variables examined were quantitative and objectively measurable. For each vector, the following three-step process was carried out to make the indicator selection process as objective and rigorous as possible (the chart on page 29 summarizes the selection process):

Step one is to, first, identify a "wish list" of optimal variables, assuming a world of perfect data availability, then identify all reputable sources of data. The wish list consists of those variables considered the most important and meaningful for measuring the achievement in a given development category.

THE DEVELOPMENT WEB

Each "vector" represents a different focal area of development progress.

As a nation achieves better performance, it moves outward on each vector (axis).

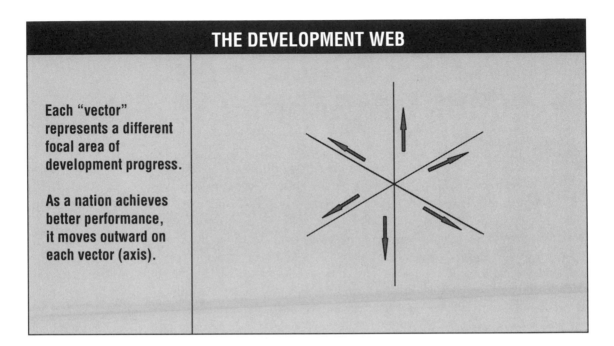

THE DEVELOPMENT WEB

THE DEVELOPMENT WEB

Functional focuses/vectors in the development web

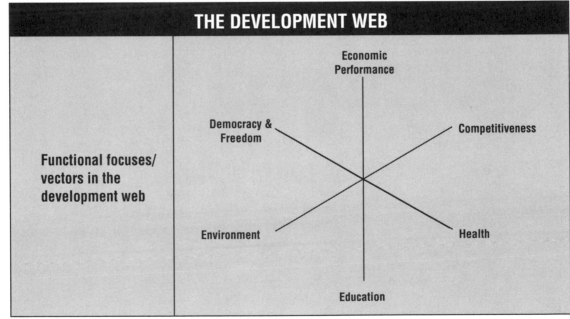

GLOBAL Benchmarks

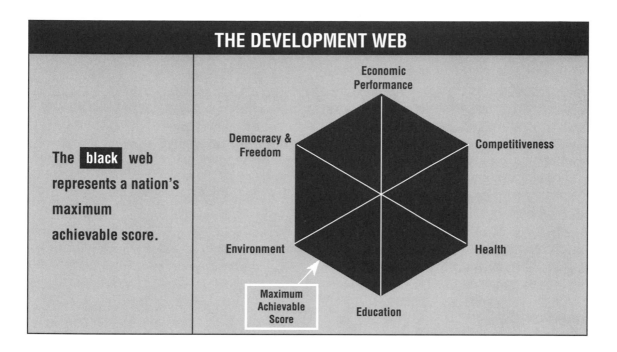

THE DEVELOPMENT WEB

The **black** web represents a nation's maximum achievable score.

Economic Performance

Democracy & Freedom

Competitiveness

Environment

Health

Maximum Achievable Score

Education

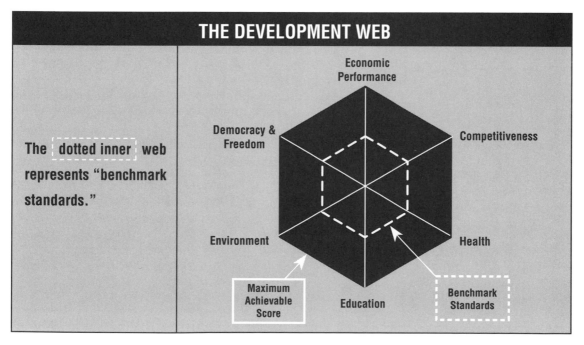

THE DEVELOPMENT WEB

The **dotted inner** web represents "benchmark standards."

Economic Performance

Democracy & Freedom

Competitiveness

Environment

Health

Maximum Achievable Score

Education

Benchmark Standards

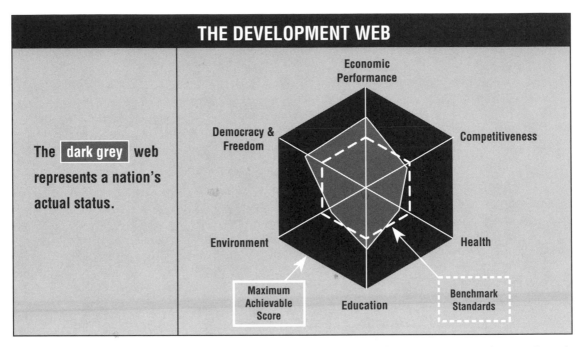

THE DEVELOPMENT WEB

The dark grey web represents a nation's actual status.

Economic Performance

Democracy & Freedom

Competitiveness

Environment

Health

Maximum Achievable Score

Education

Benchmark Standards

Step two is to, first, match available data against the wish list to develop a "working list" of variables, then subject the available data to a rigorous screening process using six key criteria: (1) reliability and accuracy—data must come from reputable sources and be viewed as generally accurate; (2) acceptability—variables should be generally accepted and commonly used as indicators of progress by specialists in a given development domain; (3) neutrality—variables should be as unbiased as possible, neither favoring nor disfavoring certain groups of countries based on their development characteristics; (4) comparability—data for a given variable must be available from a single reliable source or from various organizations of similar caliber; (5) extent of coverage—data for each variable should cover a large number of countries (in several instances, meaningful variables

have been excluded because the data apply only to a fraction of the countries considered); (6) potential for updating over time—since a principal intended usage of the development web is to track countries' progress in different development vectors over time, data produced by one-time studies are not considered useful.

Step three is to, first, have functional specialists review initial variable selection and recommend rejection or addition of variables, then refine and complete the list of indicators.

From an initial 115 variables considered, 48 were eventually selected to make up the six vectors. The information sources consulted, the indicators selected, and the data sources are discussed below by vector.[1]

[1]Full details of the sources mentioned below are provided in the reference list at the end of the book.

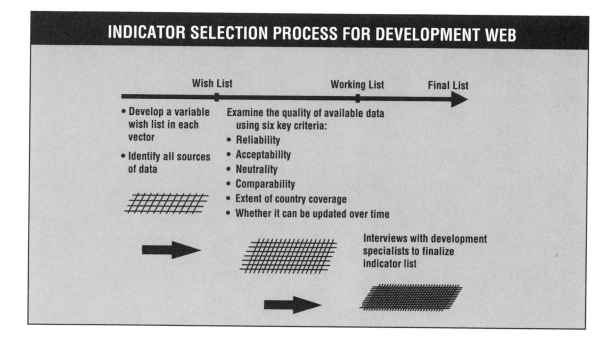

INDICATOR SELECTION PROCESS FOR DEVELOPMENT WEB

Wish List   Working List   Final List

- Develop a variable wish list in each vector
- Identify all sources of data

Examine the quality of available data using six key criteria:
- Reliability
- Acceptability
- Neutrality
- Comparability
- Extent of country coverage
- Whether it can be updated over time

Interviews with development specialists to finalize indicator list

Economic Performance

The economic performance vector is dominated by traditional growth indicators. To arrive at the variables for this vector, data from a number of sources, including the World Bank, the International Monetary Fund (IMF), the United Nations, the International Labor Organization (ILO), and the International Finance Corporation, were reviewed. Data for the final selection of indicators are drawn mostly from World Bank and IMF publications.

Average annual GDP growth, 1990–94. This is a traditional growth indicator that measures the rate of expansion of an economy. The 1990–94 annual average provided by the World Bank's *World Development Report 1996* offers the most comprehensive country coverage.

While the focus on 1990–94 data allows international comparison of the most recent growth rates, to some extent it also biases against those solid long-term economic performers that have been particularly affected by the worldwide recession in the early 1990s.

Average annual GNP growth per capita, 1985–94.[2] This indicator is widely used to measure the average increase in the amount of economic resources available to a nation's citizens. The data source is the *World Development Report 1996.*

Per capita GNP measured by purchasing power parity, 1994. The inclusion of this variable

[2]GNP comprises GDP plus net factor income from abroad. See World Bank (1996c, p. 224).

allows the model to take into account cumulative past economic achievements. For example, countries that have attained high living standards are less likely to achieve the high growth rates presented by developing countries starting from a low economic base. This measure of wealth to a certain degree offsets the lower growth rates achieved by industrialized countries. Purchasing power parity is used instead of unadjusted per capita GNP in order to allow for price-level adjustments in individual countries. After reviewing several sources, it was decided that the *World Development Report 1996* provides the most comprehensive country coverage for this variable.

Average annual growth of gross domestic investment, 1990–94. While some may argue that this could serve as an input variable for the competitiveness foundations vector, it is included as an outcome variable of economic performance, indicating an economy's capacity to invest in future growth. Data source is the *World Development Report 1996.*

Average annual growth of exports, 1990–94. This classic measure of economic performance has become especially important as individual countries increasingly integrate with the global economy. In addition, export growth is a powerful indicator because exports provide a wide range of direct benefits (for example, employment, income, foreign exchange) as well as multiplier effects for domestic growth. The data source is the *World Development Report 1996.*

M2 (money + quasi money) as a percentage of GDP, 1994. This is a widely used measure of the depth of capital markets, especially for developing countries, where stock market capi-

talization may not be relevant or meaningful. "Money" includes currency outside banks and demand deposits outside the central government; "quasi money" includes time and saving deposits and the foreign currency deposits of residents. However, using this indicator somewhat penalizes industrialized countries because their citizens invest a larger proportion of their financial resources in the stock markets. Data for this indicator are drawn from the *World Development Report 1996*, which derives its estimates from the IMF's *International Financial Statistics Yearbook.*

Gross international reserves measured in months of import coverage, 1994. Import coverage of reserves serves as a proxy indicator of external financial resources and stability. Countries that have inadequate international reserves are often vulnerable to external shocks and are more prone to balance of payments problems. This indicator has been calculated by the World Bank using IMF data and is presented in the *World Development Report 1996.*

Competitiveness Foundations

Competitiveness is a function of many factors, in particular, economic capacity and stability. Most of the indicators in this vector are chosen to reflect these foundation characteristics. Among the data sources consulted are the IMF's *Government Finance Statistics Yearbook*, the United Nations Development Programme (UNDP), the World Bank, the Fraser Institute, the Organization for Economic Cooperation and Development (OECD), the United Nations Educational, Scientific, and Cultural Organization (UNESCO), the SRI Commercial Policy Model, the ILO, the Heritage Foundation, Standard & Poor's and Moody's country ratings, the World Intellectual Property Organization, and the United Nations International Development Organization.

Gross domestic saving as a percentage of GDP, 1994. This variable measures the extent to which a nation is deferring current consumption to invest in future consumption—an important foundation indicator of future economic capacity. The data source is the *World Development Report 1996.*

Openness of economy (exports as a percentage of GDP), 1994. This is a proxy indicator of a nation's international competitiveness. It should be noted that this variable can be somewhat biased against larger economies, where high export volumes could be eclipsed by relatively large internal markets. The data source is the *World Development Report 1996.*

Foreign direct investment as a percentage of GDP, 1993. This variable is chosen to gauge both economic capacity and the revealed competitiveness of a nation in attracting foreign investment. To a considerable extent, foreign investment flows represent a vote of confidence by the international investment community in a nation's economic foundations. For developing countries, this indicator is calculated using net foreign direct investment from the *World Development Report 1995* (the 1996 issue does not provide an update of this indicator). Data for industrial countries are from OECD sources.

Government budget surplus (or deficit) as a percentage of GDP, latest three years available. This indicator captures the stability of an economy from the perspective of fiscal management. A fiscally irresponsible government inevitably creates macroeconomic problems such as inflationary pressures (which raise costs and reduce price competitiveness), the crowding out of private investment, and the risk of currency devaluation. The data source is the IMF's *Government Finance Statistics Yearbook 1995* (the 1996 yearbook does not include these data).

Standard & Poor's long-term sovereign bond rating, 1997. Sovereign ratings by internationally accredited rating agencies are good indicators of the soundness of a nation's policy, regulatory, tax, foreign exchange, and financial systems. This variable uses Standard and Poor's long-term sovereign rating for foreign currency denominated debt. Since Standard and Poor generally only rates sovereign debt at a country's request, a number of countries in the web model are not rated. In the web scoring system, it is assumed that nonrated countries do not have policy and macroeconomic environments conducive to borrowing in international financial markets. This assumption may bias against a small number of nonrated countries that have relatively favorable macroeconomic environments but have not established an international "credit history."

Average annual rate of inflation, 1984–94. This is a commonly used indicator of overall economic stability. If a nation's prices rise more rapidly than those of its competitors, its exports lose competitiveness in global markets. While there is considerable debate over the trade-offs between inflation control and employment generation, especially in the United States, economists generally agree that high levels of inflation perpetuate inflationary expectations, which could be economically, socially, and politically destabilizing. The data source is *World Development Report 1996*.

R&D scientists and engineers per million persons, latest available data. In a global economy increasingly driven by technological advances, maintaining and creating dynamic competitiveness depends critically on the amount of human resources devoted to research and development. Analysts of science and technology structures typically use this variable as a macro-level indicator of national commitment to technology development. Data source is the *UNESCO Statistical Yearbook 1996*.

R&D technicians per million persons, latest available data. This supplements the preceding indicator, to measure relative magnitudes of technology infrastructure. The data source is the *UNESCO Statistical Yearbook 1996*.

Foreign exchange freedom, 1995. Foreign exchange freedom is an essential component of a sound economic foundation. Its absence creates distortions in an economy, ultimately reducing the potential efficiency gains and enhancements of competitiveness that are achieved through international exchange. This indicator is derived from four components of the Fraser Institute's Index of Economic Freedom: the freedom of citizens to own a foreign currency bank account domestically, the freedom of citizens to maintain a bank account abroad, the difference between the official exchange rate and the black market rate, and restrictions on the freedom of citizens to engage in capital transactions with foreigners.[3] Countries that are not included in the Fraser Institute's index are rated based on information in

the IMF's *Annual Report on Exchange Arrangements and Exchange Restrictions 1996*.

Infrastructure indicators. The competitiveness foundations vector also includes four infrastructure indicators from the *World Development Report 1995*, the most recent issue in which such data were published. *Production of electricity (kilowatt hours per person)* indicates the amount of available power supply and usage. *Electricity power system loss (percent of total output)* is a good proxy for the efficiency of power generation systems. *Telephone main lines (per thousand persons)* gauges the development of the telecommunications system. *Road density (kilometers per million persons)* is used to measure the development of a nation's ground transportation network.

Health

A number of development and health organizations provide rich data sources and extensive country coverage on this area. This vector incorporates standard yardsticks, such as life expectancy, as well as indicators in the key health areas monitored by international donor and health organizations: child health and survival, maternal health, prevention of unintended pregnancies, and control of HIV transmission. It also includes overall population growth as both an input and an output indicator. To arrive at the final selection of indicators, data from a number of sources were reviewed, including the UNDP, the U.S. Agency for International Development's (USAID) Demographic Health Surveys, the United Nations Children's Fund (UNICEF), the Population Reference Bureau, the Center for Disease Con-

[3]Gwartney, Lawson, and Block (1996).

trol at the World Health Organization, and the World Bank.

Life expectancy at birth, 1994. This widely available indicator is often used to measure the overall conditions and progress achieved in the health area. While some may argue that it is too highly correlated with infant mortality rates to be meaningful, it is included in this vector because it is a standard measure of health. The data source is the *World Development Report 1996.*

Contraceptive prevalence, latest available data. This is an input indicator that gauges the extent to which women are able to prevent unintended pregnancies, including whether they have access to contraceptive resources and are educated to use them. This indicator measures the percentage of married women aged fifteen to forty-nine currently using contraception. Data sources are the Demographic and Health Surveys (DHS) and the UNDP's *State of the World's Children 1996.*

Total fertility rate, 1994. This indicator, which measures the average number of children born to a woman in her lifetime (assuming that she lives to the end of her childbearing years), is used as a proxy for success in preventing unwanted pregnancies. It is implicitly assumed that women will bear fewer children if they are able to prevent unwanted pregnancies. However, a very low fertility rate may indicate other demographic problems for a nation. The scoring system for this indicator has been adjusted to reflect these assumptions and considerations. Data sources are the *State of the World's Children 1996* and the Population Reference Bureau.

Percentage of births attended by trained health professionals, latest available data. This variable measures an input to overall maternal health. A higher percentage of births attended by trained health professionals is usually associated with lower maternal and infant mortality rates, as well as fewer obstetrical and gynecological problems after childbirth. As used here, trained health professionals include physicians, nurses, midwives, trained primary health care workers, and trained traditional birth attendants. The data source is *State of the World's Children 1996.*

Maternal mortality rate, 1993. This indicator is defined as the number of maternal deaths from pregnancy-related causes per 100,000 live births. It is drawn from both the *State of the World's Children 1996* and the *World Development Report 1996.*

Infant mortality rate, 1994. This is defined as the number of deaths of infants under one year of age per 1,000 live births. The infant mortality rate is one of the most widely used indicators of overall national health conditions. Data sources are the *State of the World's Children 1996* and the *World Development Report 1996.*

Under-five mortality rate, 1994. This is defined as the number of deaths of children under five years of age per 1,000 live births, or the probability of dying between birth and exactly five years of age. This is an important indicator of children's vulnerability. Data sources are the *State of the World's Children 1996* and the *World Development Report 1996.*

Percentage of one-year-olds immunized against measles, latest available data. This is an input indicator to gauge the vulnerability of infants to contagious diseases. The data source is the *State of the World's Children 1996.*

Percentage of one-year-olds immunized against tuberculosis, latest available data. This supplements the preceding variable as an input indicator to measure infants' vulnerability to disease. The data source is the *State of the World's Children 1996.*

Annual natural rate of population increase, latest available data. As an input indicator, rapid population growth signals unsustainable demand on a nation's health and other social systems. As an output indicator, population growth is often a proxy for overall progress in health and income, because population growth rates level off or even decline as nations achieve higher levels of development. The data source is the Population Reference Bureau.

HIV prevalence among adults, 1995 (percent of population over eighteen years old). This is an outcome variable to measure the control of HIV transmission. Data have been estimated and reported by the World Health Organization to give an indication of the magnitude of the HIV/AIDS pandemic.

Education

The education vector consists of both output and input indicators. Most of the variables selected are commonly used measures of results as well as processes considered by education specialists to be important determinants of national levels of education. The main sources consulted are the UNDP, UNICEF, and the World Bank.

Adult illiteracy rate, 1995. This is the principal "results" measure for this vector. The *World Development Report 1996*, the data source used here, defines it as "the proportion of population fifteen years and older who cannot,

with understanding, read and write a short, simple statement on their everyday life."

Enrollment indicators, latest available data. Three enrollment indicators are included in the education vector: primary-level enrollment, secondary-level enrollment, and tertiary-level enrollment. These are gross enrollment ratios, defined as the total enrollment, regardless of age, divided by the age group that officially corresponds to a specific level of education. Ideally one would use the net enrollment ratio, calculated by using only that portion of the enrollment which corresponds to the age group of a given educational level. However, recent net enrollment ratios are available only for just over half of the countries in the web model. In all cases the data source is the *UNESCO Statistical Yearbook 1996.*

Percentage of primary school children reaching grade five, latest available data. This is one of the most telling variables for assessing the quality of an education system. High dropout rates are usually associated with high illiteracy. This variable measures the percentage of the children entering the first grade of primary school who eventually reach grade five. The data source is the *State of the World's Children 1996.*

Primary repeaters as a percentage of primary enrollment, latest available data. This important indicator of the quality of the primary education system is calculated using gross primary school enrollment figures. Data source is the *UNESCO Statistical Yearbook 1996.*

Secondary repeaters as a percentage of primary enrollment, latest available data. This important indicator of the quality of the secondary education system is calculated using gross secondary school enrollment figures. The data source is the *Human Development Report 1995.*

Environment

The selection of variables for the environment vector proved to be a challenge. For example, from an environmental standpoint it would be desirable to have low levels of effluents. But effluents are a natural by-product of increased development. In addition, the available data concentrate on the volume of effluents but do not take into consideration treatment and recycling. Generally, data for treatment and recycling are compiled only in industrial countries. Another set of important input variables that would be useful but are extremely difficult to measure across countries relates to governments' environmental policies and their enforcement. Consequently, the environment vector is dominated by output variables, supplemented by several proxy indicators to gauge public involvement and government commitment to environmental management.

Data from a variety of sources were reviewed for reliable indicators with wide country coverage, including the World Resources Institute's *World Resources* and *1994 Information Please Environmental Almanac*, the UNDP, the Office of Environmental Technology Exports of the U.S. Commerce Department, World Watch, Greenpeace, United Nations Environmental Program (UNEP) Environmental Data Report, the U.S. Environmental Protection Agency, and the *World Directory of Environmental Organizations*.

Access to safe water, 1993. This is an important output variable related to several different aspects of the environment, including safe water supply, waste and sewage treatment, and agricultural and industrial pollution. The most recent data are obtained from the *World Development Report 1996*, which defines this variable

as "the percentage of the population with reasonable access to safe water supply (including treated surface water or untreated but uncontaminated water, such as from springs, sanitary wells, and protected boreholes)."

Per capita carbon dioxide emissions, 1992. This is an output variable to gauge air quality. Data are obtained from the *World Development Report 1996*, which draws from data compiled and tabulated by the World Resources Institute, the United Nations Statistical Division, and the Carbon Dioxide Information Analysis Center of the Oak Ridge National Laboratory.

Other greenhouse gas emissions per capita, 1991. This is also an output indicator for air quality. The most comprehensive and up-to-date information is provided in the World Resource Institute's *World Resources 1996–97*. Per capita levels are calculated by SRI.

Number of environmental nongovernment organizations registered, 1996. This is a proxy indicator for public involvement in environmental policymaking. The data source is the 1997 *World Directory of Environmental Organizations*.

Participation in global environmental conventions, 1993. This input indicator is included as a signal of a government's commitment to environmental management. The most recent list available is in *World Resources 1994–95*.

Urban center solid wastes per capita, 1993. This variable measures the amount of urban waste that must be disposed of by incineration or in landfills. It does not take into account waste treatment or recycling. Ideally, it would be desirable to have data for the amount of untreated wastes per capita, but such data are generally not collected in developing countries. The weighting system for this vector takes into consideration the biases that may result from including this variable. The data source is the *1994 Information Please Environmental Almanac*.

Percent change in forest and woodland, 1983–93. As used here, forest and woodland includes land under natural or planted stands of trees, as well as logged-over areas that will be reforested in the near future. This indicator is included as a proxy for deforestation and reforestation. The data source is *World Resources 1996–97*.

Democracy and Freedom

While the environment vector is problematic from a technical standpoint, the democracy and freedom vector is sensitive and politically charged. Indexes of political freedom are, by definition, more subjective than economic or social data. This vector includes only three variables, two of which are drawn from *Freedom in the World: Annual Survey of Political Rights and Civil Liberties, 1995–1996,* published by Freedom House. The third variable is from *Economic Freedom of the World 1975–1995*, published by the Fraser Institute. For some countries, the original ratings have been adjusted to reflect the current political situation. A large number of other variables were considered but rejected in the three-step screening process described above. Most were excluded because of inadequate country coverage. Other major reasons for exclusion were lack of regular reporting and bias toward or against a particular group of countries.

Freedom House and the Fraser Institute are the most objective data sources providing extensive country coverage and quantitative ratings. Data from a number of other sources were considered, including the U.S. Department of State, Human Rights Watch, Amnesty International, the ILO, and the UNDP. Some of these sources were rejected for inadequate country coverage or objectivity, and since most of them do not provide quantitative ratings, it would be difficult to use their data in the web model.

Civil liberties, 1996. Freedom House defines civil liberty as the "freedom to develop views, institutions and personal autonomy apart from the state."[4] The degree of freedom present in each country was determined using a checklist of these liberties. Each country was then assigned a score from 1 to 7, with 1 being the most free and 7 representing nations characterized by repression and a total lack of civil liberty.

Political rights, 1996. Freedom House defines political rights as those which "enable people to participate freely in the political process. . . . A system is genuinely free or democratic to the extent that the people have a choice in determining the nature of the system and its leaders." As for civil liberties, a checklist was used to rate countries on scores from 1 to 7. Category 1 includes those countries that come closest to the ideals suggested by the checklist, beginning with free and fair elections. Category 7 includes those countries where "political rights are absent or virtually nonexistent due to the extremely oppressive nature of the regime or extreme oppression in combination with civil war."[5]

Equal protection under the law and access to a nondiscriminatory judiciary, 1995. This indicator, provided by the Fraser Institute, is adapted from a subcomponent of the civil liberties checklist used for the Freedom House rat-

[4]Kaplan (1996, p. 530).
[5]Kaplan (1996, p. 530).

GLOBAL Benchmarks

ings. (Separate ratings for subcomponents are not available in the Freedom House publication.) It is included as an additional variable because a sound judiciary structure that enforces the law is vital to safeguarding democracy and freedom.

SCORING SYSTEM FOR VARIABLES

Data for 108 countries were collected for each of the forty-eight variables in the six vectors. A scoring system was then designed whereby indicators for each variable are assigned scores ranging from 0 to 4. These are defined as the *base scores* for a variable. For each variable, the base scores are determined by ranges set according to acceptable standards of well-being or measurements of progress. The chart on page 38 illustrates how the base score for a particular variable was derived, with examples from specific countries. This scoring process was repeated for all forty-eight variables, and to the extent that data are available, the 108 selected countries received base scores across the six development categories. The scoring system for each vector is described in appendix C.

WEIGHTING SYSTEM FOR VARIABLES

Following the scoring process, a weighting system was applied to the indicators in each vector. The weighting system is designed so that the sum of the maximum weighted base scores for each vector equals 100. The weights for each variable were determined by several factors:
• the relative importance of the variable in determining the overall achievement in that vector;
• the quality of the data obtained for that variable; and
• the available country coverage.
For example, if two variables in a given vector display similar quality and importance, a higher weighting would be given to the variable for which data are available for a wider range of countries. Similarly, if two variables are deemed equally important and given similar country coverage, a higher weight is assigned to the indicator for which data are deemed more accurate. (see appendix B for the weighted scores for each variable.)

All indexes incorporate some form of weighting, either explicit or implicit. The assignment of weights for different variables requires judgments that can be interpreted as being subjective. The web model weighting system was developed through a form of interpolation. Consideration is given to the quality and coverage of data, the importance of an indicator relative to others within the vector, academic literature, and discussions held with development specialists. The weighting systems for the variables of the six vectors are presented in appendix D.

SAMPLE VARIABLE IN THE HEALTH VECTOR: INFANT MORTALITY RATE IN 1993

	Scoring System	
	Range	Base Score
	$X \geq 100$	0
	$50 \leq X < 100$	1
	$25 \leq X < 50$	2
	$10 \leq X < 25$	3
	$X < 10$	4
Country	Infant Mortality per 100,000 Live Births	Base Score
Australia	7	4
Argentina	24	3
Dominican Republic	40	2
Haiti	85	1
Cambodia	115	0

SCORING PROCESS FOR THE DEVELOPMENT WEB

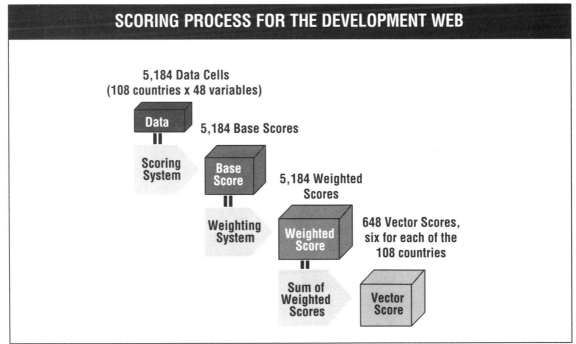

5,184 Data Cells
(108 countries x 48 variables)

Data

5,184 Base Scores

Scoring System

Base Score

5,184 Weighted Scores

Weighting System

Weighted Score

648 Vector Scores, six for each of the 108 countries

Sum of Weighted Scores

Vector Score

GLOBAL Benchmarks

SUMMARY

The process of determining the vector scores for each country is illustrated in the following figure. In sum, the web team created a database consisting of nearly 5,200 data cells, from which 648 vector scores were calculated for 108 countries—that is, 6 vector scores for each country.

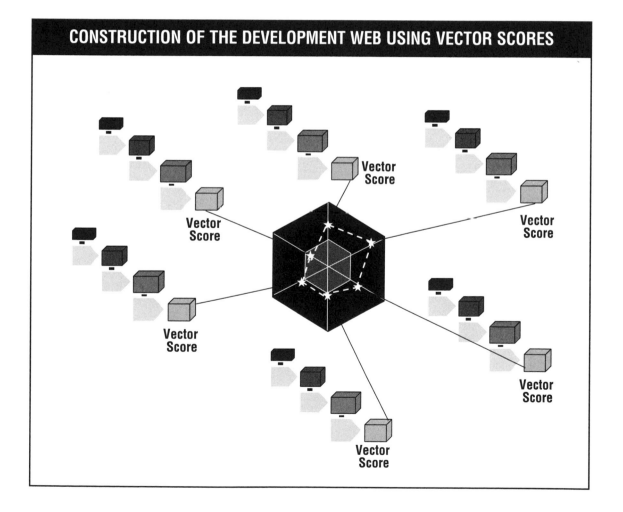

CONSTRUCTION OF THE DEVELOPMENT WEB USING VECTOR SCORES

Chapter 5

SUMMARY FINDINGS

This chapter presents the analytical results of the web development model. A total of 108 countries have been assessed using the development web model, and the resulting scores are analyzed and presented from three perspectives. The first set of analyses focuses on the individual vectors, including the distribution of scores and the average scores received by regional groupings of countries within the vector. The second part of the analysis has a regional focus, with individual development webs constructed for each region to illustrate their average development performance. Finally, the authors also took a more qualitative approach, seeking common patterns of development experience and performance among countries, and developed several "typologies" of performance based on the actual scores of countries in the different development vectors. These three sets of summary findings are presented below.

REGIONAL SCORES AND DISTRIBUTIONS

The development web scores are strongly consistent with the common perception among development economists regarding development performance, at least at the regional level. For purposes of comparison, the 108 countries are assigned to seven regions: Africa (denoted by "AFR" on the accompanying charts), the newly industrializing countries of Asia ("NICs"), Asia excluding the NICs and Japan, industrialized—or industrial—countries ("ICs"), Latin America and the Caribbean ("LAC"), the Middle East ("ME"), and middle-income Europe ("MIE").[1] The charts in this chapter present average regional scores as well as distributions of scores for all countries within each vector.

In the economic performance and competitiveness foundations vectors, the Asian NICs receive the highest scores, as a group. For most other vectors, industrialized countries are the top performers. African countries tend to rank in the bottom in most development categories, while countries in non-NIC Asia, Latin America, middle-income Europe, and the Middle East mostly fall somewhere in between. Exceptions to these general findings can be found in the environment and democracy and freedom vectors. Middle-income European countries, on average, receive the highest scores on Environment, performing slightly better than the industrial countries. And Middle Eastern countries attain the lowest scores on Democracy and Freedom.

[1]Africa includes Benin, Botswana, Burkina Faso, Burundi, Cameroon, Cape Verde, Central African Republic, Congo, Côte

Economic Performance

The strong showing of the Asian NICs, which average a nearly perfect score of 92, attests to their aggressive economic strategies and resulting gains.[2] Somewhat surprising is the fact that non-NIC Asia is the second highest regional performer, with 73. This is due to the strong growth of Malaysia, Thailand, China, Indonesia, and other nations that were starting from low bases and, more important, benefited from the overall rapid expansion in the region. While the standard growth indicators for this group generally match or exceed those for the Asian NICs, their Economic Performance scores have been hurt by relatively low levels of per capita income.

Latin America and the Caribbean (56), middle-income Europe (47), the Middle East (43), and the industrial countries (48) all measure in the middle of the scale on Economic Performance. At the bottom of the ranking is Africa (27).

The economic performance histogram, which shows the global distribution of scores by scoring decile, generally indicates a standard distribution, with the exception that a relatively large number of countries fall in the lowest decile (that is, score between 0 and 10). Almost all of these are African nations. The four highest-scoring countries in the top decile (91–100) are Malaysia, Hong Kong, Singapore and Thailand.

---

d'Ivoire, Djibouti, Ethiopia, Ghana, Kenya, Madagascar, Malawi, Mali, Mauritania, Mauritius, Morocco, Mozambique, Rwanda, Senegal, Sierra Leone, South Africa, Sudan, Swaziland, Tanzania, Togo, Tunisia, Uganda, Zambia, and Zimbabwe. The Asian NICs include Hong Kong, Korea, and Singapore (Taiwan is omitted because of the lack of comparable economic data from international organizations); and Asia excluding the NICs and Japan includes Bangladesh, Bhutan, Cambodia, China, Fiji, Hong Kong, India, Indonesia, Korea, Malaysia, Pakistan, Papua New Guinea, the Philippines, Singapore, Sri Lanka, and Thailand. Industrialized (or industrial) countries include Australia, Austria, Belgium, Canada, Denmark, Finland, France, Germany, Iceland, Ireland, Italy, Japan, the Netherlands, New Zealand, Norway, Portugal,

Spain, Sweden, Switzerland, the United Kingdom, and the United States. Latin America and the Caribbean includes Argentina, Bolivia, Brazil, Chile, Colombia, Costa Rica, Cuba, Dominican Republic, Ecuador, El Salvador, Guatemala, Guyana, Haiti, Honduras, Jamaica, Mexico, Nicaragua, Panama, Paraguay, Peru, Uruguay, and Venezuela. The Middle East includes Bahrain, Egypt, Iran, Iraq, Israel, Jordan, Kuwait, Lebanon, Saudi Arabia, Syria Arab Republic, and the United Arab Emirates. Middle-income Europe includes Cyprus, Greece, Hungary, Poland, Romania, and Turkey.

[2]Due to insufficient data, scores on Economic Performance were not calculated for Cambodia, Cuba, Djibouti, Iraq, or Lebanon.

ECONOMIC PERFORMANCE

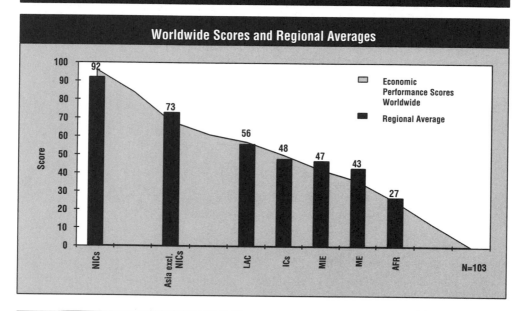

Worldwide Scores and Regional Averages

Score

- Economic Performance Scores Worldwide
- Regional Average

92 73 56 48 47 43 27

NICs — Asia excl. NICs — LAC — ICs — MIE — ME — AFR

N=103

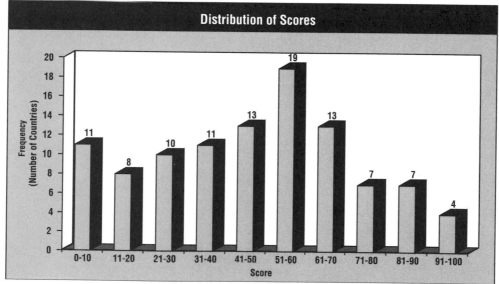

Distribution of Scores

Frequency (Number of Countries)

11 8 10 11 13 19 13 7 7 4

0-10 11-20 21-30 31-40 41-50 51-60 61-70 71-80 81-90 91-100

Score

Competitiveness Foundations

Average regional scores on Competitiveness Foundations in most cases closely track those on Economic Performance.[3] Once again, the Asian NICs (82) top the list. The two exceptions to the close relationship between competitiveness foundations and economic performance are the industrial countries (70) and the non-NIC Asian countries (45).

In the case of industrial countries, competitiveness foundations are stronger than economic performance. This indicates the fact that as mature economies, they can achieve only moderate growth, despite their relatively strong economic capacity and stability. Industrial countries generally score relatively high on competitiveness foundations indicators such as inflation rates, long-term sovereign bond ratings, infrastructure, and concentrations of scientists, engineers, and technicians. Their lower scores in such competitiveness indicators as the level of foreign direct investment and the ratio of exports to GDP primarily reflect the structure of mature economies.

Non-NIC Asia shows the opposite pattern. On average these countries perform better economically than their competitiveness foundations would suggest, demonstrating that growth can take place in the process of building capacity and achieving stability. Many of these countries have relatively high saving rates and levels of foreign direct investment. However, other foundation indicators, such as inflation rates and, in some cases, foreign exchange freedom are weak. Still other weak foundation indicators generally are closely tied to low per capita incomes, such as infrastructure and the concentration of scientists, engineers, and technicians in the population.

The global distribution of Competitiveness Foundations scores by decile is more lumpy than that for Economic Performance, particularly at the lower end of the scale, but it still resembles a fairly standard curve. The two countries measuring in the 90s are Singapore and the Netherlands.

[3]In this vector data coverage is weak for thirteen countries: Bahrain, Bhutan, Cambodia, Cape Verde, Cuba, Fiji, Guyana, Iraq, Lebanon, Sudan, Swaziland, Syria, and Zaire. Competitiveness Foundations scores for these countries are calculated based on those indicators for which data are available, and therefore may be biased upward or downward, depending on the indicators used.

COMPETITIVENESS FOUNDATIONS

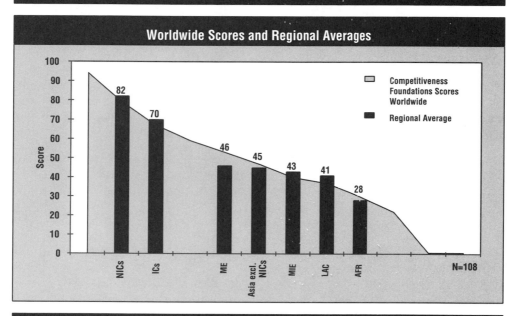

Worldwide Scores and Regional Averages

Score

Competitiveness Foundations Scores Worldwide

Regional Average

NICs 82
ICs 70
ME 46
Asia excl. NICs 45
MIE 43
LAC 41
AFR 28

N=108

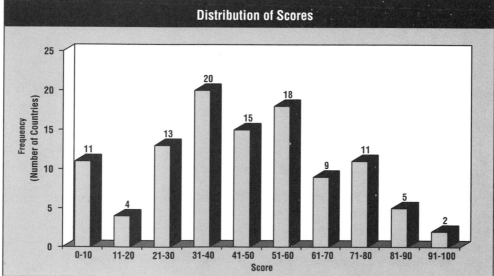

Distribution of Scores

Frequency (Number of Countries)

0-10: 11
11-20: 4
21-30: 13
31-40: 20
41-50: 15
51-60: 18
61-70: 9
71-80: 11
81-90: 5
91-100: 2

Score

Health

The health vector, like the education vector, displays considerable variation among regions. The industrial nations top the list in Health, on average receiving a nearly perfect score (96). The Asian NICs also score well (90), followed by middle-income Europe (80). Falling in the middle range are the Middle East (60), Latin America and the Caribbean (58), and non-NIC Asia (43). As in other vectors, Africa (20) scores much lower than other regions. The regional ranking by average scores on Health suggests that health conditions have a strong relationship with per capita incomes as well as with the overall level of economic development. This is to be expected, since a more materially wealthy society would have more public and private resources to spend on health.

The global distribution of health vector scores is quite uneven among deciles and does not represent a normal distribution. Of the thirteen nations in the lowest decile, all but two—Bhutan and Cambodia—are in Africa. A large number of countries (twenty-three) score in the highest decile. Among these, all but four are industrial economies; and the exceptions—Israel, Singapore, Hong Kong, and Cyprus—are considered high-income countries by the World Bank, as are most of the industrial countries.

GLOBAL **Benchmarks**

HEALTH

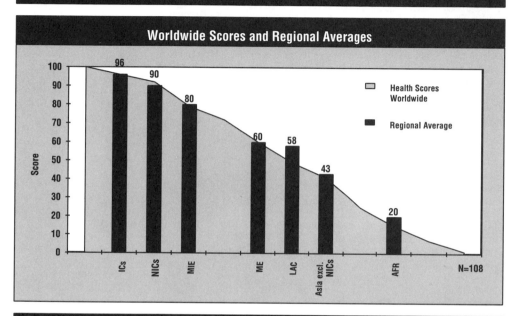

Worldwide Scores and Regional Averages

Score

Health Scores Worldwide

Regional Average

96 — ICs
90 — NICs
80 — MIE
60 — ME
58 — LAC
43 — Asia excl. NICs
20 — AFR

N=108

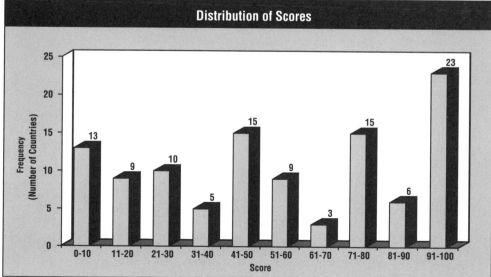

Distribution of Scores

Frequency (Number of Countries)

Score	Frequency
0-10	13
11-20	9
21-30	10
31-40	5
41-50	15
51-60	9
61-70	3
71-80	15
81-90	6
91-100	23

Education

Regional performance on Education mirrors that on Health. In fact, the scores of all regions on Education are within 4 points of their respective scores on Health. The ability of a society to invest resources in education, as in health, is strongly tied to its relative wealth and per capita income. The synchronization of these two vector scores also supports the view that education is an important determinant of health performance (and vice versa).

Of all the web vectors, Education exhibits the most even global distribution among deciles. Among the twenty nations in the highest decile, only South Korea and Greece are not classified as industrial countries. Again, African countries dominate the lowest decile, but several countries from non-NIC Asia, the Middle East, and the Caribbean also fall in this group.

EDUCATION

Worldwide Scores and Regional Averages

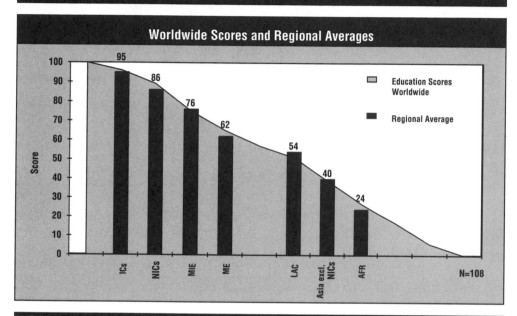

Distribution of Scores

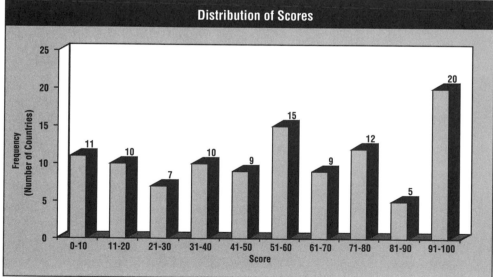

Environment

As noted in the previous chapter, this measure is complicated by the nature of the variables (for example, by the fact that effluent levels rise with increased development). An important observation is that this is the only vector in which no region achieves a high score. Middle-income Europe achieves the highest average score (62), despite the common view that some of these countries are confronting substantial pollution. The region's overall Environment score might be explained by the fact that most of these countries are sufficiently developed to provide basic amenities such as safe water but are not as industrialized or urbanized as the industrial countries, so that they score relatively well on indicators such as carbon dioxide and other greenhouse gas emissions.

The industrial nations are next on the list, with an average score of 60. Most of them score low (0 or 1) on indicators such as carbon dioxide emission and urban center solid wastes. If other desirable variables, such as pollution abatement, recycling, waste treatment, and the enforcement of environmental regulations, could be included, the industrial nations would be likely to receive higher scores in the environment vector. The remaining regions cluster around the 50-point mark.

The global distribution of scores on Environment displays the most interesting shape: all the scores are clumped under a "normal" curve in the middle deciles. No countries score in either the top two or the bottom two deciles.

ENVIRONMENT

Worldwide Scores and Regional Averages

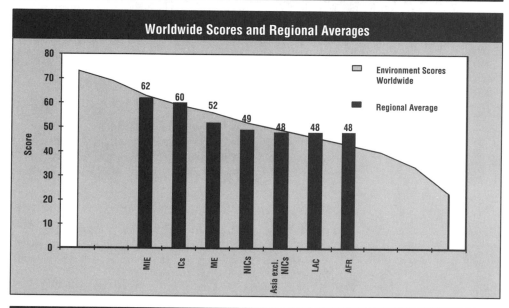

Distribution of Scores

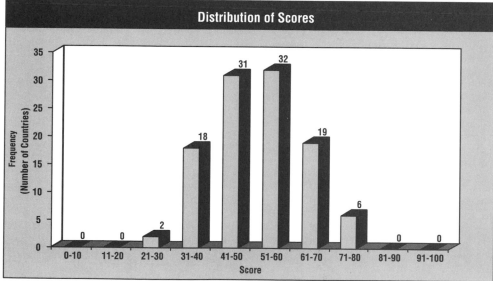

Democracy and Freedom

Performance in the political arena shows the greatest variability of all the development vectors. The industrial nations exhibit the strongest regional score, with 95. This is followed by middle-income Europe, with 70. In the middle of the scoring range are the Asian NICs (50) and Latin America and the Caribbean (52). The lowest regional scores are recorded for Africa (34), non-NIC Asia (32), and the Middle East (18).

The histogram of the global distribution of Democracy and Freedom scores is remarkable. Specifically, relatively large groups of countries fall at either end of the spectrum (top and bottom deciles), as well as in one central decile (between 41 and 50), and relatively few nations fall in the intervening deciles.

DEMOCRACY AND FREEDOM

Worldwide Scores and Regional Averages

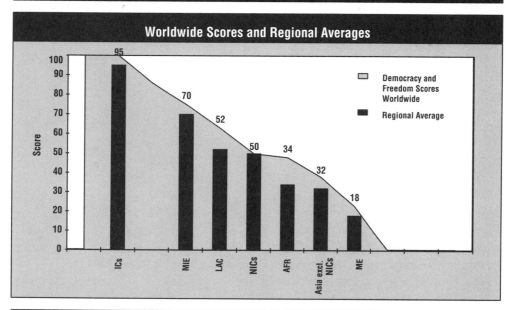

Distribution of Scores

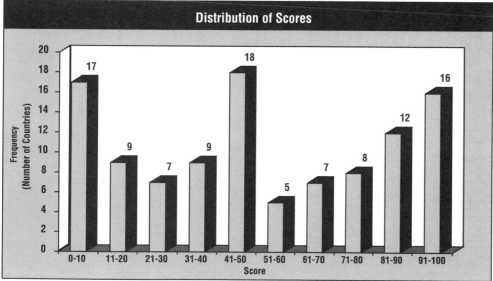

REGIONAL WEBS

Combining vector scores in the development web, one can see that the global mean scores for all six vectors are close to 50. Most vectors have high scores of 100 or in the high 90s. The exception is Environment, where the highest score is only 73.

Industrialized Countries

Among industrial countries, the regional score for Economic Performance is just above the world average. In every other vector regional scores are significantly higher than the world averages. The highest scores are in the education, health, and democracy and freedom vectors.

Developing Countries

For developing countries, the average scores in most vectors are below the world averages.[4] The only exception is on Economic Performance, where the score is the same as the world average. The highest average scores are in the environment vector.

Asian NICs

The three Asian NICs included in the web model achieve very high scores on Economic Performance, Competitiveness, Health, and Education. The region's lowest scores are in the environment

---

[4]This group includes countries in all the regions defined above with the exception of the industrialized countries; the Asian NICs are included.

---

and the democracy and freedom vectors, both of which are close to the world averages.

Non-NIC Asia

The Economic Performance score for non-NIC Asia is well above the world average. Other vector scores are either at or slightly below the world averages. The lowest score is on Democracy and Freedom. In this vector the average score is lowered by scores of zero for several countries in the region; other countries' scores range from the 30s to the 60s.

Middle-Income Europe

For middle-income Europe, scores on Economic Performance and Competitiveness are close to the world averages. Other vector scores are substantially above the world averages. On Economic Performance and Environment, middle-income Europe has average scores similar to those of industrialized countries. Other vectors scores are much lower than the averages for industrialized countries.

Latin America and the Caribbean

Scores for the Latin America and Caribbean region closely track the world averages in most vectors. The region performs substantially above the world average on Economic Performance, slightly above average on Health and Democracy and Freedom, average on Education, and slightly below average on Competitiveness Foundations and Environment.

International Comparison		
Vector	Indust. Countries	World Average
Economic Performance	48	47
Competitiveness	70	45
Health	96	55
Education	95	54
Environment	60	52
Democracy & Freedom	95	50

INDUSTRIALIZED COUNTRIES

International Comparison		
Vector	Dev. Countries incl. Asian NICs	World Average
Economic Performance	47	47
Competitiveness	39	45
Health	45	55
Education	45	54
Environment	50	52
Democracy & Freedom	39	50

DEV. COUNTRIES INCL. ASIAN NICs

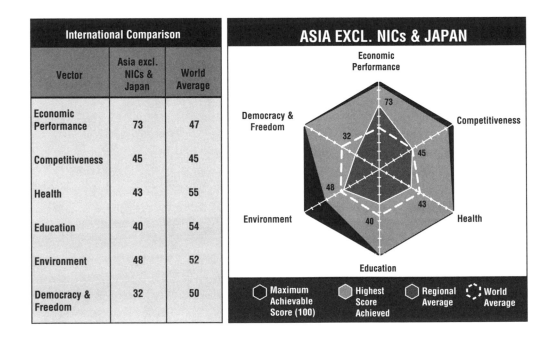

International Comparison		
Vector	Asian NICs	World Average
Economic Performance	92	47
Competitiveness	82	45
Health	90	55
Education	86	54
Environment	49	52
Democracy & Freedom	50	50

ASIAN NICs

Economic Performance 92

Competitiveness 82

Democracy & Freedom

50

49

Environment

Health 90

86 Education

Maximum Achievable Score (100) — Highest Score Achieved — Regional Average — World Average

International Comparison		
Vector	Asia excl. NICs & Japan	World Average
Economic Performance	73	47
Competitiveness	45	45
Health	43	55
Education	40	54
Environment	48	52
Democracy & Freedom	32	50

ASIA EXCL. NICs & JAPAN

Economic Performance

73

Democracy & Freedom

32

Competitiveness

45

48

43

Environment

40

Health

Education

Maximum Achievable Score (100) — Highest Score Achieved — Regional Average — World Average

GLOBAL Benchmarks

International Comparison

Vector	Middle-Income Europe	World Average
Economic Performance	47	47
Competitiveness	43	45
Health	80	55
Education	76	54
Environment	62	52
Democracy & Freedom	70	50

MIDDLE-INCOME EUROPE

Maximum Achievable Score (100) · Highest Score Achieved · Regional Average · World Average

International Comparison

Vector	Latin America & Caribbean	World Average
Economic Performance	56	47
Competitiveness	41	45
Health	58	55
Education	54	54
Environment	48	52
Democracy & Freedom	52	50

LATIN AMERICA & CARIBBEAN

Maximum Achievable Score (100) · Highest Score Achieved · Regional Average · World Average

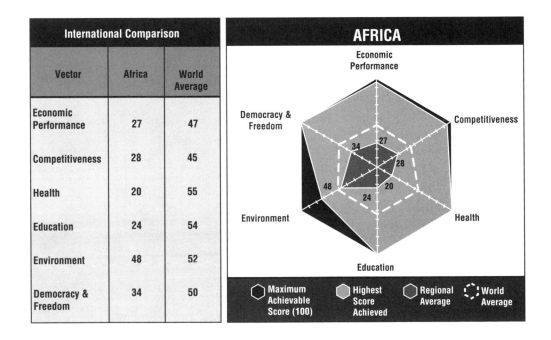

International Comparison		
Vector	Middle East	World Average
Economic Performance	43	47
Competitiveness	46	45
Health	60	55
Education	62	54
Environment	52	52
Democracy & Freedom	18	50

MIDDLE EAST

Economic Performance

Democracy & Freedom

43

18

52

Environment

62

60

Competitiveness

46

Health

Education

Maximum Achievable Score (100) · Highest Score Achieved · Regional Average · World Average

International Comparison		
Vector	Africa	World Average
Economic Performance	27	47
Competitiveness	28	45
Health	20	55
Education	24	54
Environment	48	52
Democracy & Freedom	34	50

AFRICA

Economic Performance

Democracy & Freedom

34

27

28

48

24

20

Environment

Competitiveness

Health

Education

Maximum Achievable Score (100) · Highest Score Achieved · Regional Average · World Average

GLOBAL Benchmarks

Middle East

Vector scores for the Middle East are mostly close to the world averages, except for low scores in Democracy and Freedom. The average score on Democracy and Freedom has been depressed by the zeroes scored by several countries in this region. The remaining countries in the Middle East have Democracy and Freedom scores ranging from the low teens to the low 70s. The region earns above average scores on Health and Education.

Africa

Africa receives low scores in all vectors except environment, on which the regional score is only slightly below the world average. Africa performs especially poorly in the health and education vectors.

Summary

The results of the web model indicate that while balanced development can be achieved, it is not easy to do so. Out of 108 countries included in the model, only 2 rank among the top 20 in at least five vectors—Austria and Switzerland—and neither country is among the top 20 on Economic Performance. Seven other countries rank among the top 20 in at least four vectors, but none of these have high scores on Economic Performance either. All 9 of these countries with more balanced development are high-income countries and members of the Organization for Economic Cooperation and Development (OECD). It may be more difficult for them to achieve the high growth rates possible for countries that are starting from a lower per capita income base.

The web model also shows how countries' development could be unbalanced. For example, the United Arab Emirates, where per capita income is among the highest in the world, ranks third worldwide in Competitiveness Foundations, is in the top third in Health, ranks above average in Education, but is in the bottom third in Economic Performance, Environment, and Democracy and Freedom.

Perhaps more important, the web model demonstrates that countries can develop in a somewhat balanced fashion even at modest levels of per capita income. For example, Costa Rica, with a per capita income of $2,610 in 1995 (compared with the world average of $4,880), ranks in the top third in four vectors: economic performance, health, environment, and democracy and freedom. Likewise Sri Lanka, with a per capita income of only $700 in 1995, ranks in the top half in the economic performance, health, education, and environment vectors.

The development web analysis confirms that each country's experience of economic development is unique. Historical, political, social, and economic factors combine to determine development policies and outcomes. However, the web analysis can uncover common themes or characteristics among certain countries. The following section discusses some country "types" identified through the web model by combining their vector performance with the defining characteristics of their development.

TYPOLOGIES OF DEVELOPMENT PERFORMANCE

Since development performance is the sum of a country's particular conditions, traditions, historical experiences, and development strategies, each country should be approached and analyzed individually to ensure that its singular circumstances are adequately taken into account. Nevertheless, similarities and common groupings can provide terms of reference for analysis.

The development experiences and performances of different countries can be categorized in various ways. For example, nations often undergo similar phases of economic and social performance as a result of regional or functional similarities. Geographic clusters of performance include the recovery of Western European economies in the post–World War II period, the stagnation of Latin American nations in the 1970s, and the explosive growth of the Asian NICs in the 1960s and 1970s. Functional clustering of performance can be tied to socialist versus capitalist orientation, import substitution versus export promotion strategies, and so forth.

The web model of socioeconomic performance reveals a number of patterns of performance among nations. These can be considered "typologies," since they indicate classifications of achievement. The typologies described below are driven by the actual scores of countries in the different development vectors. However, they closely track the experiences of various nations as explained by traditional development analysts, indicating that the development web results are consistent with the literature.

It is important to keep in mind that some nations do not fit into any typology, while a number of countries may exhibit characteristics of more than one typology. Moreover, there are anomalies and aberrations caused by unique circumstances, and it would be inappropriate to force countries to fit into one or another typology.

The following typologies have been identified:

● Capitalist industrialized countries have achieved high standards of living over many years of development. Educational and health standards are high. These nations place a premium on market-led growth, which has created strong competitiveness foundations. Growth performance is moderate because of the plateaus of output already reached, and environmental performance is muted owing to the major levels of effluents produced.

● Socially oriented industrialized countries are similar to capitalist industrialized nations with the exception of placing stronger emphasis on government-supplied education and health services, with high standards. The price of stronger government intervention is often lower economic growth and competitiveness.

● Newly industrializing countries are known for very strong growth performance, achieved through activist government efforts to stimulate competitiveness as well as major investment in education. Protecting the environment has often taken a back seat to the goal of rapid growth. These countries are rapidly becoming able to afford higher standards of living for the majority of their populations.

● Aspiring NICs have emulated the NICs in promoting investment and exports and establishing strong competitiveness foundations. They lag in economic stability and social performance but are rapidly closing the income gap through rapid growth.

- "Typical" developing countries tend to be characterized by periods of rapid growth followed by instability and contraction. Many are dualistic economies, with the rich outnumbered by the poor. These countries often score at or near the global averages in all the development web vectors.

- Highly challenged nations face serious economic and social problems. They are often subject to severe economic and political instabilities, which preclude systematic efforts to achieve sustained growth. Political leaders tend to funnel government resources toward maintaining support among entrenched elites rather than toward alleviating poverty or stimulating economic expansion. These countries score poorly in Health and Education.

Capitalist Industrialized Countries

The industrialized nations can be divided into two typologies with regard to their basic orientation and socioeconomic performance: capitalist and socially oriented. Capitalist industrialized countries have achieved high levels of economic development driven primarily by market forces, whereas socially oriented industrialized countries place a higher priority on social welfare provided primarily through government services, often at the expense of growth. In the capitalist industrialized countries, governments employ a relatively hands-off, laissez-faire approach to economic matters, and many social services are delivered by the private sector. Both types of country score very well on Health, Education, and Freedom and Democracy, but capitalist industrialized nations on average tend to score higher on Competitiveness and Economic Performance than do socially oriented nations.

The United States is presented as an example of a capitalist industrialized country. Others that fit this typology include Australia, Germany, Ireland, Japan, and the United Kingdom.

The United States. Throughout their history, the people of the United States have generally sought to minimize government intervention in the economy. The dominant philosophy holds that the private sector is able to deliver goods and services more efficiently than the government. During the eighteenth and nineteenth centuries, government involvement in business activity was minimal, consisting primarily of the imposition of import taxes to finance government operations and the support of such infrastructure development as roads, railroads, and canals.

The first half of the twentieth century witnessed increased government activity to regulate business. Legislation primarily focused on antitrust laws and efforts to protect the rights of labor. In the second half of the century, there has been a notable increase in government efforts to ensure equal rights and improve opportunities for minorities and women, and to protect consumers and the environment.

Government involvement in the economy peaked during the 1970s. Since that decade a counterswing has sought to remove government regulations and oversight and place responsibility increasingly on industry to police itself. Subsidies created to protect certain sectors, such as agriculture and shipping, are now generally seen as counterproductive and are being stripped away. Deregulation was a dominant theme during the Reagan administration and continues to remain politically popular.

A unique aspect of the U.S. economy is the extremely low level of government ownership or management of productive enterprise, even in such sectors as telecommunications, transportation, energy, and banking, which have significant government involvement in many industrialized nations. Historically, relations between business and government can be characterized as arm's length, often distant, even hostile at times. There has generally been a lack of the close-knit cooperation between business and government that is present in countries such as Japan. Nevertheless, in recent years there has been a shift toward increased partnership between the public and private sectors.

The United States was the only major industrial economy left intact after World War II. Through the implementation of the Marshall Plan and its own demand for world products, the United States acted as the economic driver that rebuilt many other economies. The country was able to continue stable economic growth until the late 1960s, when its military intervention in Vietnam overheated the U.S. economy. Problems continued into the 1970s, as major economic disruptions were caused by inflationary pressures and the oil shocks caused by the Organization of Petroleum Exporting Countries (OPEC). Since the early 1980s the United States has experienced an unprecedented period of economic stability, due in large part to effective monetary policy.

Although its size relative to the world economy has diminished over the past several decades, as other nations have recovered and grown, the United States remains the leading economic power. The country has all the characteristics of an advanced major economy: a declining manufacturing base, a large service sector, and a very productive agricultural sector. The American economy is exceptionally diversified and is self-sufficient in most raw materials. Leading industries include steel, motor vehicles, aerospace, telecommunications, chemicals, electronics, and computers. The economy is noted for strong technological capabilities and the mobility of labor and capital. Although the United States is the largest trading nation, the external sector (as a percentage of total GNP) is small relative to those of other developed economies.

The federal budget deficit experienced unparalleled growth during the 1980s, largely as a result of tax cuts and a significant increase in military spending. This large deficit caused financial markets to demand higher domestic interest rates, which, in turn, pushed up the value of the dollar. By the mid-1980s, the appreciated dollar had combined with strong domestic demand to produce a surge in import volumes and a significant trade deficit. Fiscal policy in the 1990s has been constrained by the effects of the policy shifts of the 1980s. The reduction of the massive budget deficit has become a critical political and economic issue. Although the deficit is large in absolute terms, it has fallen as a percentage of GDP, from 4.7 percent in 1992 to 2.3 percent in 1995.

The Federal Reserve System performs the role of central banker. Its board of governors regulates bank credit and monetary policy,

Summary Findings

principally through open-market operations in government securities and the manipulation of the federal funds rate. The Federal Reserve is a further example of the American philosophy of limited government involvement in the economy. It was established in 1913 to be independent from government, although its governors are appointed by the president and must be confirmed by the Senate.

Universal heath coverage is a relatively new concept in the United States, in contrast with most western European nations. The first nationwide hospital insurance bill was introduced in the Congress in 1942 but was rejected.[5] Discussions of various forms of national health insurance over the next two decades culminated in 1965 with the Johnson administration's Great Society initiative and the enactment of the medicare and medicaid programs. These programs represented a compromise between those who wanted universal national health insurance and those who wanted the private sector to continue to be the primary source of insurance coverage. Medicare provides health insurance for citizens aged sixty-five years and older, while medicaid provides medical care for low-income families and welfare recipients. Private medical insurance has remained essential for those who do not qualify for either program.

The medicare and medicaid programs have given the federal government an institutional interest in health care cost containment, as it has become the single largest health insurer. The 1970s were marked by a rapid expansion in

health care costs and strategies for their containment. The National Health Planning Act of 1974 created a system of state and local health planning agencies supported by federal funds. Costs continued to rise, however: currently the United States spends more on health care services than does any other nation, and on average more than twice as much per person than other OECD countries do. Yet the United States still lacks universal coverage and faces problems in geographic maldistribution of providers, gaps in the continuity of care, and high rates of inappropriate utilization of health services. Paradoxically, the vast majority of the population that has health care coverage has access to high-quality care and advanced medical technology and benefits from a system that vigorously promotes biomedical research and development.

Like other industrialized nations, the United States offers thirteen years of publicly supported schooling, from kindergarten through grade twelve. The public school system, which is mostly managed by localities, predominates in the provision of education at the elementary and secondary levels. By and large, it provides a strong education through grade twelve.

As to higher education, the United States arguably has the most extensive system of public and private universities and colleges in the world. First-rate research facilities, high-quality faculty, extensive educational opportunities, and, for some, generous scholarships have attracted hundreds of thousands of undergraduate students from other nations. This strong system of higher education, which produces both a high-quality labor force and the human

[5]See Organization for Economic Coordination and Development (1994).

resource base for state-of-the-art basic and applied research, contributes significantly to the nation's continued competitiveness, especially in technology sectors. The principal drawback of the U.S. higher education system is its high cost compared with that in other industrial nations.

Socially Oriented Industrialized Countries

Socially oriented industrialized countries have achieved a high level of economic development and have chosen to place a higher priority on socioeconomic welfare than on market-driven growth. The governments of such countries play a more activist role than those in other industrialized countries do, not so much in controlling the economy but in financing and delivering services for their citizens. Consequently, in terms of socioeconomic performance, socially oriented industrial countries are characterized by extremely high scores on Health, Education, and Democracy and Freedom but only moderate scores on Economic Performance, despite relatively strong scores on Competitiveness Foundations.

Sweden is presented as an example of a socially oriented industrialized country. Other nations that fit into this typology include Canada, Denmark, Finland, France, and Norway.

Sweden.[6] Perhaps the most striking feature of Swedish economic policy is the long-standing and pervasive commitment to economic equality. This

[6]See Bengtsson (1994); Bosworth and Rivlin (1987); Schnitzer (1970); Organization for Economic Cooperation and Development (1994, 1996).

commitment is primarily carried out through government spending programs and policies related to taxation and wage determination.

Sweden's strong wage policies were originally formulated in the 1950s as a means of improving both egalitarianism and economic growth. Wage bargaining is highly centralized, and the number of bargainers is small. The strategy of compressing wage scale variations by raising wages at the lower end of the scale was designed to shift the industrial structure toward capital-intensive, high-productivity industries. As a result, wage differences across occupations, industries, and skill levels have been significantly reduced.

Sweden's progressive tax system has further contributed to income equalization. Tax rates are very high by international standards. The net result of taxing and redistributing massive amounts of income is that very little correlation remains between incomes before and after taxes and transfers. Differences in standards of living among upper- and lower-income Swedes are remarkably narrow.

Sweden is also distinguished from other developed nations by the extraordinary lengths to which its government will go to reduce unemployment. The country's strong history of low unemployment, however, comes at a price. Large numbers of workers who would otherwise be jobless are enrolled in training programs and provided with jobs in the public sector. Such policies have served to disguise unemployment and have aggravated the budget deficit. These programs alone cost nearly 3 percent of GDP in the 1980s and have contributed to declining rates of productivity growth that are unmatched by other industrialized countries.

Since the 1970s Swedish economic growth has generally been below the OECD average. Slow GDP growth and the fall in the value of the krona in the early 1990s has resulted in a marked decline in overall living standards. Measured by the OECD standard of income per capita and purchasing power, Sweden's world ranking has declined from one of the top three in the 1970s to eleventh in the 1990s. In terms of income distribution, however, Sweden remains near the top.

Although nearly all of Swedish industry is privately owned, the public sector is still very large in terms of employment and spending. The state is an important player in the economy, intervening in industry not so much through direct ownership as through the fiscal system. The public sector accounts for a large share of GDP. OECD statistics indicate that the Swedish government represents about two-thirds of spending and 58 percent of income. The corresponding ratios for the United States are 33 percent and 31 percent, respectively. Only the other Scandinavian countries and France have comparably high ratios.

Throughout the twentieth century, Sweden has used revenue from taxation to build up an extensive welfare system. In recent years, however, a rising budget deficit, increasing social spending costs, and more intense international competition have shifted the orientation of the nation's economic policy toward the reduction of state spending. This shift is most visible in the welfare system since 1991. In addition, many key sectors of the economy, including banking, telecommunications, and public utilities, have been deregulated in the hope of making them more competitive.

In an economy that for many years enjoyed full or near full employment, the rise of joblessness since 1992 has become a major economic concern. The country's existing labor market programs, designed for small levels of frictional unemployment, have met with only limited success. Historically, public intervention in the labor market in Sweden has been particularly strong. Public consumption as a share of GDP is the highest among OECD nations. In 1994 some 40 percent of the labor force worked in the public sector.

Although consumer price inflation in Sweden has dropped in the 1990s, it has remained consistently above the European OECD average since the 1970s. High wages are the result of a labor market that remains highly regulated. Recent wage increases have been made with little reference to unemployment or productivity.

Sweden's commitment to social welfare dates back several hundred years. Since medieval times Swedish kings and governmental bodies have provided certain basic forms of social services. Relief for the poor was a major parliamentary issue as far back as 1847. The Health and Medical Services Act of 1982 provides health care to all citizens on equal terms. Health services are not free, although they are heavily subsidized through a statutory general health scheme. In 1993 Sweden's health and medical services cost $14 billion—about 7.5 percent of GDP. Reductions in central government funding have prompted measures to raise efficiency and cut costs. Indeed, it is believed that cuts so far have been achieved without a decline in health care standards, because funding reductions have been offset by increases in productivity and medical advances. Despite funding decreases, Sweden maintains an excellent health care system.

Swedish citizens are served by a strong and high-quality educational system. Schooling is compulsory between the ages of seven and sixteen. Most students pursue another two or three years of vocational and preuniversity training. Currently, one-third of these upper-secondary graduates continue to higher education. Most higher education institutions are funded by the central government. Tuition is free, and students receive government assistance to meet their costs. As universities expand and the employment rate drops, the number of people moving on to higher education is increasing. More than one-fourth of the Swedish labor force has had some form of higher education, and three-fourths have completed upper-secondary school, placing Sweden above the OECD average in the labor force educational level. Universal enrollment and heavy subsidies from both local and central governments have made Sweden's educational system one of the best in the world.

All Swedish citizens aged eighteen years or older are entitled to vote in parliamentary elections, which are conducted on the basis of proportional representation. Voter turnout in Sweden is traditionally very high, standing at about 86 percent to 91 percent of the electorate since 1982. Sweden's constitution emphasizes civil liberties. It was the first country in the world to include, as early as 1766, a "freedom of the press" act as part of its constitution. The protection of the rights of the individual and very high voter participation contribute to Sweden's perfect score on Freedom and Democracy.

Newly Industrializing Countries

The newly industrializing countries have achieved an unprecedented level of economic development performance, transforming their countries from poor, backward economies to highly advanced industrial giants. Most analyses that present growth strategies to developing nations use the NICs as models. These countries are characterized by extremely high scores on Economic Performance and very strong levels on Competitiveness. NICs usually place a high priority on education and have achieved major progress in standards of health. Rapid industrial expansion, however, has often been at the expense of the environment. The development of democracy has differed among these nations. Some, such as South Korea, have taken significant steps toward establishing a multiparty democracy, while others, such as Singapore, maintain a one-party authoritarian regime. The NICs share a common emphasis on economic growth and prosperity as the driving force behind state policy.

In undertaking significant policy reforms, these nations have usually suffered painful adjustment periods as they have shifted out of import substitution policies to open trade and investment regimes that would integrate them with the global economy. Reducing the role of government in the economy in order to promote productivity has also caused difficulties. However, many sectors of these economies have experienced strong growth, which has more than offset the losses in income and employment opportunities in previously protected or government-operated activities. Experience has shown that the benefits of change have far exceeded the costs. The populations of the NICs have witnessed enormous increases in standards of living and socioeconomic well-being.

Two examples of NICs are presented. South Korea represents the four East Asian "tigers," which have become the envy of developing countries in the region and throughout the world. Several East Asian NICs have pursued a development strategy patterned roughly after that of Japan, including concerted government intervention. In Chile, a more recent Latin American example, the government has taken a more hands-off stance and a more pure free market approach. Other NICs identified by the web analysis include Argentina, Hong Kong, Malaysia, Mauritius, and Singapore. Taiwan would also be classified in this group, but due to major gaps in comparative data it is not quantitatively rated in the web model.

Republic of Korea.[7] The experience of the Republic of Korea (South Korea) is a prime example of how a relative latecomer to economic development can rapidly accelerate growth rates. South Korea has modernized its institutions, and even its ideologies, by imitating those of more advanced countries, benefiting from their technological heritage and condensing the longer development process of industrialized nations.

In 1962 South Korea was one of the poorest countries in the world, with a per capita GNP of just $100, and annual per capita GNP growth had stood at less than 1 percent since the end of the Korean War in 1953. Its industrial base and exports were negligible. The economy was in a severe decline, subsisting largely

on American economic aid. Nevertheless, some noticeable preparations for growth were made during the presidency of Syngman Rhee (1948–60): education was improved, as was the basis for import substitution in light industries. After a brief and unsuccessful attempt at democracy between April 1960 and May 1961, Korea was ruled by President Park Chung Hee until his assassination in October 1979. During this period, the economy, led by the government, began to make great progress.

South Korea has achieved high growth rates by adopting an export-led strategy, which has allowed the country to make the fullest possible use of its substantial endowment of human resources and to compensate for its shortage of natural resources. The export-led growth strategy was implemented by an energetic government in close collaboration with business and labor. The favorable external factors surrounding South Korea after the Korean War, including U.S. economic aid in the 1950s, a stable global free trade regime, and strong demand for labor-intensive products in the industrialized countries, strongly supported South Korea's development efforts.

Virtually all policy measures at the disposal of the government were directed toward assisting business. These included not only traditional monetary and fiscal measures but also policies on labor, foreign trade, agriculture, and finance. The government placed a high priority on installing sufficient infrastructure: roads, ports, and communications systems were established, often ahead of demand. The government also established the basic institutional framework necessary to carry out the economic plan, including laws and regulations

[7]See Cho (1994); Cole (1980); Kuznets (1994); Kwon (1990); World Bank (1993a).

favoring the expansion of foreign capital and investment. This export-led growth strategy worked because priorities and means combined to induce investment in the labor-intensive industries in which Korea had a comparative advantage.

The initial successes of such policies in the 1960s kindled a "can-do" spirit among the Korean people, whose enthusiastic support created the foundations for future economic successes. Despite little tradition of entrepreneurship, vigorous entrepreneurship emerged in the 1960s and 1970s, contributing significantly to the economy's growth. Korean entrepreneurs were aided by several factors. During the early period of development, capital and technology could be easily imported, and the low costs of labor and capital raised profit margins. In addition, the government offered entrepreneurs monetary, fiscal, and other subsidies to reduce the risk of investments.

The government intensified its development efforts in the 1970s. It targeted heavy industries such as iron and steel, shipbuilding, nonferrous metals, chemicals, machinery, and electronics, partly to foster defense industries and partly to strengthen and deepen the industrial structure by establishing upstream industries. These policies, however, resulted in an unbalanced industrial structure and a built-in system of inflation.

During the 1980s, government priorities shifted from the maximization of exports and industrialization to price stabilization through direct control of wages and restructuring of industries. Although the government attempted to correct the excesses and distortions of the previous decades, it was only moderately successful in controlling inflation and restructuring industry. The 1990s have seen Korean manufacturers of labor-intensive goods move upmarket or shift low-end, labor-intensive production to low-cost manufacturing locations such as Thailand and Vietnam. Between 1991 and 1995, South Korea sustained an average annual rate of real GDP growth of 7.5 percent, close to its long-term average over the past three decades.

Education has always been a priority in South Korea. By 1970, primary school enrollment stood at 100 percent. Gross secondary school enrollment had risen to 92 percent by 1993. More remarkable, higher education enrollment shot up from 16 percent in 1970 to 48 percent in 1993, ahead of Japan, the United Kingdom, and Germany, although still behind France and the United States. Recently, the Korean education system has been criticized for overemphasizing rote learning at the expense of analytical thinking and creativity. Critics also point to the excessive emphasis placed on gaining entrance to the elite universities, forcing students to study day and night. However, the government's priority on basic as well as higher education has been instrumental in creating an educated and more adaptable work force, which is key to maintaining long-term dynamic competitiveness.

Health indicators are improving in South Korea. Average life expectancy was fifty-seven years in 1965 but had risen to over seventy-one years by 1994. The primary reasons are improvements in the supply of drinking water, sanitation, housing, diet, and medical services. While in 1963 there were thirty-eight hospital beds per 100,000 people, by 1993 there were 286.

Reflecting rapid industrial growth and a growing number of motor vehicles, emissions of carbon dioxide per head have more than doubled since 1980. Although still below U.S. levels, emissions in South Korea are beginning to approach the levels in Japan. Fresh water supply remains sustainable, thanks to the continental climate and plenty of precipitation. Deforestation is not a significant problem.

One of the most striking aspects of the Republic of Korea's development has been its recent steps toward democratization. Recent political developments support the theory that economic development often leads to the rise of a middle class, which inevitably demands increased political participation and government accountability. The February 1988 constitution limited presidents to a single five-year term and revoked the president's power to dissolve the National Assembly. In 1990 the opposition coalition, the Democratic Liberal Party, was victorious in the cleanest elections in the nation's history. In 1995 President Kim Young Sam's administration initiated criminal proceedings against two former presidents, Roh Tae Woo and Chun Doo Hwan, offering the possibility of reforming a system characterized by corrupt links between business and politics.

Chile.[8] In comparison with the East Asian NICs, Chile is a relatively new example of success. It abandoned import substitution and other restrictive economic policies in the mid-1970s, and since then has enjoyed high levels of export diversification and expansion, fueling economic growth rates of almost 7 percent a year since 1984. Chile also boasts health and education conditions far above typical developing country standards, and government spending continues to focus on social programs aimed at alleviating poverty.

Chile's economic reforms took place under General Augusto Pinochet, who came to power in 1973 after President Salvador Allende's experiment with socializing the economy produced massive economic dislocation and contraction. Pinochet early on sought guidance from a team of University of Chicago–trained economists, who aimed to transform the state's role from being the main producer and distributor of goods to facilitating private sector activity. Among the first reforms was to reduce import tariffs, some of which were as high as 750 percent, to a uniform rate of 10 percent by 1979. Subsidies and price controls were discarded, the government budget deficit was brought down from the 24 percent of GDP sustained under Allende, and a stabilization plan was introduced to eliminate hyperinflation. In 1976 the government dramatically liberalized the foreign investment regime and strengthened guarantees on private property rights that encouraged mining investment. Labor reform designed to increase the flexibility of Chile's labor market reduced government mandates and payroll taxes. The tax system was simplified, and other reform measures instituted a value-added tax and lowered income and corporate taxes to encourage investment and production over consumption. In 1981 the pension system was privatized, sharply increasing national saving.

However, in 1982 the government was forced to devalue the currency in the face of a

[8]See Economic Intelligence Unit (1996–97); Pan American Health Organization (1994); World Bank (1996b).

dramatic reversal in the country's terms of trade and the drying up of foreign credit. The result was a massive weakening of many of the country's most important banks and corporations, which had significant amounts of dollar-denominated debt. Subsequently, an appreciating currency, the continued entry of cheap foreign imports, and excessive deregulation forced many industries into bankruptcy in 1982. Unemployment increased markedly, and the economy contracted by 14 percent. The economic contraction generated strong public criticism within Chile, which forced the military regime to halt the reform effort temporarily. The worst of the crisis was over by 1985, and reforms began anew with the reprivatization of the banks and corporations rescued during the crisis, as well as the privatization of energy companies and the telecommunications monopoly. Tariffs, which had been increased to 35 percent during the crisis, were lowered again to 11 percent, and the central bank was given full control over monetary policy.

When Pinochet came to power, he was at first supported by the major political parties of the right and center. But certain important segments of society soon began to oppose him, and then all political activity was banned. The parties of the left were largely destroyed, their leaders either put in jail, killed, or exiled. Pinochet was thus able to follow the path of economic reform with little opposition, even though the social costs of dislocation were particularly high in the mid-1970s.

A dramatic change in political attitudes took place in the late 1980s. Fueled by the desire to live under civilian authority and by a growing recognition of the benefits brought about by economic liberalization and growth, Chilean society gained a new pragmatism that favored compromise rather than the ideological antagonism characteristic of the previous thirty years. New democratically elected governments since 1990 have continued the country's liberal economic program but shifted government resources toward social programs to combat poverty.

Orthodox monetary and fiscal policies, market liberalization, and increasing investment in human capital and infrastructure are currently the key characteristics of the Chilean economy. Monetary policy is in the hands of an independent central bank that seeks OECD levels of inflation. Foreign exchange operations are unregulated. The exchange rate is allowed to float within a band defined in comparison with a basket of currencies. Chile has had budget surpluses since 1987, and debt payments constituted only 3 percent of government expenditures in 1996. Public sector employment is less than 7 percent of total employment, and the public sector's proportion of GDP stands at 5.7 percent, far below that in the United States.

Liberalization has resulted in the expansion of traditional export industries, such as mining and fishing, as well as new industries producing wine, fruit, and cellulose. Tourism has also flourished. This diversified export sector has been the main driver behind the economic expansion over the past ten years: exports grew from 29 percent of GDP in 1985 to 38 percent in 1995.

The volume and quality of investment in Chile are high because of financial liberalization. Gross capital is estimated to have reached 29 percent of GDP in 1996. The domestic saving rate is also high by Latin American standards, hovering around 25 percent of GDP in the 1990s. As a result the country is financially self-sufficient. Much of the saving has been achieved through the privatized pension system, which is now being duplicated in many other countries. Chile also has a sophisticated capital market, including venture capital resources. The country's stability has in turn encouraged foreign direct investment, which has also accelerated economic development.

Chile continues to integrate with the global economy. Its export markets are varied. Within the Latin American region, it pursues integration through trade accords such as Mersocur, which also includes Argentina, Brazil, Paraguay, and Uruguay.

One of the government's main priorities is the eradication of poverty. The poorest have been given wider access to training, education, health care, housing, and basic infrastructure (water, electricity, paved roads) as well as microenterprise credit. The proportion of the population living in poverty in Chile was lowered to 28 percent in 1994 from 45 percent in 1987.

While the country currently has an elected government, democracy is not perfect in Chile. Under the 1989 constitution written by the military government, Pinochet remained the commander-in-chief of the armed forces until he stepped down in March 1998 and became a senator for life. A number of senators are not elected by the citizens of Chile, and four of these are chosen by the armed forces. The military also has a constitutionally mandated presence in the National Security Council, which deals with high-level matters regarding national security and the constitution. This body also nominates two of the seven members of Chile's Constitutional Tribunal, which rules on the constitutionality of laws and executive decrees. The judiciary is independent and is known for being one of the most corruption-free systems in Latin America. However, its slow and complicated procedures tend to give the advantage to those who can afford the best legal advice.

Chile's Education score of 71 compares well with the Latin American average of 56. Ninety-nine percent of Chilean children are enrolled in primary school, of whom 95 percent reach the fifth grade. However, as in the rest of Latin America, the quality of education is not equivalent to that in developed and the Asian newly industrializing countries. Poor teaching methods and the low number of annual school hours are major contributing factors.

Chile has some of the best health conditions in Latin America. Health spending shifted from curative to preventive measures in the 1970s and 1980s, allowing health standards to go up while spending decreased. Initiatives focused on investment in water and sewage infrastructure, free vaccination programs, and the extension of mother and child health programs, particularly for the poor. Public hospitals and health services need much improvement, however, despite increasing budgets in the 1990s. As in other NICs, resources are not always efficiently used in the public sector. Chile provides health care coverage through a mixed private-public system. All workers are required to pay 7 percent of wages to the health insurance program of their choice, whether the national public provider or one of the more than thirty private providers. Most poorer individuals participate in the government plan.

Like other rapidly growing countries, Chile is often criticized for putting growth ahead of environmental protection. Air pollution due to heavy vehicle traffic is at dangerous levels in and around the main urban areas. Santiago, in particular, suffers from severe air pollution during the winter as a result of thermal inversion and the lack of winds. Laws designed to cut down industrial emissions are not always enforced. Water pollution is also a threat, mostly because raw sewage and unprocessed industrial waste are dumped in the country's lakes and rivers.

Aspiring NICs

This group consists of developing economies on their way to becoming the newly industrializing countries of the future. Aspiring NICs score very well on Economic Performance, although on average their Competitiveness scores are well below those of the NICs. Most of these nations, however, need to achieve considerable improvements in Health, Education, Environment, and Democracy and Freedom, on which they generally score closer to the world averages than to the industrialized nations.

We choose Botswana as the case study of an aspiring NIC because it is not commonly thought of as such. It is important to recognize that aspiring NICs represent a diverse collection countries from Africa, Asia, and Central and South America. Other examples include China, Colombia, Costa Rica, El Salvador, Indonesia, the Philippines, Sri Lanka, Thailand, and Uruguay.

Botswana.[9] When it gained independence from Britain in 1966, Botswana was one of the world's poorest countries. Most observers believed there was little hope that it would become any less dependent on international aid. Yet from 1965 to 1985, Botswana experienced the most rapid growth of GNP per capita of any country in the world (8.3 percent). Accompanying the growth of real output, formal sector employment grew at 9.6 percent per year, and its measures of real welfare, such as life expectancy and infant mortality, improved to become among the best in Africa. The five-year drought of 1982–87, perhaps the most protracted during that period in Africa, produced a relatively small increase in malnourishment and had little measurable effects on death rates. Overall, the contrast with experience in much of the rest of sub-Saharan Africa could hardly be greater.

The structural changes in Botswana's economy and society have been almost as dramatic as its GDP growth. As employment has shifted away from agriculture, the population has rapidly urbanized, wage employment in nonagricultural sectors has grown, ratios of both investment and saving to GDP have increased dramatically, the share of visible exports in GDP has risen sharply, and the country's substantial reliance on grant aid to balance both government budgets and external payments has been transformed to a position of substantial external financial assets.

At independence, large-scale cattle ranching was the mainstay of Botswana's economy. However, the growth of diamond output and the exploitation of copper-nickel reserves since 1971 have led to significant expansion of the economy, even though it remains considerably undiversified. Agriculture and mining now

---

[9]See Harvey and Lewis (1990); Hope (1997); Perrings (1996); Stedman (1993); World Bank (1989).

dominate, with mining having overtaken agriculture as the largest contributor to GDP. Manufacturing has also grown rapidly, though from a very small base.

The rapid increase in diamond export revenues during the 1980s enabled the government to finance major infrastructure projects and pursue significant improvements in the welfare system. The economy, however, remains extremely vulnerable to external forces, particularly fluctuations in the world diamond market.

An essential component in Botswana's economic growth has been the pragmatic leadership of the government. Throughout the first two decades of independence, the government exhibited a coherent view of development and priorities, which it adjusted to meet changing realities and circumstances. Prudent advice from outside economic advisors, many from Williams College in the United States, contributed to sound policymaking. The government made efforts to anticipate both problems and opportunities. In advance of major drought cycles, studies were commissioned and institutions were developed to minimize the impact of future droughts. The government also pursued sophisticated foreign exchange management policies to create realistic annual spending projections. Finally, it chose projects carefully, based on economic and social returns, and allowed few "white elephant" or prestige projects.

Botswana's political record is equally remarkable. In five national elections between 1965 and 1984, the Botswana Democratic Party won large majorities against several opponents in a multiparty system. On two occasions a serving vice president of the country was defeated in a reelection bid. Botswana does not hold political prisoners, has maintained freedom of speech, association, religion, and the press, and has appointed a small number of its minority white population, as well as black citizens from a variety of the country's ethnic regions, to senior political and administrative posts without any quota-based system of representation.

This impressive economic and political performance was achieved under strained circumstances. Not only were the beginnings mostly disadvantageous—a four-year drought, virtually no infrastructure, and only a handful of university and high school graduates—but, in addition, landlocked Botswana was surrounded by white minority regimes in Namibia, South Africa, and Southern Rhodesia (now Zimbabwe), which were hostile to the country's nonracial approach to politics and government.

Botswana has a well-developed decentralized primary health care system, with nineteen district health teams. In 1993 there were 16 general hospitals, 14 primary hospitals, 201 clinics, 313 health centers, 364 doctors (2.4 per 10,000 people), and 3,355 nurses (22.4 per 10,000 people). Although severe malnutrition is rare, undernutrition is becoming increasingly serious due to the droughts of the past decade. Moreover, the incidence of AIDS is increasing. An estimated 10 percent of the total population is infected with HIV. Children make up almost one-fifth of all HIV-positive cases, while women outnumber men by 30 percent. A National AIDS Prevention and Control Program has been established, and the National AIDS Committee promotes education and prevention measures.

Since independence the provision of education has increased dramatically. In 1994,

310,000 children attended 670 primary schools. Secondary-level enrollment was 86,700 in 1994, two-thirds in government or grant-aided schools and the rest in private schools. The government has made a long-term commitment to universal access to secondary education by implementing a large school-building program and abolishing fees for publicly provided secondary education. In 1994 over 10,000 students were enrolled in tertiary-level education.

"Typical" Developing Countries

While all nations are unique and should be viewed as such, this typology captures the characteristics of many "middle-of-the-road" developing countries that are neither strong nor poor performers but have endured the trials and tribulations of the development process with uneven results. Many industrialized and newly industrializing countries presented characteristics of this typology earlier in their development histories. Several "typical" developing countries have passed through a phase in which the state sector expanded to dominate the economy. Others have attempted to use protectionist and import substitution policies to boost economic growth, and have not yet changed these policies as their benefit has declined. A large number are currently undertaking policy reform and economic restructuring, and some are becoming better positioned for a stage of economic take-off as a result.

The Dominican Republic serves as a case study of a "typical" developing country. Of the many other nations that fall in this category, examples include Bolivia, India, Pakistan, Papua New Guinea, and Peru.

Dominican Republic.[10] The Dominican Republic is "typical" in a sense that its development web scores are reasonably close to world averages in every vector. Its Economic Performance score is relatively high, as a result of unusually strong economic growth in the 1990s. Its scores on Education and Environment are slightly below the world averages.

The experience of the Dominican economy during the past five decades can be described as a series of growth and stagnation cycles. During the 1950s, it expanded relatively rapidly, as a result both of the early positive effects of the Dominican import substitution industrialization strategy and of strong global demand for Dominican commodities to supply postwar reconstruction. From the late 1950s through the mid-1960s, growth slowed due to instabilities resulting from political conflict and civil war. In the following decade the economy returned to rapid growth owing to the combination of a return to political stability and a favorable external environment. The key engine of growth was exports, which enjoyed prevailing high world prices.

Economic growth rates dropped sharply in 1976–84, as a result of inadequate adjustment to the OPEC oil crisis and the subsequent decline in global economic activity. Gains from the import substitution policy, which heavily protected domestic industry, began to fall off rapidly. The nation's terms of trade deteriorated rapidly, and the public sector deficit rose sharply. The years between 1984 and 1991 represent a period of fundamental adjustment. The peso was devalued, monetary policies were

---

[10]See SRI International (1996); World Bank (1995a, 1996b).

tightened, and energy prices were raised. However, the government continued to swing between the desire to achieve stability and the politically driven need to stimulate demand and output. Per capita output and living standards actually declined in the latter half of the 1980s. The only major positive development during this period was the rapid growth of free-zone assembly operations and tourism, both of which have become mainstays of the economy.

In response to the economic crisis, the government introduced an emergency stabilization initiative: the New Economic Program (NEP) in August 1990. The NEP incorporated a set of strong stabilization measures, including fiscal and monetary restraint, exchange rate unification, and trade and financial market liberalization. The economy reacted rapidly and positively. The fiscal deficit was eliminated in 1991, inflation fell to moderate levels, and the exchange rate stabilized. Output also increased in 1991, after having declined for the previous two years. However, these gains were not sustained, and conditions deteriorated in 1993–94. In the period leading up to the 1994 election, the government's structural reform program stalled, the flexible exchange rate regime was abandoned, and financial policies weakened. Since 1994 real GDP has been growing moderately, in the 4–5 percent range.

The long-run growth of the Dominican economy has been modest by international standards. Over the past thirty years, real output has expanded by an average of 5 percent annually. Given the rapidly growing population, this represents real growth of about 2 percent in per capita GDP. Such a rate of growth, while reasonable, is not sufficient to propel the economy to higher absolute or relative plateaus of development within a reasonably short time frame, much less to reduce the incidence and level of poverty. With a per capita output of U.S. $1,492 in 1995, the Dominican Republic ranks among the world's low-middle-income countries. At the historical growth rate of about 2 percent, it would take more than thirty years for the Dominican Republic to double its 1995 per capita income level.

The social sectors in the Dominican Republic have long suffered from neglect, inadequate funding, and mismanagement. Public spending has tended to gravitate toward high-profile projects, often chosen for political reasons rather than for yielding high social returns. For example, in 1994, 35 percent of the total education budget was spent to construct new schools, even though observers agree that the most pressing needs of the public schools system are increased teacher compensation and training and adequate materials and facilities for existing schools. While primary education spending is quite progressive, a high percentage (30 percent) of the government subsidy to universities benefits only the wealthiest 20 percent of the population. Inadequate resources and misplaced priorities in the Dominican education system are manifested in high dropout rates; the primary school completion rate is one of the lowest in the world. In the web model, the Dominican Republic's score in the education vector is below both the world and the regional averages.

Government expenditures on public health as a percentage of GDP were lower than on education, averaging 2 percent in the 1990s. This is low by developing country standards and is one of the lowest levels of health spending in the Caribbean and in the world. As in education, insufficient resources have led to an acute shortage of public health care services. While the government has opted to provide widespread health care, quality is poor and there are serious problems with service delivery. The approximately 5,000 doctors in the nation's Social Security Health Care System average only 1.9 appointments per day. Most devote the majority of their time to private hospitals or private practices because of the poor compensation they receive in the public system. Public hospitals suffer severe shortages of essential hospital equipment and basic materials and supplies, such as bed sheets, syringes, and medicines. In general, health indicators have improved over the past ten years in the Dominican Republic, but overall standards remain below those of many countries in Latin America. The initiatives with the greatest impact have been preventive measures and programs directed at vulnerable groups, including mothers and children, especially those living in remote rural regions.

Since achieving independence, first from Spain in 1821 and then from Haiti in 1844, the Dominican Republic has endured a history of dictatorship, political assassination, and conflict. President Joaquin Balaguer ruled the country for twenty-two years of the thirty years between 1966 and 1996. The 1996 elections put Leonel Fernandez and his Dominican Liberation Party at the head of a coalition government. There is no clear linkage between democratization and economic and social development in the Dominican Republic. However, it is likely that public discontent with widespread poverty and the lack of economic opportunity has strengthened the citizens' determination to give another party a chance to improve the situation. As its democratic institutions mature, constituent groups in the Dominican Republic are expected to become more vocal in their demands for increased public spending on essential social services.

Highly Challenged Nations

This typology contains countries at the lowest levels of development. They are typically characterized by ongoing political strife or civil war, totalitarian political regimes, and the absence of law and order. Their governments are unable or unwilling to provide even the most basic social services or infrastructure. The extent of economic instability is sufficient to preclude normal financial and real market functions. Productive private investment remains low, and employment opportunities are very limited. Their poor political and economic conditions often isolate these nations from international trade, investment, and finance.

With some exceptions, highly challenged countries tend to score below the world average in all the categories analyzed in this study. Poverty is widespread, and social performance is abysmal, with rampant disease, lack of access to health and education services, poor sanitation, and generally dismal standards of living. Such countries pose the greatest challenge to development practitioners.

Rwanda is presented as an example of a highly challenged nation. Others that fall into this category include Burundi, Cameroon, Cambodia, Haiti, and Malawi.

Rwanda.[11] This small, densely populated, resource-poor, landlocked country in Central Africa has been beset for decades by chronic poverty and ethnic conflict between the Tutsi and Hutu peoples. Years of tribal violence came to a head in April 1994, when an airplane carrying the presidents of Rwanda and Burundi was shot down under suspicious circumstances, killing both. In retaliation for the assassination of the ethnic Hutu president, Rwanda's Hutu extremists, supported by the government-controlled army, set out to exterminate the Tutsi population as well as moderate leaders within their own ranks. An estimated 500,000 people were killed in the violence. The Rwandese Patriotic Front (RPF), composed mainly of Tutsis, responded by ousting the government and driving the Hutu militia groups and the army out of the country. Nearly 2 million Hutus were forced from their homes and sought refuge in neighboring Congo, Burundi, and Tanzania.

A new government dominated by the RPF was formed in July 1994 following the Arusha accords. Although the fighting has stopped, nearly 1.7 million Rwandese remain in refugee camps because they are afraid to return to their homeland. The Rwandese government and the international community continue efforts to aid and facilitate the return of the refugees.

Even before the outbreak of violence in 1994, Rwanda was among the poorest nations in Africa. The economy was predominantly rural, with 95 percent of the population deriving their livelihood from subsistence agriculture. The civil war has had devastating effects on the economy. Real GDP declined by nearly one-half in 1994;

it has recovered partially since that time. In 1995 agricultural and industrial output were still at only 67 percent and 40 percent of prewar levels, respectively. Rwanda's once promising tourism sector also collapsed as a result of the fighting. Foreign assistance amounted to 172.5 percent of imports, equivalent to U.S. $56 per capita, in 1995. External debt outstanding was equivalent to U.S. $1 billion at the end of 1995, almost 80 percent of Rwanda's GDP. Scheduled debt obligations represent nearly half of exports of goods and nonfactor services.

Rwanda has not always had poor development performance. During the 1960s and 1970s, the country experienced relatively high rates of economic growth (5 percent a year on average) owing to political stability, prudent economic and fiscal management, high coffee prices, and high levels of external assistance. This generated budget surpluses and large external reserves. The Rwandan government invested heavily in infrastructure, improving roads, telecommunications, and air transport facilities, as well as social conditions. Until the mid-1980s, Rwanda was able to meet the food needs of its growing population.

The economic situation began to deteriorate in the 1980s as coffee prices fell, arable land became more scarce, and public spending grew less efficient. Between 1979 and 1990, the Rwandese franc was allowed to appreciate in real terms, even though terms of trade were deteriorating. The sharp fall in world coffee prices in 1987 precipitated the currency's decline. The government responded to the fall in world coffee prices by increasing controls over the economy rather than adjusting to the external environment and maintaining compet-

[11]See World Bank (1995b, 1996a, 1996b).

itiveness. In 1990, with the aid of the World Bank and the International Monetary Fund, the Rwandan government embarked on an economic reform program to stabilize the economy and enhance competitiveness, improve resource allocation, and lay the policy framework for sustainable growth and poverty reduction. The ambitious program was ultimately derailed by the events of 1994.

Rwanda's social indicators, once above sub-Saharan African averages, began to deteriorate significantly in the late 1980s. In 1992 life expectancy was only forty-nine years, and health conditions were continuing to spiral downward. Maternal mortality remains high because of the high incidence of pregnancy, insufficient maternal care, and increasing malnutrition. An estimated 20 percent of newborns are underweight. The 1991 Demographic and Health Survey shows that 45 percent of Rwandan children suffer from chronic malnutrition, which has contributed to an increased infant mortality rate. Other evidence indicates a high prevalence of parasitic infestation and diarrhea.

Rwanda is among the countries most badly affected by the AIDS epidemic. A survey in 1986, relatively early in the history of the disease, estimated HIV infection rates in urban areas at 18 percent for the general population and 30 percent for adults between the ages of twenty-six and forty. The problem continues to intensify. As many as 30 percent of pregnant women attending prenatal clinics in Kigali are HIV positive, and 90 percent of all deaths among women of childbearing age in urban areas are caused by AIDS. Rwanda has over 60,000 AIDS orphans.

Before the civil war, primary school enrollment was only 65 percent in Rwanda, and the proportion continues to decline. The problem is compounded by the low transition rate from primary to secondary education (8 percent). It is nearly impossible for the average poor household to afford to send all of its children to primary school. And with restrictions on labor mobility and the low transition rate to secondary school, parents see little advantage in sending their children to primary school.

Agricultural productivity has not been able to keep up with population growth. As a results, the periodic famines have become increasingly frequent and the well-being of the population is highly vulnerable to slight changes in prices and weather. The rapid population growth and very high population density have led to dramatic deforestation, as people attempt to create more arable land and settle on very steep hilltops. Additional environmental problems include dangerous landslides caused by settlement on overly steep slopes and respiratory illnesses resulting from poor ventilation and indoor cooking fires.

Chapter 6

COUNTRY WEBS

his chapter presents development web scores and accompanying analysis for 100 countries. Initially, 108 countries were rated under the web model. However, owing to the lack of data and information, it is not possible to compute meaningful vector scores and construct development webs for eight countries: Bahrain, Bhutan, Cyprus, Iraq, Sudan, Swaziland, Syria, and the United Arab Emirates.

Countries are listed alphabetically below. For each country, a table indicates its scores on the six development progress vectors, along with those of its region or grouping. Web diagrams depict several sets of vector scores: the country's scores, the highest scores achieved by any country for each vector, the maximum achievable score (100 for each vector), and world average scores. In this way individual countries can be benchmarked against a range of standards: region or grouping, best practice, and world average.

Each country's development web is accompanied by a discussion of its conditions and how they are related to its vector scores. For brevity, the discussion is divided into three substantive sections: "economic development" covers the economic performance and competitive foundations vectors; "social development and the environment" addresses performance in the

health, education, and environment vectors; and the third section is devoted to the democracy and freedom vector.

A wide range of sources have contributed to the descriptive assessments. Information on the economic development of individual countries is drawn primarily from the following (see the reference list at the end of the book for details): Asian Development Bank, *Asian Development Outlook 1995 and 1996*; Economist Intelligence Unit, *EIU Country Reports*; and World Bank, *Adjustment in Africa: Lessons from Country Case Studies, The East Asian Miracle: Economic Growth and Public Policy*, and *Trends in Developing Economies*.

Sources for the descriptions of social developments include Organization for Economic Cooperation and Development (OECD), *Education at a Glance: OECD Indicators* and *The Reform of Health Care Systems: A Review of Seventeen OECD Countries*; Pan American Health Organization, *Health Conditions in the Americas;* and World Bank, *Trends in Developing Economies*.

Discussions of environmental conditions are primarily drawn from World Bank, *Trends in Developing Economies;* and World Resources Institute, *1994 Information Please Environmental Almanac*.

Descriptions of political conditions, levels

of freedom, and civil liberties are drawn primarily from *Freedom in the World: Annual Survey of Political Rights and Civil Liberties*, published by Freedom House.

Several important points should be kept in mind regarding individual country scores and descriptions of performance. The vector scores do not encompass all possible factors that might influence a nation's achievement in a given area. For example, economic performance can be affected by geographic location, and health conditions depend in part on the prevalence of infectious disease. Competitiveness can hinge in part on the degree to which economic activities are carried out by private firms as opposed to state-owned enterprises. In some cases important determinants are not quantifiable, while in others, comparative data simply do not exist for a large number of countries.

Vector scores are meant to provide a measure of overall performance in each functional area, and on balance the scores achieve that end. Nevertheless, national leaders and development practitioners should recognize that high scores do not suggest that all is necessarily well in a given area.

Every country faces problems and challenges in each economic, social, and political sphere. Conversely, low scores do not indicate an absence of positive developments in that domain.

The country descriptions seek not only to describe the primary reasons for web score performance, but also to provide additional information on domestic conditions, developments, and the factors at work in each vector. Hence the descriptive sections may sound more "positive" or "negative" than would seem warranted by the web scores themselves. To a certain extent this is due to the fact that many sources deal with factors not explicitly scored or tend to focus on problems rather than achievements.

It is hoped that the country web scores and descriptions will be used in the manner in which the model is intended, not to assign acclaim or disapproval for national performance, but rather to offer an objective benchmark and especially to point out areas of development requiring more concerted action and progress. In this way the development web model can be applied as an analytical tool to support development initiatives.

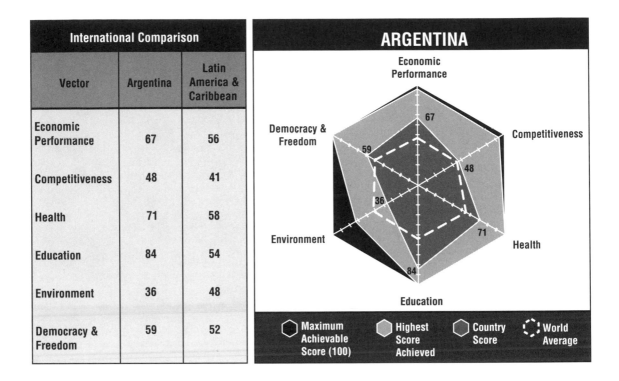

International Comparison		
Vector	Argentina	Latin America & Caribbean
Economic Performance	67	56
Competitiveness	48	41
Health	71	58
Education	84	54
Environment	36	48
Democracy & Freedom	59	52

ARGENTINA

Economic Performance

Competitiveness

Health

Education

Environment

Democracy & Freedom

67 59 48 36 71 84

○ Maximum Achievable Score (100) ○ Highest Score Achieved ○ Country Score ⬡ World Average

ARGENTINA

Economic Development. Once among the world's most prosperous economies, Argentina has experienced slow and sometimes negative economic growth for over four decades, since the 1940s. Throughout the 1970s long-term growth declined sharply, and in the second half of the 1980s Argentina suffered its longest economic stagnation of the century.

Since 1991 the government has sustained structural adjustment reforms that have progressively improved economic foundations. The Law of Convertibility, enacted in April 1991, established a bold framework for maintaining convertibility of the domestic currency with the U.S. dollar. Since then economic stability and competitiveness have improved, with tight monetary discipline to contain inflation. Argentina achieved an impressive average annual rate of GDP growth of 6.7 percent from 1990 to 1994.

Argentina scores 67 on Economic Performance, higher than the regional average of 56. On Competitiveness its score is hurt by the triple-digit average inflation rate over 1984–94 as well as by its relatively low exports-to-GDP ratio. The country scores 48 on Competitiveness, compared with an average of 41 in Latin America and the Caribbean.

Argentina

Social Development and the Environment. Public services such as health, education, and social services, in which the state has traditionally played a leading role, have steadily deteriorated during the extended period of economic stagnation and decline. Public sector financing of social services has eroded since 1982 as a result of economic instability, inflation, and the adjustment measures of the 1980s. Economic, political, and institutional changes have led to an increase in poverty, a drop in "formal" industrial employment, increasing losses in the efficiency, effectiveness, and equity of public spending on social needs, and a reduction in the coverage and quality of public services. The shortage of housing in urban areas, especially around Buenos Aires, has given rise to shantytowns, which raise health and other social risks.

Argentina scores 71 on Health, which is higher than the regional average but falls short of scores achieved by several Latin American countries that have lower levels of per capita income, including Chile, Uruguay, Costa Rica, and Cuba. On Education Argentina receives a score of 84, the highest in the region.

The heavy concentration of population and industrial activities in urban centers, especially around Buenos Aires, has led to acute problems of air and water pollution and solid waste disposal. Increased use of pesticides and fertilizers in farming areas has also polluted rivers. Over 25 percent of the urban population and over 80 percent of the rural population do not have access to safe water. Argentina scores 36 on Environment, below the regional average of 48.

Democracy and Freedom. Argentina is a democracy in which citizens have the right to change their government. However, democratic institutions have been challenged by President Carlos Menem's attempts to suspend the constitution and rule by decree. The judiciary has not earned the trust of Argentinean citizens in upholding the law and bringing about justice. Journalists critical of the government are sometimes targets of harassment and intimidation by security forces. Argentina scores 59 on Democracy and Freedom, compared with a regional average of 52.

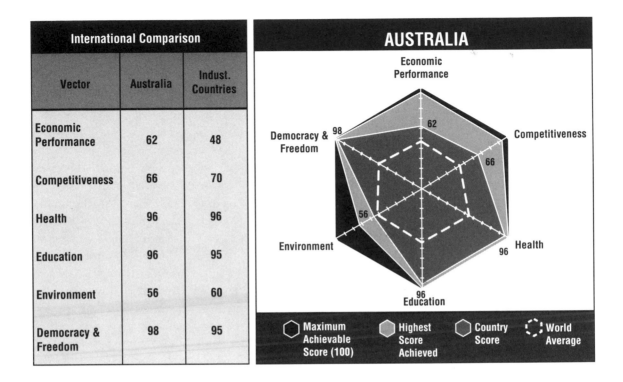

International Comparison		
Vector	Australia	Indust. Countries
Economic Performance	62	48
Competitiveness	66	70
Health	96	96
Education	96	95
Environment	56	60
Democracy & Freedom	98	95

AUSTRALIA

Economic Development. Australia has a relatively prosperous capitalist economy, with a per capita GNP comparable to that of the western European countries. Rich in natural resources, Australia is a major exporter of agricultural products, minerals, metals, and fossil fuels. Of the top twenty-five exports (by value) in 1995, twenty-one were primary products. Because of its dependence on the export of primary products, the economy is subject to big swings as prices and demand in the world market fluctuate.

During the 1990s, Australian policymakers have begun a major transition away from an economic structure dominated by commodity sales, import substitution, and protectionism. Import tariffs have been reduced significantly and many government-owned enterprises have been privatized or deregulated, including airlines, natural gas, water, electricity, and telecommunications. Airports and ports have also been privatized, and the state-owned railroad has recently been offered for sale to the public.

Australia scores 62 on Economic Performance, compared with the industrialized country average of 48, boosted by a healthy 3.4 percent GDP growth rate as well as an impressive 7.6 percent export growth rate between 1990 and 1994. Its score of 66 on Competitiveness is just below the industrialized country average.

Social Development and the Environment. Australia is a highly literate society where education is compulsory between the ages of six and fifteen years. Education policy emphasizes equality in the provision of resources within the public system and of assistance to low-income students in private schools. About three-quarters of all students complete the final (twelfth) year of secondary education. Over the past ten years, the number of students enrolled in higher education has increased 63 percent, while the number undertaking postgraduate studies has increased 178 percent. Australia's Education score of 96 is above the industrialized country average.

Australia's health indicators are comparable to those of other OECD members. In 1984 Australia implemented a universal health program, known as medicare, that provides access to free hospital care and to medical care and prescription medicines at reasonable prices. The program has caused a major shift in funding sources for health care and a marked change in the government's role in public health financing. On Health Australia scores 96, which is the industrialized country average.

Australia's environmental problems are mainly related to land degradation and the protection of endangered species. Overgrazing, destruction of native vegetation, and urbanization have resulted in salinization and erosion. Many unique plants, mammals, birds, and fish are at risk of extinction, primarily because of the loss of natural habitats. Industrial activities have also caused high levels of greenhouse gas emissions. Australia scores 56 on Environment, just below the industrialized country average of 60.

Democracy and Freedom. Australia is an established democracy where fundamental freedoms are guaranteed by law and respected in practice. The judiciary is fully independent of the executive branch. Major outstanding issues mostly relate to the indigenous population, including land rights and the continued disparity in social well-being between native and nonnative groups. Australia receives a score of 98 on Democracy and Freedom, above the industrialized country average of 95.

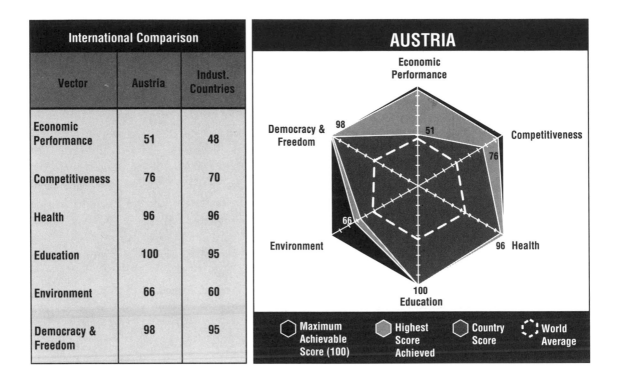

International Comparison		
Vector	Austria	Indust. Countries
Economic Performance	51	48
Competitiveness	76	70
Health	96	96
Education	100	95
Environment	66	60
Democracy & Freedom	98	95

AUSTRIA

Economic Performance

98 Democracy & Freedom   51   Competitiveness
                                76

66 Environment   96 Health

100 Education

⬡ Maximum Achievable Score (100) ⬡ Highest Score Achieved ⬡ Country Score ⬡ World Average

AUSTRIA

Economic Development. Austria boasts a prosperous and stable economy. A sizable proportion of industry is still in the hands of the state, but a privatization program is under way. Thanks to an excellent endowment of raw materials, a technically skilled work force, and strong links to German firms, Austria has occupied specialized niches in European industry and services (tourism, banking) as well as agriculture. Following the fall of communism in eastern Europe and German unification, exports to Germany have risen sharply and exports to eastern Europe have also increased.

Austria's economic problems include an aging population, the high level of state subsidies, and the struggle to keep welfare benefits within budget capabilities. Economic growth has been fairly slow in the 1990s, with real GDP growing at only 1.6 percent per year over 1990–94. In the competitiveness vector Austria receives high scores in the areas of saving, exports, and credit ratings. However, it has less than half as many scientists and engineers per million persons as Germany, the United States, Japan, Finland, or Norway.

Austria scores 51 on Economic Performance and 76 on Competitiveness, just above the averages for industrialized countries.

Social Development and the Environment. Austria has an excellent education system and scores 100 in the education vector. Attendance at the extensive network of state institutions is free, and the government provides family allowances and free transportation to students up to the age of twenty-seven, as well as direct grants, talent scholarships, subsidies for study abroad, and subsidized health insurance for students. In 1993 the total expenditure on education represented 5.3 percent of GDP. Adult illiteracy is minimal, and more than 40 percent of the population goes on to higher education.

Health care services are provided by both state and private institutions, financed chiefly from public funds. Central to Austria's health care system is a compulsory social insurance scheme, which provides health coverage for 99 percent of the population. Overall health indicators are very good. Infant mortality is only 6 per 1,000 live births, and life expectancy has risen to seventy-seven years. Austria's Health score of 96 is in line with the industrialized country average.

Forests cover about 38 percent of Austria's territory, and one of the country's chief environmental problems is forest degradation, including severe defoliation caused by a combination of air and soil pollution. Industry has recycled raw materials since 1973, and municipalities are now beginning to recycle solid waste. Austria receives a score of 66 on Environment, above the average for industrialized countries.

Democracy and Freedom. Austria is an established democracy; voting is compulsory in some provinces. Fundamental rights are guaranteed by the constitution and protected in practice. A notable exception is the restriction placed on Nazi organizations, which are illegal. Freedom of expression is respected, with the exception of publicly denying the Holocaust and justifying Nazi crimes. In other aspects the media are generally free. Austria scores 98 on Democracy and Freedom, just above the industrialized country average of 95.

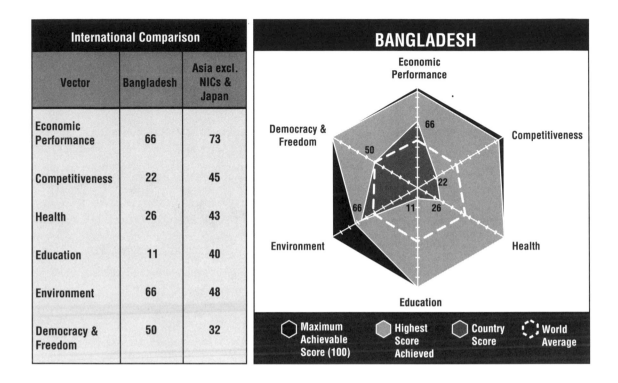

International Comparison		
Vector	Bangladesh	Asia excl. NICs & Japan
Economic Performance	66	73
Competitiveness	22	45
Health	26	43
Education	11	40
Environment	66	48
Democracy & Freedom	50	32

BANGLADESH

Economic Development. Bangladesh is one of the poorest countries in the world, with a per capita income of U.S. $240 in 1995. It has limited natural resources and a population density three times that of India or China. Rapid population growth has strained its economic resources. The country is also highly vulnerable to weather shocks, including cyclones and floods.

Bangladesh has made important strides in improving its economic foundation and performance in the past decade. Since 1991 the country has implemented a structural adjustment program (financed by the International Monetary Fund) aimed at stimulating private sector growth, improving fiscal and monetary management, reforming public enterprises, and liberalizing the trade regime. Bangladesh achieved a healthy annual GDP growth of 4.2 percent and an impressive export growth of 11.7 percent from 1990 to 1994. Bangladesh scores 66 on Economic Performance and 22 on Competitiveness, in both cases below the Asia average.

Social Development and the Environment. The overriding goal in terms of social development in Bangladesh is the alleviation of poverty. Since independence in 1971, the country's population has increased by some 45 million, severely hampering poverty alleviation efforts. Rapid population growth has greatly increased the number of rural, landless households and of the urban poor and has stretched social services.

Literacy, health, and nutrition indicators, although still low, have shown impressive gains over the past two decades. There have also been sustained improvements in infant mortality rates, life expectancy, and gross primary school enrollment rates. However, the adult literacy rate is among the lowest in the world, and primary and secondary enrollment rates remain significantly lower than for countries at similar income levels. Programs to expand and improve the quality of primary education are being implemented, many funded by donor agencies. There has also been a rapid expansion of funding for girls' education. Bangladesh receives 26 on Health, much lower than the Asia average of 52. It scores 11 on Education, the lowest in Asia after Bhutan and Pakistan.

Environmental problems in Bangladesh are mostly related to water, whether too plentiful, too scarce, or too polluted. Serious and recurring flooding in the coastal areas has killed or displaced thousands of people in recent years. Deforestation in the Himalayas has aggravated floods in the wet season and reduced water supply in the dry season. Many Bangladeshis lack access to potable water. Since most of its water-related environmental problems are ignored by the web model, Bangladesh receives a relatively high score of 66 on Environment.

Democracy and Freedom. While the citizens of Bangladesh have the democratic means to change their government, political processes such as rallies and elections are frequently disrupted by violence. The rule of law is weak, and law enforcement groups and the military are often suspected of rights violation. The torture of suspects and the abuse of prisoners by the police are serious problems. The safety of journalists who criticize the government, the military establishment, or fundamentalists is often threatened.

Women are discriminated against in many aspects of society, including health care, education, and employment. Domestic violence against women, largely related to dowry disputes, is common. While religions other than Islam are allowed to practice freely, there is some tension with the Hindu minority. Bangladesh scores 50 on Democracy and Freedom, which is the world average.

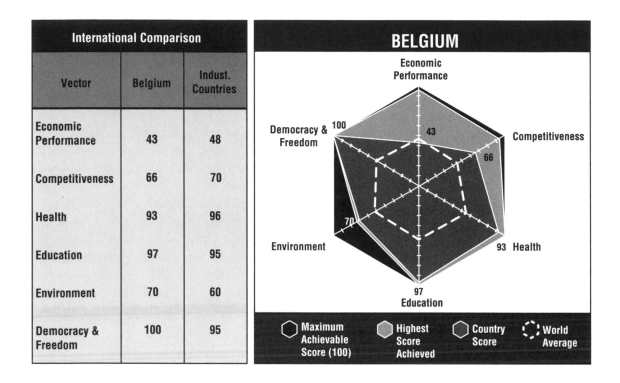

International Comparison		
Vector	Belgium	Indust. Countries
Economic Performance	43	48
Competitiveness	66	70
Health	93	96
Education	97	95
Environment	70	60
Democracy & Freedom	100	95

BELGIUM

Economic Performance — Competitiveness — Health — Education — Environment — Democracy & Freedom

100 — 43 — 66 — 93 — 97 — 70

Maximum Achievable Score (100) · Highest Score Achieved · Country Score · World Average

BELGIUM

Economic Development. This relatively small, private enterprise–oriented economy has capitalized on its central geographic location, highly developed transport network, and diversified industrial and commercial base. Industry is concentrated in the northern part of the country. With few natural resources, Belgium imports most of its essential raw materials. The Belgian economy is highly dependent on international trade. In 1994 export goods and nonfactor services represented 69 percent of GDP, the highest level among industrialized countries.

During the 1990s, the Belgian economy has been marked by slow growth, with real GDP growing by only 0.9 percent a year over 1990–94. Growth rates in gross domestic investment were negative over this period, averaging –1.7 percent annually. In the competitiveness foundation vector, gross domestic saving is high, standing at 23 percent of GDP in 1994. Belgium scores 43 on Economic Performance, just below the average for industrialized countries. On Competitiveness it scores 66, also below the industrialized country average, mainly because of its persistent budget deficit, which ran at 6.4 percent of GDP in 1991–94.

Social Development and the Environment. Belgium is a highly educated society, with free compulsory schooling for twelve years. Higher education is subject to payment and registration fees. Since 1990 there has been a marked increase in the number of students enrolled in higher education. Belgium's Education score of 97 is higher than the average among industrialized countries. Its Health score of 93 is slightly below the industrial country average, mainly because of its relatively low rates of child immunization.

The major environmental problems are related to pollution from industrial activities. Fines for polluting are so low that many companies would rather pay them than treat their effluents adequately. Belgium is also the home of a number of the smokestack industries that contribute to Europe's air pollution. Belgium scores 70 in the environment vector, a relatively high score compared with the industrialized country average of 60, mainly because of the low reported levels of per capita emission of other greenhouse gases.

Democracy and Freedom. Governments are democratically elected in Belgium; nonvoters can be fined. Each language group (that is, Dutch, French, and German) is granted considerable autonomy within its own region. Most fundamental freedoms are guaranteed by law and respected in practice. Belgium scores a perfect 100 on Democracy and Freedom.

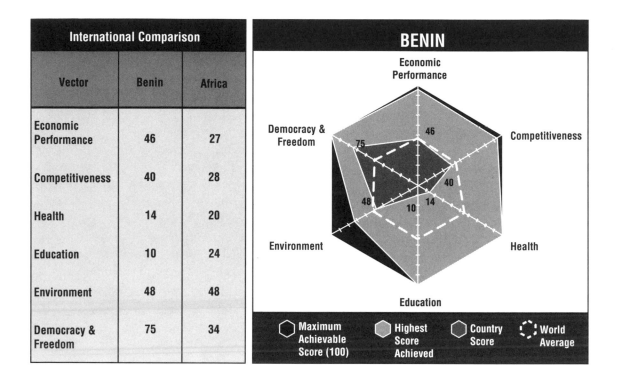

International Comparison		
Vector	Benin	Africa
Economic Performance	46	27
Competitiveness	40	28
Health	14	20
Education	10	24
Environment	48	48
Democracy & Freedom	75	34

BENIN

Economic Performance

Democracy & Freedom

Competitiveness

Environment

Health

Education

Maximum Achievable Score (100) Highest Score Achieved Country Score World Average

BENIN

Economic Development. Benin, a small country with a population of 5 million, is highly dependent on its primary commodities and tertiary activities. Cotton is a major contributor to GDP and is the largest export commodity. The government's socialist economic policies since the mid-1970s plunged the country into nearly two decades of economic stagnation and decline. Between 1980 and 1993, GDP per capita fell at a rate of 0.4 percent per year. In 1989 Benin embarked on a new, market-led reform program, which was renewed for 1991–93. These reforms aimed at improving fiscal and monetary discipline, privatizing state-owned enterprises, reducing price controls, liberalizing the trade regime, and reorienting public expenditure toward essential social services. The government also undertook a comprehensive tax reform program that simplified tax rates and reduced corporate income taxes.

Benin receives scores of 46 on Economic Performance and 40 on Competitiveness, which compare favorably with the Africa averages of 27 and 28, respectively.

Social Development and the Environment. Despite poor social indicators, the adjustment program has brought about some improvements in living standards. Higher cotton production and producer prices have raised rural incomes. The reorientation of government expenditure to health, education, rural development, and infrastructure has helped to reduce poverty and improve the living conditions of the poor. However, the high fertility rate (an average of seven births per woman) and high population growth rate (3.1 percent) will continue to challenge poverty reduction efforts. Benin scores 14 on Health and 10 on Education, below the Africa averages of 20 and 24, respectively.

In recent years widespread drought, population pressure, poor land management, and forest fires have seriously degraded extensive areas of Benin, especially in the north. The rate of deforestation in the 1980s was progressing at three times the average for Africa. Illegal hunting threatens to exterminate some important protected species. Limited access to safe drinking water and inadequate sanitation services, especially in the rural areas, are major causes of disease. Benin receives a score of 48 on Environment, which is the average for Africa.

Democracy and Freedom. Benin held its first free, multiparty election in 1991. Most fundamental freedoms are guaranteed in the constitution and respected in practice. The local press operates with considerable freedom, and foreign periodicals circulate freely. The judiciary is generally considered independent, although inadequate staffing resources have limited its efficiency. Workers' rights to organize and join unions, strike, and bargain collectively are respected. Benin receives a score of 75 on Democracy and Freedom, more than twice the Africa average.

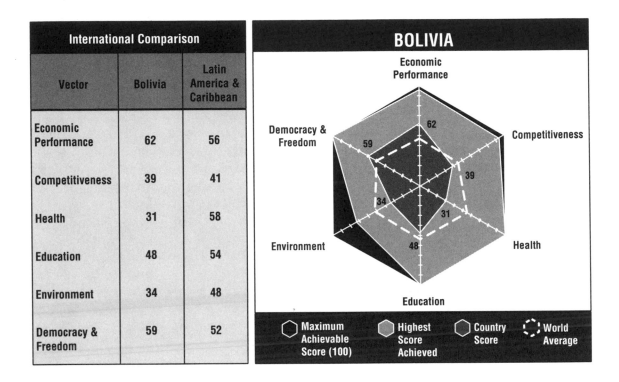

International Comparison		
Vector	Bolivia	Latin America & Caribbean
Economic Performance	62	56
Competitiveness	39	41
Health	31	58
Education	48	54
Environment	34	48
Democracy & Freedom	59	52

BOLIVIA

Economic Development. With estimated per capita income of U.S. $800 in 1995, Bolivia is one of the poorest countries in Latin America. In the face of a mounting economic crisis and rapidly deteriorating economic and social conditions, the government implemented a series of stabilization measures beginning in 1985 and succeeded in bringing about modest improvements in the 1990s. Comprehensive reform programs cover all economic sectors, including the financial sector, public enterprises, trade procedures, financial systems, the regulatory and legal frameworks, and social sectors. While the exploitation of Bolivia's rich mineral resources has been dominated by public enterprises, private sector participation has been encouraged and is now increasing.

Bolivia scores 62 on Economic Performance, above the regional average of 56, because of its favorable growth rates in GDP, exports, and domestic investment between 1990 and 1994. Bolivia receives a score of 39 on Competitiveness, indicating that competitiveness foundations are still weak.

Social Development and the Environment. While social conditions have improved since the late 1980s, an estimated 70 percent of the country's population continue to live in poverty. Poverty is especially acute in rural areas. Bolivia's health indicators are among the worst in the region. In recent years the government has placed increased emphasis on social sector development, poverty alleviation through community involvement in essential services, and investment in human development. The economic stabilization program has also helped to improve the relative position of the poor. Bolivia scores 31 on Health, the second lowest score in Latin America and the Caribbean, after Haiti. On Education it scores 48, just below the regional average of 54.

Deforestation is a major environmental concern in Bolivia. Indiscriminate clearing, inefficient use of land, and poorly planned road construction may soon deplete the eastern lowlands of valuable resources. Water pollution threatens public health. Pollutants discharged by industry and from illegal cocaine production are contaminating irrigation and drinking water. Only a quarter of the urban population and 30 percent of the rural population in Bolivia have access to safe water. Bolivia scores 34 on Environment, which is lower than the regional average.

Democracy and Freedom. Bolivian citizens can change their government through democratic elections. The constitution protects fundamental freedoms, including those of expression, religion, and the right to organize political parties, civic groups, and labor unions. The judiciary has been weakened by corruption and the influence of drug traffickers. In recent years there have been increasing reports of torture, brutality, and abuse committed by domestic law enforcement agencies. Bolivia scores 59 on Democracy and Freedom.

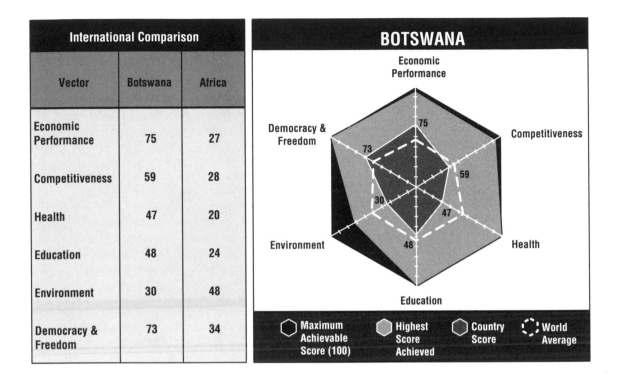

International Comparison		
Vector	Botswana	Africa
Economic Performance	75	27
Competitiveness	59	28
Health	47	20
Education	48	24
Environment	30	48
Democracy & Freedom	73	34

BOTSWANA

Economic Performance

Democracy & Freedom

Competitiveness

Environment

Health

Education

Maximum Achievable Score (100) Highest Score Achieved Country Score World Average

BOTSWANA

Economic Development. Botswana is one of the most successful economies in sub-Saharan Africa, owing to its open and market-oriented economic policies and prudent macroeconomic and fiscal management. In 1995 its per capita income reached U.S. $2,800, placing it ahead of Russia, Poland, Venezuela, and Turkey. Over 1984–94, per capita GDP grew at an impressive annual rate of 6.6 percent. The country is blessed with vast mineral resources—in particular, diamonds—which account for a significant portion of total exports and government revenues.

In recent years Botswana's central bank has used monetary tools effectively to discourage consumption, control inflation, and stabilize government revenues in the face of export booms. The government has maintained a fiscal surplus, averaging 11 percent of GDP over 1990–93. Botswana scores 75 on Economic Performance, one of the highest scores in Africa. On Competitiveness it receives a score of 59, which is the highest score attained by any African country.

Social Development and the Environment. As one of the richest countries in sub-Saharan Africa, Botswana has some of the best social indicators in the region, ranging from life

GLOBAL Benchmarks

expectancy and child mortality to primary school enrollment and completion rates. However, the fertility rate remains high, at 4.7 children per woman. Botswana scores 47 on Health and 48 on Education, the highest and second highest scores, respectively, in sub-Saharan Africa.

Overgrazing is one of the most serious environmental problems, threatening to degrade over half of the country's land area by early next century. Industrial development has led to problems of air and water pollution, as well as solid wastes in urban areas. Reported per capita levels of greenhouse gas emissions are high. Botswana receives a score of 30 on Environment, the lowest in Africa.

Democracy and Freedom. Botswana gained independence from Britain in 1966 and has since been ruled by elected governments. It is considered one of Africa's freest countries. The country has maintained a good human rights record. Rights concerns are mainly related to the treatment of its Baswara minority and inequality for women. While unions exist, the rights to strike and to bargain for wages are restricted. Botswana scores 73 on Democracy and Freedom, more than twice the Africa average of 34.

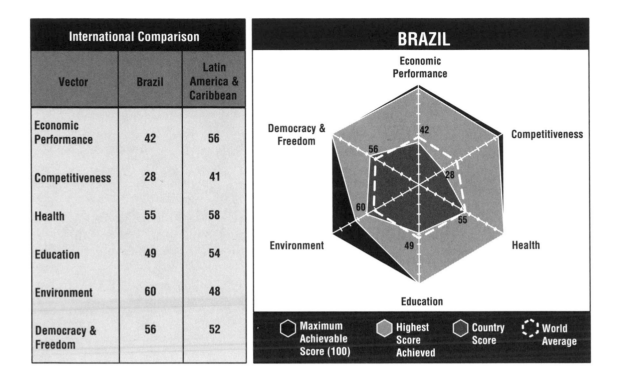

International Comparison		
Vector	Brazil	Latin America & Caribbean
Economic Performance	42	56
Competitiveness	28	41
Health	55	58
Education	49	54
Environment	60	48
Democracy & Freedom	56	52

BRAZIL

Economic Development. In the late 1960s Brazil was hailed as a "miracle economy," blessed with double-digit growth rates and rapid economic transformation, financed largely by foreign loan capital. Since 1980, however, its economic performance has been poor, considering its potential: growth has been slow and income distribution has worsened. Real per capita income actually declined throughout the 1980s. The problems were mainly triggered by the oil shocks caused by the Organization of Petroleum Exporting Countries, increases in real interest rates, the debt crisis (which affected most Latin American countries in the 1980s), and sharp cutbacks in Brazil's access to foreign loan and investment capital, combined with domestic problems such as inadequate public finance management and high inflation.

The government that came into power in March 1990 undertook significant structural reforms, including trade liberalization, deregulation, and privatization. In recent years the country has been put back on a modest growth path, with GDP growing at an average rate of just over 2 percent and exports rising at 9 percent between 1990 and 1994. Brazil scores 42 on Economic Performance and 28 on Competitiveness, low scores compared with the regional averages and higher only than those for Haiti, Guyana, Nicaragua, and Cuba.

Social Development and the Environment. Brazil's political and economic situation is reflected in its social conditions. Unemployment rates have remained high, at 12–14 percent of the work force, and a 1992 study showed that the mean monthly income of an average worker in metropolitan São Paulo had been halved since 1985. The economic downturn has also increased the incidence of poverty, which is estimated at about 45 percent of the population.

Despite financial crises, Brazil's government maintained a constant level of spending on social goods and services between 1984 and 1994. Infant mortality fell steadily during the 1980s. Nearly one-third of Brazil's adult population is illiterate. Brazil scores 55 on Health and 49 on Education, both slightly below the average for Latin America and the Caribbean.

Deforestation is a serious environmental problem, resulting in the loss of millions of acres of tropical forest every year. Cutting and burning accelerated during the mid-1980s but are now being brought under control. Brazil scores 60 on Environment, a relatively high score owing to the reportedly high percentage of the population with access to safe water. However, water pollution remains a problem in some localized areas, exacerbated by the dumping of untreated sewage and industrial wastes.

Democracy and Freedom. Brazilian citizens can change their government in democratic elections. The constitution guarantees most fundamental freedoms. However, in recent years, deteriorating police discipline and escalating drug-related violence have encouraged crime and a climate of impunity. Brazil's police force has a reputation for violence and corruption, and the military police are routinely accused of human rights violations. The current climate of insecurity is aggravated by a weak judiciary, which is overwhelmed by the lack of resources and vulnerable to corruption. Forced prostitution, domestic violence, and the presence of street children and violence against them are serious social problems. Brazil scores 56 on Democracy and Freedom.

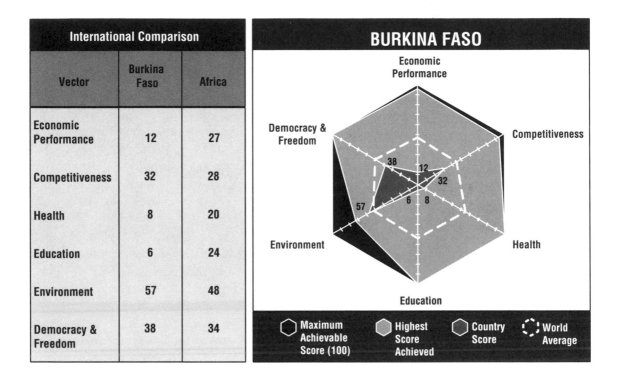

International Comparison		
Vector	Burkina Faso	Africa
Economic Performance	12	27
Competitiveness	32	28
Health	8	20
Education	6	24
Environment	57	48
Democracy & Freedom	38	34

BURKINA FASO

Economic Performance
Democracy & Freedom
Competitiveness
38 12
32
57 6 8
Environment
Health
Education

○ Maximum Achievable Score (100) ○ Highest Score Achieved ○ Country Score ⟡ World Average

BURKINA FASO

Economic Development. Burkina Faso, with a per capita income of U.S. $230 in 1995, is one of the poorest countries in the world. It is poorly endowed with natural resources, has extremely limited rainfall, and has no coastal access. The majority of its population is engaged in agricultural activities, both crops and livestock. Burkina Faso is a member of the West African Communauté Financière Africaine (CFA) zone, which devalued its currency against the French franc in 1994.

A population growth rate of almost 3 percent per year is creating severe pressure on already marginal land resources in Burkina Faso. The main development challenge is to reduce poverty and improve living standards and social conditions through accelerated economic growth and investment. Burkina Faso scores 12 on Economic Performance, about half the Africa average, and 32 on Competitiveness, just above the Africa average.

Social Development and the Environment. Burkina Faso's high population growth rate has made reducing poverty and improving social conditions a serious challenge. The country's social indicators are among the worst in the world, ranging from school enrollment to life expectancy and access to clean drinking

Burkina Faso

water. High child and infant mortality rates are caused by widespread contagious disease and unhygienic conditions. The most pressing health problem is the proliferation of AIDS; an estimated 7 percent of the adult population is infected with HIV. The government has developed a health strategy that focuses on decentralizing activities to fifty-three health districts, each covering a population of about 200,000. Burkina Faso scores 8 on Health and 6 on Education, among the lowest scores in Africa.

Despite poor agricultural conditions, Burkina Faso is primarily an agricultural economy. However, the lack of rainfall, population pressure, overfarming, and overgrazing have contributed to land degradation over an increasing area. Burkina Faso scores 57 on Environment, a relatively high score among African countries, mainly as a result of low levels of emission of carbon dioxide and other greenhouse gases.

Democracy and Freedom. The constitutional rights of citizens of Burkina Faso to change their government through multiparty elections have not been realized in practice. Recent presidential and legislative elections were not considered free and open. However, the country has made some democratic gains in recent years, mainly reflected in its freer and more independent media. The judiciary is independent, but effectiveness is constrained by the lack of resources and training. Traditional courts operate in many rural villages, and their ruling often discriminates against women. Female genital mutilation remains common despite a government campaign against the practice. Burkina Faso scores 38 on Democracy and Freedom, just above the regional average of 34.

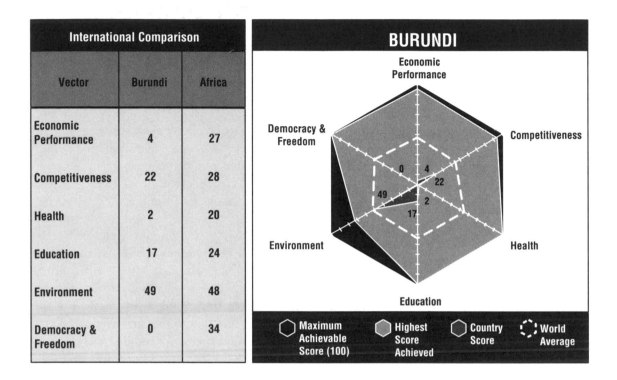

International Comparison		
Vector	Burundi	Africa
Economic Performance	4	27
Competitiveness	22	28
Health	2	20
Education	17	24
Environment	49	48
Democracy & Freedom	0	34

BURUNDI

- Maximum Achievable Score (100)
- Highest Score Achieved
- Country Score
- World Average

BURUNDI

Economic Development. Burundi is a small, landlocked, low-income country, with a per capita GDP only of U.S. $160 in 1994. Population is growing at the rapid annual rate of 3 percent, putting severe strain on a country where population density is already ten times the average for sub-Saharan Africa. Agriculture contributes above half of GDP, employs 90 percent of the population, and accounts for 80 percent of export earnings. Coffee is the dominant crop.

Over the period 1989–93, the government undertook a series of economic reforms, including introducing a new labor code, banking law,

and central bank legislation. It has promoted exports through a free-trade zone created in 1992 and has provided export incentives such as duty drawbacks, transportation subsidies for exporters, and liberalization of foreign exchange accounts for exporters. Political instability and ethnic strife have caused major economic disruptions in Burundi over the past several years. GDP fell an average of 1.4 percent per year over 1990–94, when the economic situation was made worse by disinvestment and declining exports. Burundi scores 4 on Economic Performance, one of the lowest in the world. It scores 22 on Competitiveness, just below the Africa average.

Burundi

Social Development and the Environment. As one of its poorest nations, Burundi has some of the worst social indicators in the world. The economic disruption caused by the ethnic strife has worsened social conditions and increased poverty. Nearly 16 percent of the population is displaced, dispersed, or in refugee camps. Since 1993 social indicators have also deteriorated, including immunization rates, malnutrition, and primary school enrollment. Official estimates indicate that between 15 percent and 20 percent of the urban population could be infected with HIV. Burundi receives a score of 2 on Health and 17 on Education.

High population density and rapid population growth have led to very intensive land use, including both grazing and farming. The need for new farmland and for fuel wood threatens to deforest the entire country in the near future. Soil degradation has been exacerbated by the displacement of population as people have moved to more marginal land for subsistence farming. Burundi receives a score of 49 on Environment, just above the average for Africa.

Democracy and Freedom. Burundi's citizens elected the president and legislature freely in the country's first multiparty election in 1993. Sporadic waves of ethnic violence have plagued Burundi since it gained independence from Belgium in 1962. Violence escalated in 1994 as the anti-Tutsi genocide in Rwanda spilled over the border to Burundi. The country has traditionally maintained a delicate balance among its ethnic groups. However, the murder of President Melchior Ndadaye in October 1993 and his political successor Cyprien Ntaryamira in April 1994 plunged the country into political chaos. A coalition government was formed in 1995 under a power-sharing arrangement among the major parties. Civilian control over the military is weak. Journalists often refrain from critical reporting for fear of violent reprisals. The judiciary is barely functioning and is widely distrusted as an institution to uphold justice. Burundi receives a score of 0 on Democracy and Freedom.

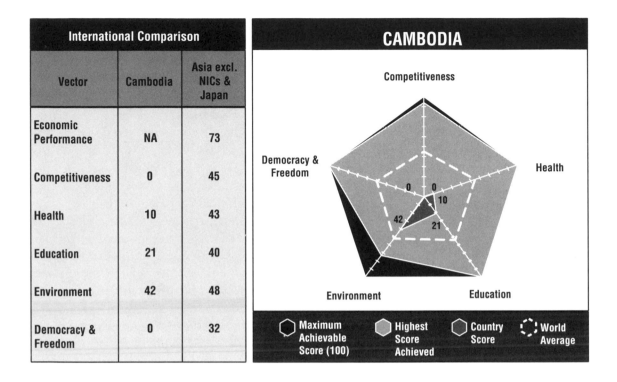

International Comparison		
Vector	Cambodia	Asia excl. NICs & Japan
Economic Performance	NA	73
Competitiveness	0	45
Health	10	43
Education	21	40
Environment	42	48
Democracy & Freedom	0	32

CAMBODIA

Competitiveness

Democracy & Freedom · Health

0 0
10
42 · 21

Environment · Education

◯ Maximum Achievable Score (100) ⬡ Highest Score Achieved ⬡ Country Score ⬡ World Average

CAMBODIA

Economic Development. Cambodia is one of the poorest nations in the world. For decades its economy has been ravaged by war and internal strife. Its per capita income in 1995, at U.S. $260, was lower than it had been in the 1960s. In the past several years relative stability has allowed the economy to grow at moderate rates, albeit from a low base, improving living conditions. It is estimated that over 1991–95, the economy grew at an annual average rate of 6 percent. Cambodia has also achieved some important success in macroeconomic stabilization, including raising government revenues and bringing down triple-digit inflation to less

than 10 percent in 1995. Due to the lack of data, Cambodia cannot be scored on Economic Performance. On Competitiveness it is the only country in Asia to score 0.

Social Development and the Environment. Occupation by Vietnam and the recent civil war have disrupted all aspects of life in Cambodia for over two decades. The country's social indicators are among the worst in Asia. Maternal, infant, and child mortality rates are very high, reflecting the inadequacy of health services, particularly in rural areas. Cambodia's population is also among Asia's most illiterate, due in large part to the flight and massacre of many of its educated citizens during the Khmer Rouge's reign (April 1975–December 1978). Cambodia scores 10 on Health, the second lowest in Asia after Bhutan. It receives a score of 21 on Education, ranking above Bangladesh, Bhutan, and Pakistan in Asia.

The environmental damage caused by the Cambodian civil war will be felt for years to come. The most pressing environmental problems facing the country are inadequate supply of safe water, deforestation and loss of habitats from bombing during the Vietnam war, and soil erosion caused by the shifting cultivation practiced by its farmers. Cambodia receives a score of 42 on Environment, mainly because of low reported levels of air pollution; otherwise, this is a relatively high score considering the extent of its environmental problems.

Democracy and Freedom. In May 1993 Cambodian citizens voted in the country's freest election, after two decades of turmoil that included the bloody rule of the Khmer Rouge, invasion and occupation by Vietnam, civil war, and border insurgencies. However, Cambodia's transition to democracy continues to be rocky. The government routinely cracks down on opposition groups and the media. Under a power-sharing agreement reached in 1993, Prince Norodom Ranariddh became the First Prime Minister and Hun Sen, leader of the former Communist Cambodian People's Party, became Second Prime Minister. However, this arrangement collapsed when Hun Sen ousted Ranariddh during a violent coup in July 1997. Civil liberties are severely restricted in Cambodia. Expressing political opinions against the government can bring harassment and attacks. There is no independent judiciary in practice. Large number of Cambodians still live in areas controlled by the Khmer Rouge, which refused to participate in the 1993 elections or to demobilize its army. Both the national army and Khmer Rouge soldiers terrorize civilians with banditry, extortion, and other abuses, especially in the countryside. Cambodia scored 0 in Democracy and Freedom.

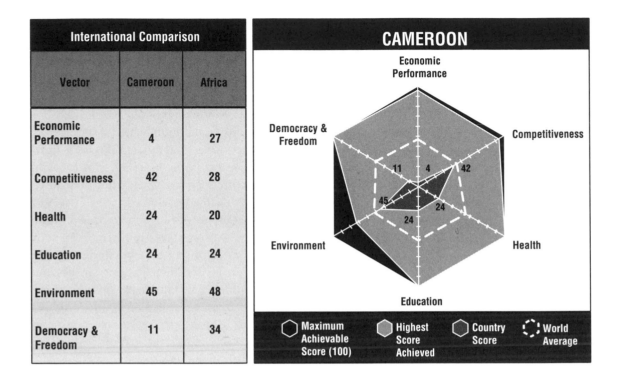

International Comparison		
Vector	Cameroon	Africa
Economic Performance	4	27
Competitiveness	42	28
Health	24	20
Education	24	24
Environment	45	48
Democracy & Freedom	11	34

CAMEROON

Economic Performance

Democracy & Freedom

Competitiveness

Environment

Health

Education

Maximum Achievable Score (100) · Highest Score Achieved · Country Score · World Average

CAMEROON

Economic Development. For over two decades, from 1960 to 1985, Cameroon was a high-growth economy, with real growth averaging 7 percent per year. The country possesses abundant natural resources, a diversified production base, and a well-developed infrastructure. Until 1978 agriculture was the main source of export earnings. Soon afterward, oil production and revenues began to drive national economic growth. As with many oil-exporting countries, however, the money generated by the oil bonanza was not wisely invested. The petroleum boom led to higher expenditures on the civil service, wage inflation, subsidies to ineffi-

cient public enterprises, and investments in several capital-intensive projects with low or negative rates of return.

After 1986, Cameroon suffered a series of external shocks as world prices for oil, coffee, and cocoa, its primary commodities, fell. In 1988 the government adopted a structural adjustment program supported by the IMF. However, the economic reforms were not followed through because of the lack of government commitment amid political instability. Output declined by 4.1 percent annually from 1990 to 1994. GDP per capita fell even more sharply, by 6.9 percent per year, during this period. Cameroon receives a score of 4 on Economic Performance, one of the lowest in the world. It scores 42 on Competitiveness, above the Africa average.

Social Development and the Environment. While Cameroon continues to compare favorably with its sub-Saharan neighbors on social conditions, a decade of economic decline has taken its toll. Poverty has been increased and spread to the urban areas. Malnutrition is widespread, particularly among rural women and children. These conditions, combined with very high rates of adult female illiteracy and poor health care delivery, have resulted in high maternal and infant mortality. AIDS is also emerging as a serious health risk. Cameroon scores 24 on Health and 24 on Education, in line with the averages for Africa.

In recent years Cameroon's forests and wildlife have been increasingly threatened by commercial logging, deforestation, and poaching. Malaria remains the country's most critical health issue and is estimated to affect over 90 percent of the population. Cameroon scores 45 in Environment, which is comparable to the regional average.

Democracy and Freedom. The citizens of Cameroon do not live under a democratic regime. The 1992 legislative and presidential elections were riddled with fraud and irregularities. President Paul Biya continues to rule by decree. The legislature has little power in reality, and judiciary is dominated by the executive. The broadcast media are monopolized by the government. Current legislation authorizes prepublication censorship and allows the government to seize and ban articles that conflict with "the principles of public policy." Cameroon receives a score of 11 on Democracy and Freedom, well below the regional average of 34.

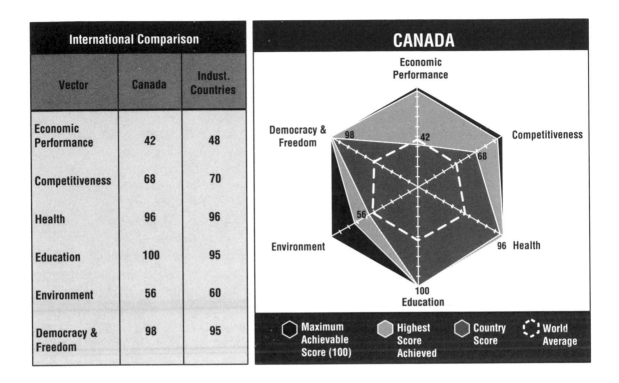

International Comparison		
Vector	Canada	Indust. Countries
Economic Performance	42	48
Competitiveness	68	70
Health	96	96
Education	100	95
Environment	56	60
Democracy & Freedom	98	95

CANADA

Economic Performance

Democracy & Freedom — 98 — 42

Competitiveness — 68

Environment — 56

Health — 96

Education — 100

Maximum Achievable Score (100) · Highest Score Achieved · Country Score · World Average

CANADA

Economic Development. As an affluent, high-technology, industrial society, Canada closely resembles the United States in its per capita output and market-oriented economic system. It has vast natural resources, including minerals, forests, petroleum, and natural gas. With its natural resources, skilled labor force, and modern production systems and infrastructure, Canada has excellent economic prospects.

After nearly a decade of sluggish growth, the economy in Canada has been gathering momentum in the early 1990s. Underlying this development has been the strength of the economy of its largest trading partner—the United States—and a decline in inflation that has allowed Canadian interest rates to fall. Canada is strong in the competitiveness vector, with high levels of saving, a relatively high level of exports, and a good sovereign bond rating. The only exception is the government budget deficit, which has averaged 3.7 percent of GDP over 1989–95.

Canada scores 42 on Economic Performance and 68 on Competitiveness, both very near the averages for the industrialized countries.

Social Development and the Environment. Canada has an excellent educational system. Schooling is compulsory through age sixteen.

Public education is provided free to all citizens and permanent residents through secondary school. Education is the responsibility of each of the country's ten provinces and two territories. Canada spends 7.4 percent of GDP on education, which is among the highest levels of spending in the industrialized world. Overall, Canada scores a perfect 100 on Education.

Canadians enjoy publicly funded universal health services. The 1980s was a decade of radical restructuring for the Canadian health care system, with shifts in priorities and the recognition of the need to contain costs without sacrificing quality. Canada's Health score of 96 is in line with the industrialized country average.

Canada's environmental problems are shared by many industrial countries. Much of Canada's acid rain originates from the United States. Metal smelting, energy generation, and emissions on both sides of the border have degraded part of Canada's forests. Canada scores 56 on Environment, below the industrialized country average mainly because of high reported levels of greenhouse gas emissions.

Democracy and Freedom. Canada has a strong tradition of democracy. The country has nearly 100 percent effective voter registration. The media are generally free, with the exception of the unevenly enforced "hate laws." Civil liberties are guaranteed in the Charter of Rights. There are some rights issues regarding land claims by native Indians, which have led to litigation and strained relations between these peoples and the government. Canada scores 98 on Democracy and Freedom, above the industrialized country average.

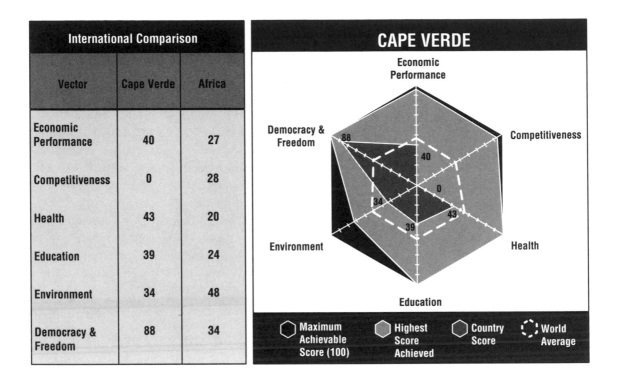

International Comparison		
Vector	Cape Verde	Africa
Economic Performance	40	27
Competitiveness	0	28
Health	43	20
Education	39	24
Environment	34	48
Democracy & Freedom	88	34

CAPE VERDE

Economic Development. Cape Verde is a small archipelago with little arable land. Prolonged cycles of drought aggravate a serious shortage of fresh water. Faced with austere living conditions and limited economic opportunities at home, Cape Verdeans have frequently emigrated. It is estimated that twice as many citizens of Cape Verde live abroad as at home. The close ties of expatriate Cape Verdeans with their homeland are evidenced in significant remittances, which averaged about 12 percent of GDP between 1990 and 1995.

Cape Verde has developed a reputation for sound management of macroeconomic condi-tions and public finances, responsible use of foreign aid for development and infrastructure, and good debt repayment. The country has also maintained healthy foreign exchange levels, and the balance of payments has usually been in equilibrium.

Cape Verde scores 40 on Economic Per-formance, well above Africa's average of 27. It receives 0 on Competitiveness, as data on most of the major indicators are not avail-able; the web score for Competitiveness does not reflect the country's improving condi-tions in economic policies and competitive-ness foundations.

Cape Verde

Social Development and the Environment. Cape Verde's social indicators are impressive relative to those of its sub-Saharan African neighbors. It has universal primary school enrollment, an adult literacy rate much higher than Africa's average, low rates of infant mortality and fertility, and an average life expectancy of sixty-five years. These achievements are the result of active grass-roots and nongovernmental organizations, donor involvement, and prudent allocation of public resources to social programs. Cape Verde scores 43 on Health, more than double the average for Africa. On Education the country scores 39, much higher than the Africa average of 24.

Centuries of intense land exploitation for fuel, construction materials, grazing, and agriculture have destroyed most of the natural vegetation in Cape Verde. The country now lacks natural water supplies and suffers from chronic drought and periodic famines. Cape Verde receives a score of 34 on Environment, below the Africa average of 48.

Democracy and Freedom. In 1991 Cape Verdeans held their first democratic legislative elections after sixteen years of single-party Marxist rule. The president and members of the National People's Assembly were elected through universal suffrage in free and fair voting. The judiciary is independent and efficient. The police force is accountable to the civilian government. Freedom of expression, of the press, and of assembly are guaranteed in law and respected in practice. Minority religious groups face no restrictions. Cape Verde scores 88 on Democracy and Freedom, one of the highest in Africa.

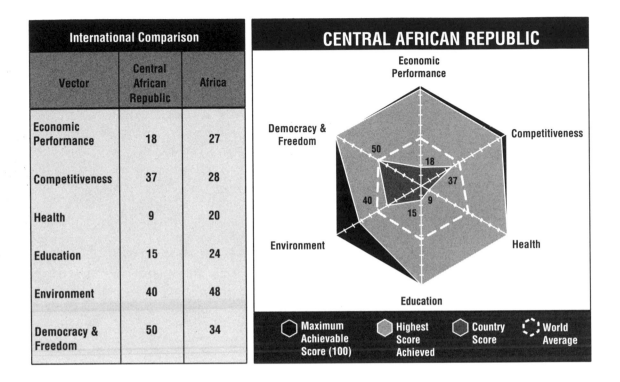

International Comparison		
Vector	Central African Republic	Africa
Economic Performance	18	27
Competitiveness	37	28
Health	9	20
Education	15	24
Environment	40	48
Democracy & Freedom	50	34

CENTRAL AFRICAN REPUBLIC

Economic Development. With a per capita income of only U.S. $330 in 1995, the Central African Republic is among the least developed countries in the world. Landlocked in the heart of Africa, it covers a vast but sparsely inhabited territory. The country's rich natural resources are mostly unexploited. Two-thirds of the population are subsistence farmers. About 60 percent of export earnings come from diamond mining. The major export crops are timber, coffee, and cotton.

Real per capita GDP fell during a decade of economic stagnation and decline in 1985–94. Investment growth declined at a rate of 9 per-

cent over 1990–94. In 1994 the republic and a group of CFA countries realigned parity with (that is, devalued against) the French franc. The boost in exchange rate competitiveness, as well as rising commodity prices, brought about significant improvements in the Central African Republic's economic indicators in 1995 and 1996. It scores 18 on Economic Performance owing to poor economic performance indicators for the early 1990s. It fares better on Competitiveness, scoring 37, which is much above the regional average of 28.

Social Development and the Environment. Poverty is pervasive in the Central African

Central African Republic

Republic, and social indicators are below the averages for Africa. Life expectancy, at forty-nine years, is among the lowest in Africa. Women are particularly socially disadvantaged and have less access to education and employment than men do. The incidence of contagious diseases, parasites, and malnutrition is very high. The spread of AIDS is especially alarming; the rate of increase in HIV infections is estimated at close to 6 percent throughout the 1990s. Illiteracy rates are also very high, estimated at 40 percent among those over fifteen years old. The Central African Republic receives a score of 9 on Health and 15 on Education, both below the averages for Africa.

Most of the country is covered with woodlands and hosts diverse wildlife. Overgrazing of cattle is exacerbating soil degradation. Poaching has taken a toll on the wildlife, particularly on the elephant. Inadequate access to safe drinking water remains a serious problem for both urban and rural populations. The Central African Republic scores 40 on Environment, below the Africa average.

Democracy and Freedom. In 1993 the citizens of the Central African Republic elected their government in open and democratic elections for the first time. A new constitution enacted in 1994 has increased judicial and legislative autonomy and guarantees a multiparty system. However, fundamental freedoms are still restricted. The broadcast media are dominated by the state, and freedom of assembly is restricted in practice. Reform of judiciary institutions continues to lag behind democratic transition, and the judicial system remains subject to political influence. Police brutality is reported by human rights groups. Women continue to face discrimination in many aspects of society. The Central African Republic receives a score of 50 on Democracy and Freedom, above the regional average of 34.

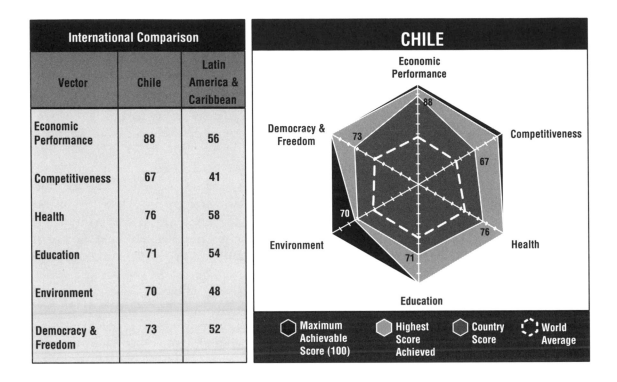

International Comparison		
Vector	Chile	Latin America & Caribbean
Economic Performance	88	56
Competitiveness	67	41
Health	76	58
Education	71	54
Environment	70	48
Democracy & Freedom	73	52

CHILE

Economic Development. Chile has one of the most stable and liberalized economies in Latin America. Since the mid-1980s Chile has sustained conservative fiscal and monetary policies, a relatively open economy, and strong debt management. In the 1980s and early 1990s, the privatization of pension funds and insurance companies helped deepen financial markets. The privatization of manufacturing and service companies, banks, and public utilities has encouraged investment and enhanced productivity and efficiency. Over this period, Chile had one of the highest growth rates in Latin America. Between 1990 and 1994, the Chilean economy posted impressive annual GDP growth of 7.5 percent, domestic investment growth of 13 percent, and export growth of 9 percent. Chilean companies and produce cooperatives have been highly successful in penetrating high-value niche markets in North America.

Chile scores 88 on Economic Performance, ranking in the top 19 of the 108 countries assessed by the web model. On Competitiveness it scores 67, much above the average of 41 for Latin America and the Caribbean.

Social Development and the Environment. Social developments in Chile have been impressive. Key social indicators, including the average life expectancy at birth, infant mortality rate, prevalence of malnutrition, educational attainment, and overall adult literacy, are closer to those of higher income economies than to those of the developing world. Chile has a long history of sustained, substantive investment in the social sectors. Since the early 1980s it has also made significant progress in the reduction of poverty. Chile scores 76 on Health and 71 on Education, among the highest scores attained by countries in Latin America and the Caribbean.

Forest products are one of Chile's major exports, and consequently the deforestation of natural forests is progressing rapidly. The country is also increasingly suffering from problems of industrial air and water pollution. Environmental policies exist, but enforcement is weak.

Chile scores 70 on Environment, a relatively high score, because of its low overall levels of greenhouse gas emissions.

Democracy and Freedom. After fifteen years of military rule, democracy was restored to Chile in 1988. Chilean citizens now can exercise their rights to change their government. Freedom of expression, freedom of media, and other civil liberties were restored by constitutional reforms in 1989. However, civilian control over the armed forces is still limited by the 1980 constitution installed under the Pinochet regime. There are reports of police abuses, but overall accountability to the civilian government is improving. Chile receives a score of 73 on Democracy and Freedom, high compared with a regional average of 52.

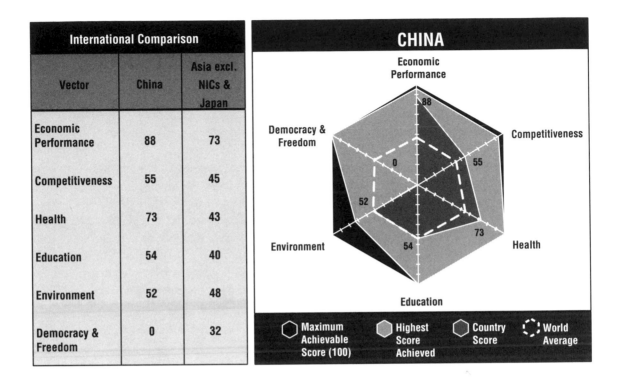

International Comparison		
Vector	China	Asia excl. NICs & Japan
Economic Performance	88	73
Competitiveness	55	45
Health	73	43
Education	54	40
Environment	52	48
Democracy & Freedom	0	32

CHINA

Economic Performance · Competitiveness · Health · Education · Environment · Democracy & Freedom

Maximum Achievable Score (100) · Highest Score Achieved · Country Score · World Average

CHINA

Economic Development. Since China began market-oriented reforms in 1978, the country's real GDP growth has averaged over 9 percent per year, the highest level in the world during this period. This remarkable achievement was the fruit of a series of key policy changes. First, the household responsibility system replaced the former commune system of agricultural production. This, accompanied by a partial liberalization of agricultural prices, provided incentives to increase agricultural production, consequently boosting rural incomes significantly. Second, the open-door policy toward trade and investment immediately encouraged

dramatic inflows of foreign investment, much of which was oriented toward export production. Exports grew at a rate of 12 percent in the 1980s and at 16 percent over 1990–94. Other key policy reforms included the introduction of special economic zones, tariff reductions, decreases in subsidies and transfers to state-owned companies, and the gradual introduction of private competition to state-owned enterprises.

China's economic performance has continued to be strong in the 1990s. From 1990 to 1994, GDP increased at a rate of 13 percent per year, and average gross domestic investment growth was 15 percent. China scores 88 on Economic Performance, ranking among the top ten nations in the world, and scores 55 on Competitiveness.

Social Development and the Environment. Since 1978 rapid economic growth has lifted over 100 million Chinese above the level of absolute poverty and improved social conditions for all. However, economic growth in the coastal areas, cities, and special economic zones have increased the rural-urban income disparity, drawing millions of rural workers to the cities as migrant workers.

For a country at its level of per capita income, China's social indicators are very strong, including life expectancy, maternal and infant mortality, and child malnutrition. It scores 73 on Health, higher than all Asian countries except the newly industrializing countries (NICs). On Education it scores 54, above the Asia average of 48. A legacy of the decades spent under the socialist system is that basic social services are available to a majority of the population. However, there are signs that the erosion of the commune system and the shrinking of the state social services sector have led to restricted access to and a decline in the quality of health care for the poor.

An emphasis on industrial development, combined with rapid urban population growth and inadequate pollution control over several decades, has created some serious environmental problems. Air pollution is severe in many cities, aggravated by the burning of coal to meet residential and industrial energy needs. More than one-third of China's rural population lacks access to safe water. China scores 52 on Environment.

Democracy and Freedom. Chinese citizens have no democratic means to change their government. The Chinese Communist Party wields ultimate power. There is no rule of law in practice. The judicial and penal systems do not respect due process rights; defendants are presumed guilty, and over 99 percent are convicted. Torture to extract confessions, the trial of dissidents as common criminals, and abuse in the prison system are common. A large number of dissidents languish in labor camps or under harsh prison conditions. Freedom of expression and association are severely restricted. All media are state controlled, and coverage must conform to government guidelines. Religious practices are limited to government-sanctioned "patriotic" churches. China's draconian one-child policy encourages the abortion of female fetuses and female infanticide. China scores 0 on Democracy and Freedom.

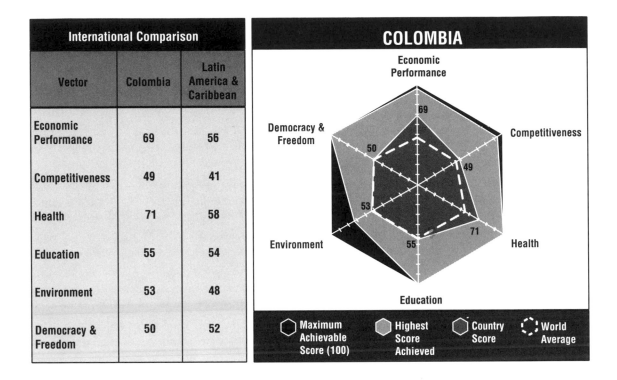

International Comparison		
Vector	Colombia	Latin America & Caribbean
Economic Performance	69	56
Competitiveness	49	41
Health	71	58
Education	55	54
Environment	53	48
Democracy & Freedom	50	52

COLOMBIA

Economic Performance — 69
Competitiveness — 49
Health — 71
Education — 55
Environment — 53
Democracy & Freedom — 50

Maximum Achievable Score (100) · Highest Score Achieved · Country Score · World Average

COLOMBIA

Economic Development. Colombia has enjoyed good economic growth and improvements in standards of living over the past three decades. Natural resources are plentiful, including agricultural land, water, energy (oil, natural gas, and coal), and minerals. Colombia's location also offers several advantages; it is close to North America and has ports on both the Atlantic and Pacific coasts. Rich physical resources, a literate and dependable work force, a robust private sector, and prudent macroeconomic management are major factors in Colombia's good economic record. Between 1990 and 1994, GDP grew at an average

annual rate of 4.3 percent, exports at 6 percent, and gross domestic investment at 21 percent. Colombia scores 69 on Economic Performance and 49 on Competitiveness, both much above the regional averages.

However, the growth of the illegal drug trade over the past twenty years has had serious economic, political, and social effects. The U.S. government's recent "decertification" of Colombia for inadequate efforts in halting the drug trade is expected to have an adverse impact on investor confidence, especially among foreign investors.

Social Development and the Environment. Solid

economic performance and a drop in population growth have facilitated substantial improvements in social conditions. Life expectancy at birth in 1995 was seventy years, compared with fifty-nine years in 1965. The adult literacy rate is close to 90 percent. However, poverty remains significant and there is inadequate access to health care and to safe drinking water in rural areas. Improving the living conditions of the poor remains a government priority, and Colombia is expected to further its gains in this area. Under the ambitious *Salto Social* programs (1994–98), the government hopes to generate more than 1.6 million jobs, increase access to primary education, expand water service, and extend health coverage to approximately 12 million poor people. Colombia scores 71 on Health and 55 on Education, both above average for Latin America and the Caribbean.

In recent years Colombia has experienced increasing deforestation, leading to the rapid dwindling of its massive timber resources. Large regions have been cleared of heavy vegetation for cattle raising, coffee production, and mining, causing soil erosion and land degradation. Colombia scores 53 on Environment.

Democracy and Freedom. Colombian citizens can elect their governments democratically. However, voter participation has been low, and there is widespread cynicism regarding the effectiveness of the political system, given the extensive corruption at all levels of government. Major drug cartels are believed to have influenced congressional reforms regarding the penal code and extradition. Civil liberties have been compromised by political and drug-related violence and the government's inability to protect its citizens, institutions, and the media from this violence. Homicide, mostly with political and drug-related motives, remains the principal cause of adult death in Colombia. Colombia scores 50 on Democracy and Freedom, below the regional average.

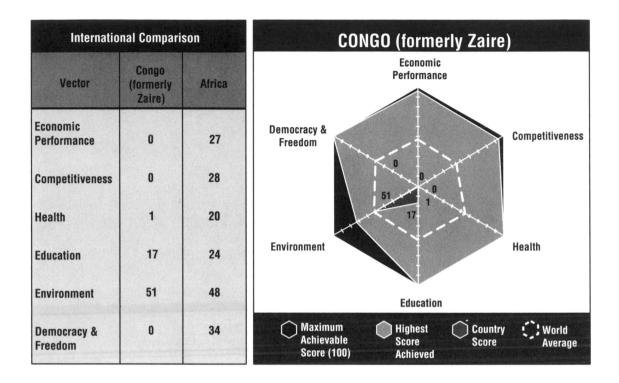

International Comparison		
Vector	Congo (formerly Zaire)	Africa
Economic Performance	0	27
Competitiveness	0	28
Health	1	20
Education	17	24
Environment	51	48
Democracy & Freedom	0	34

CONGO (formerly Zaire)

Economic Performance

Democracy & Freedom

Competitiveness

Environment

Health

Education

0 · 0 · 51 · 1 · 17

⬡ Maximum Achievable Score (100) ⬡ Highest Score Achieved ⬡ Country Score ⬡ World Average

CONGO

Economic Development. Congo (formerly Zaire) is endowed with a rich resource base, including the largest area of rain forest of any country in the world, fertile soils, ample rainfall, and varied mineral resources. Gold and diamond mining and petroleum extraction are the predominant economic activities. Since early 1990 political instability has been accompanied by declining production, investment, and fiscal mismanagement, plunging the country into a severe economic decline. Per capita GNP fell to U.S. $120 in 1995, half of the 1990 level, placing Congo among the lowest income countries worldwide. It modern econ-

omy, institutions, and human capital have suffered seriously and are rapidly eroding. The economic collapse accelerated during intensified civil strife in 1997. Structural reforms initiated by the Mobutu government in 1995 and 1996 took a back seat to the political crisis, and their impact on the economy has been minimal. Congo's dismal economic situation is reflected in scores of 0 on both Economic Performance and Competitiveness, owing to very weak indicators in all categories.

Social Development and the Environment. Congo's economic and political crises have accelerated the decline of social conditions. With the

GLOBAL Benchmarks

exception of limited humanitarian aid, financing for all social programs has been halted. There is evidence that Congo's mortality and health indicators, already among the lowest in the world, are growing worse. Contagious diseases have become more widespread as a result of inadequate preventive programs and medication. The rate of adult HIV infection is among the highest in the world. Already low primary school enrollment rates have fallen in recent years, and adult illiteracy is estimated at 33 percent. Congo receives a score of only 1 on Health. On Education it scores 17, below the Africa average of 24.

Water contamination is a major source of disease in Congo's urban areas. The discharge of untreated human waste has contaminated rivers. Poor management and limited resources for preservation has led to increasing deforestation and the loss of wildlife. Congo scores 51

on Environment, just above the Africa average of 48, primarily because of the low levels of greenhouse gas emissions associated with low levels of economic activity.

Democracy and Freedom. Citizens of Congo cannot change their government democratically; there are no freely elected representatives. The country was governed by President Mobutu Sese Seko for nearly thirty-two years, until he was ousted by rebel forces in early 1997. It remains to be seen whether the rebel leader, Laurent Kabila, will hold free and fair elections in 1999 as promised. There are allegations that Kabila's rebel forces have committed genocide against Rwandan refugees within Congo. Journalists have been intimidated, and judiciary independence under the new government is uncertain. Congo receives a score of 0 on Democracy and Freedom.

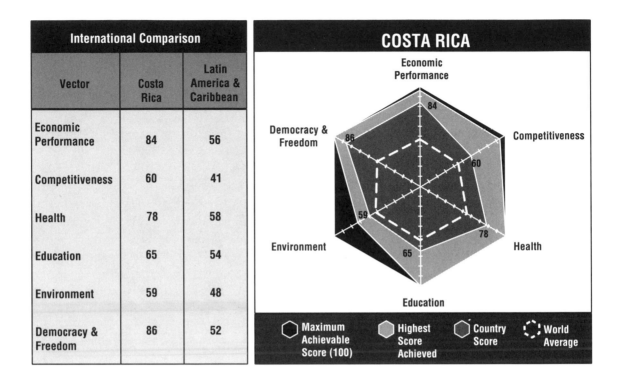

International Comparison		
Vector	Costa Rica	Latin America & Caribbean
Economic Performance	84	56
Competitiveness	60	41
Health	78	58
Education	65	54
Environment	59	48
Democracy & Freedom	86	52

COSTA RICA

Economic Performance

Competitiveness

Health

Education

Environment

Democracy & Freedom

Maximum Achievable Score (100) — Highest Score Achieved — Country Score — World Average

COSTA RICA

Economic Development. Costa Rica is one of the most stable and robust economies in Central America, with a per capita income of U.S. $2,590 in 1995. In the early 1980s its economic competitiveness was weakened by expansionary monetary policy and an overvalued exchange rate. However, by the middle to late 1980s, a series of structural adjustment and stabilization programs had succeeded in putting the economy back on track. From 1983 to 1995 the economy grew at a real annual rate of 5.4 percent. Both gross domestic investment and exports grew at an annual rate of 11 percent over 1990–94. Continuing reforms of the

public sector and the banking system are expected to fuel further economic growth. The government is also reforming the pension system to ensure an equitable and financially stable social security system. Costa Rica scores 84 on Economic Performance, the second highest score in Latin America and the Caribbean. On Competitiveness it scores 60, well above the regional average of 41.

Social Development and the Environment. Costa Rica's extensive social programs have helped to rank its social indicators among the best in Latin America. Life expectancy, infant and maternal mortality, and literacy rates are among the highest in the region. The level of human development is exceptional for a country of its level of per capita income. Although living conditions deteriorated substantially as a result of the economic crises of 1981–82, the economic recovery has since led to improvements.

Health conditions in Costa Rica have improved significantly since the 1970s. While little progress was made in the 1980s, traditional health indicators did not decline. Primary school enrollment is now almost universal. Costa Rica scores 78 on Health, ranking third in Latin America and the Caribbean, after Cuba and Uruguay. It scores 65 on Education, compared with a regional average of 54.

Costa Rica has developed one of the most ambitious conservation programs in the world and has established an extensive network of parks and nature preserves. Its major environmental problems are deforestation and soil erosion. Deforestation has been brought under better control in recent years with the development of forest plantation and agroforestry. Costa Rica scores 59 on Environment, much above the regional average of 48.

Democracy and Freedom. Costa Rica's long tradition of democracy dates back to 1899. The formation of a national army has been banned under the constitution since 1949. Citizens can elect their government through free and fair elections. Constitutional rights regarding freedom of speech and religion and the right to organize political parties are respected in practice. The judiciary is independent. There are occasional charges of human rights violation associated with the police. The press, radio, and television are generally free. Costa Rica scores 86 on Democracy and Freedom, the highest in Latin America and the Caribbean.

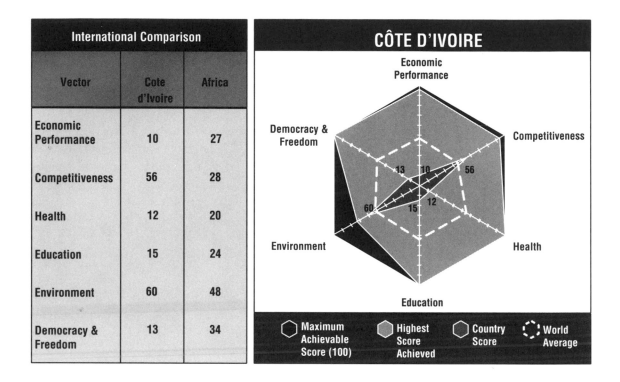

International Comparison		
Vector	Cote d'Ivoire	Africa
Economic Performance	10	27
Competitiveness	56	28
Health	12	20
Education	15	24
Environment	60	48
Democracy & Freedom	13	34

CÔTE D'IVOIRE

Maximum Achievable Score (100) · Highest Score Achieved · Country Score · World Average

CÔTE D'IVOIRE

Economic Development. Côte d'Ivoire enjoyed good economic growth in the 1960s and 1970s, when it was considered to be one of the most successful economies on the African continent. From 1980 to 1993, however, the economy grew by only 0.1 percent per year. Economic stagnation combined with a very high population growth rate of 3.5 percent per year has led to declines in the overall standard of living. By 1995 GNP per capita had fallen from over U.S. $1,000 in the 1970s to U.S. $610.

Some of Côte d'Ivoire's principal economic problems have been high external debt, unsustainable public finance deficits of up to 10 per-

cent of GDP in the 1980s, and public enterprise mismanagement. In addition, international prices for its chief export products, such as cocoa and coffee, have deteriorated sharply compared with the boom periods of 1972–74 and 1976–79. Côte d'Ivoire scores 10 on Economic Performance, well below the Africa average of 27. On Competitiveness it receives a relatively high score of 56, mainly as a result of a high saving rate, a low inflation rate, and a high ratio of exports to GDP.

Social Development and the Environment. The economic decline after 1987 caused a steady decline in per capita income as well as in social indicators. The incidence of poverty is increasing, particularly in the urban areas, in part because of the high urbanization rate, rising levels of unemployment, and a decline in real wages.

The education system continues to suffer from low enrollment, low completion rates, high repetition, and inefficient resource allocation. Primary education covers only an estimated 50 percent of school-aged children. Sixty percent of the population above the age of fifteen remains illiterate. Health care coverage reaches about 30 percent of the population and is severely inadequate in the face of severe population pressure and the high incidence of infectious diseases, in particular the rapid spread of AIDS. Infant mortality was at 90 of 1,000 live births in the early 1990s. Immunization is low relative to other nations at this income level. Côte d'Ivoire scores 12 on Health and 15 on Education, both below the average for Africa.

Côte d'Ivoire has suffered very high deforestation rates. The principal causes have been rapid population growth, shifting cultivation, logging, and forest clearance for agricultural uses. Inadequate restrictions on plantation expansion and land clearing have also have accelerated deforestation. Côte d'Ivoire receives a score of 60 on Environment, high compared with the Africa average, mainly because of good access to safe water and participation in major global environmental conventions.

Democracy and Freedom. Democratic rights were violated in Côte d'Ivoire's 1995 presidential and legislative elections, when the leading opposition candidate was prohibited from running, demonstrations were banned, and the media were intimidated. Journalists have been fined and imprisoned for "insulting the president" or "threatening public order." Freedom of association cannot be exercised in practice. Judiciary independence is undermined by the political appointment of judges; judges are not assured tenure. Legal provisions regarding due process are often ignored. Traditional courts prevail in many rural areas, especially in matters regarding the family. Côte d'Ivoire scores 13 on Democracy and Freedom, well below the Africa average of 34.

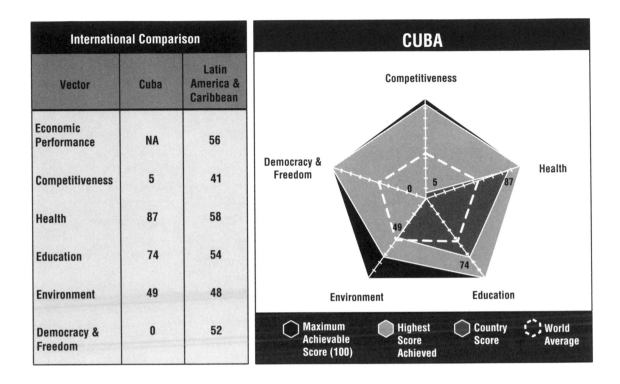

International Comparison		
Vector	Cuba	Latin America & Caribbean
Economic Performance	NA	56
Competitiveness	5	41
Health	87	58
Education	74	54
Environment	49	48
Democracy & Freedom	0	52

CUBA

Competitiveness

Democracy & Freedom

Health

0 5 87

49

74

Environment

Education

Maximum Achievable Score (100) · Highest Score Achieved · Country Score · World Average

CUBA

Economic Development. Since the collapse of the Soviet Union in 1989, the socialist-style command economy of Cuba has been hurt by the end of Soviet subsidies and their exclusive barter relationship. Because Cuba lacks established relations with most multilateral development agencies and the international financial community, only a very small amount of economic data on Cuba is available for international comparison. Cuba cannot be scored on Economic Performance, and its score of 5 on Competitiveness is probably biased downward.

Social Development and the Environment. Despite the serious economic difficulties, Cuba's health indicators continue to improve. This can be attributed to the capacity and effectiveness of the national health system, the health consciousness of the public, which considers its health care system one of the country's greatest social triumphs, and overall education levels. In addition, part of the Cuban government's social policy has been to maintain the supply of basic foods for the entire population. It ensures universal access to free education and medical care and guarantees temporary employment to any workers who are laid off. The government's efforts in protecting the most vulnerable groups of the population, including children, women, the elderly, and the sick, have helped to mitigate the social impact of the continuing economic crises. Illiteracy was eradicated in the 1970s, and 98 percent of children between ages six and fourteen are now enrolled in regular primary or secondary education. Cuba scores 87 on Health, the highest in Latin America and the Caribbean. On Education it receives a score of 74, the third highest in the region.

Deforestation is the principal environmental problem. Reforestation efforts are now underway to protect watersheds and prevent further soil erosion. Other environmental problems include inadequate treatment of solid wastes in urban areas and insufficient protection for the great variety of wildlife. Cuba scores 49 on Environment, in line with the average for Latin America and the Caribbean.

Democracy and Freedom. Cubans cannot change their government through democratic means. All political and civic organizations outside the Cuban Communist Party are illegal; political dissent is a punishable offense. The Cuban prison system holds a large number of political dissidents. The judiciary, the educational system, labor unions, professional organizations, and print and broadcast media are all controlled by the state. The government dominates most aspects of life. Cuban citizens are not free to choose their place of abode, their education, or their jobs. Attempting to leave the country without state permission is a punishable offense. Official discrimination against religious practices was lifted in 1992. Cuba scores 0 on Democracy and Freedom.

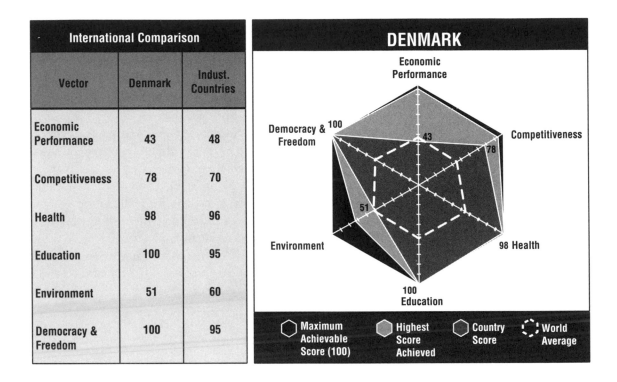

International Comparison		
Vector	Denmark	Indust. Countries
Economic Performance	43	48
Competitiveness	78	70
Health	98	96
Education	100	95
Environment	51	60
Democracy & Freedom	100	95

DENMARK

Economic Development. Denmark has been characterized by a high standard of living, a well-educated work force, and high-quality infrastructure. In 1994, with an average per capita income of U.S. $27,970, it ranked third in the world, after Switzerland and Japan. Over 1990–94, GDP growth was relatively slow, at 1.8 percent per year. Export growth has also been moderate, at only 2.7 percent. After joining the European Union in 1993, growth, investment, exports, and competitiveness all improved. Denmark scores 43 on Economic Performance, below the industrialized country average of 48.

On Competitiveness Denmark is generally strong, with high scores in saving, exports as a proportion of GDP, bond ratings, and inflation control. In addition, a relatively high percentage of the work force consists of scientists, engineers, and technicians. Denmark scores 78 on Competitiveness, ranking twelfth in the world.

Social Development and the Environment. Denmark's outstanding indicators earn a perfect score of 100 on Education. Education is compulsory for nine years, beginning at age seven, and mostly is publicly financed. Over half of Denmark's labor force holds an upper-secondary education qualification. Opening up the economy to greater international competition, especially within the European Union, has been associated with extensive initiatives to increase skill levels through education and training and to secure a better balance between supply and demand in specific skills and qualifications. The government is committed to achieving an upper-secondary completion rate of at least 90 percent by the year 2000.

For several decades the Danish health care system has been characterized by universal coverage, financing from general taxation, and public ownership and control of services. Health care is generally considered a public responsibility. All Danish citizens have equal and free access to almost all health care services, regardless of employment or financial or social status. Denmark scores 98 on Health, above the industrialized country average.

Like most other Western industrial societies, Denmark faces problems caused by hazardous wastes that were not properly disposed of. Per capita emissions of carbon dioxide and other greenhouse gases are high. Denmark scores 51 on Environment, below the industrialized country average.

Democracy and Freedom. Denmark is a strong and established democracy. The judiciary is independent, fair, and efficient. The media are mostly free, except for restrictions on broadcasts intended to incite racial hatred. All fundamental freedoms are guaranteed by law and respected in practice. Discrimination on the basis of gender, race, language, religion, or sexual orientation has been outlawed. Denmark receives a perfect score of 100 on Democracy and Freedom.

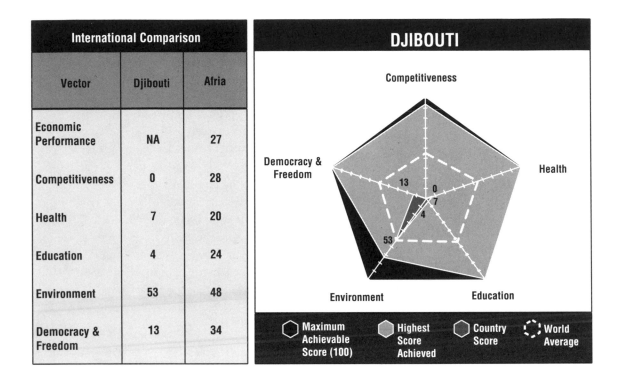

International Comparison		
Vector	Djibouti	Afria
Economic Performance	NA	27
Competitiveness	0	28
Health	7	20
Education	4	24
Environment	53	48
Democracy & Freedom	13	34

DJIBOUTI

Competitiveness

Democracy & Freedom

Health

Environment

Education

13   0   7   4   53

Maximum Achievable Score (100) Highest Score Achieved Country Score World Average

DJIBOUTI

Economic Development. Djibouti, a small city-state of only 23,200 square kilometers, occupies a strategic location in the Horn of Africa. It does not submit basic economic data to the World Bank or the IMF. World Bank estimates classify Djibouti as a low-income country, with per capita income below U.S. $725 in 1994.

The economy is highly fragile and dependent on external assistance. Agriculture and industry are both underdeveloped. The tertiary sector dominates, contributing 70 percent of GDP. Its mainstays are services provided to the local French military base and trade and transshipment with other countries. Djibouti is a regional trade center because of its port facilities, international railroad and airport, and private banking and telecommunications. Because of the lack of relevant data, Djibouti is not scored on Economic Performance. Its Competitiveness score of 0 is skewed downward, as data are lacking for most indicators.

Social Development and the Environment. Djibouti has a highly skewed income distribution. As in most other low-income countries in Africa, the level of social development in Djibouti is very low. Life expectancy at birth is only forty-nine years, infant and child mortality rates are among the highest in the world, and over half of the adult population is illiterate. Djibouti scores 7 on Health and 4 on Education, well below the averages for Africa.

Because of the high level of urbanization, Djibouti's major environmental problems are solid waste disposal and pollution by greenhouse gases. It scores 53 on Environment.

Democracy and Freedom. Djibouti does not have a democratic political system. President Hassan Gouled Aptidon has ruled the country since it gained independence from France in 1977. In both 1992 and 1993 elections were reportedly subject to fraud. Fundamental freedoms guaranteed by the constitution are mostly disregarded by the government in practice. The government routinely interferes with judiciary functions. Djibouti receives a score of 13 on Democracy and Freedom, well below the Africa average of 34.

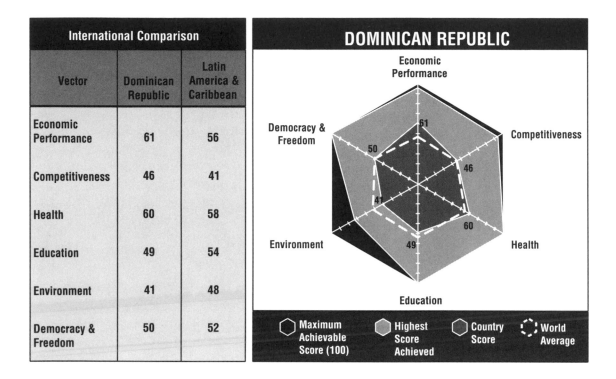

International Comparison		
Vector	Dominican Republic	Latin America & Caribbean
Economic Performance	61	56
Competitiveness	46	41
Health	60	58
Education	49	54
Environment	41	48
Democracy & Freedom	50	52

DOMINICAN REPUBLIC

Maximum Achievable Score (100) · Highest Score Achieved · Country Score · World Average

DOMINICAN REPUBLIC

Economic Development. With a population of 7.6 million, the Dominican Republic is one of the most densely populated countries in the Caribbean. Tariff protection of industry is relatively high, and key commodities are covered by price controls and import quotas. Despite recent reform efforts, the state continues to dominate the economy and owns a high proportion of manufacturing enterprises and banks and about half the arable land. Investment in infrastructure has been very low by regional standards. The state-owned power company is one of the least efficient in the world.

Nevertheless, substantial progress has been made in several areas. From 1989 to 1993, the country operated a highly successful foreign investment promotion program, attracting investment mainly to free-trade zones, where over 100,000 jobs were created. Tourism has been another flourishing segment of the economy, with steady growth in investment, employment, and foreign exchange earnings. The Dominican Republic scores 61 on Economic Performance and 46 on Competitiveness, both above the averages for Latin America and the Caribbean.

Social Development and the Environment. Over the past three decades the living conditions of

Dominican Republic

Dominicans have consistently improved. Life expectancy rose by fourteen years between 1960 and 1995, infant and child mortality declined by 60 percent, and illiteracy was halved. Nonetheless, the nation suffers from widespread poverty and highly unequal distribution of wealth. Economic stagnation, reductions in social spending, and the deterioration of basic services have exacerbated the problem. Over 1980–90, real per capita income declined 19 percent, while the average real minimum wage dropped 39 percent.

Compared with other countries at its level of development, the Dominican Republic lags in several social indicators, especially those relating to maternal and child health and education. Maternal mortality is among the highest in the region, and primary school completion rates are the lowest. Overall mortality rates and the incidence of malnutrition are particularly severe in the provinces along the Dominican-Haitian border. Insufficient investment in social infrastructure, especially water supply and sewage systems, has increased the prevalence of waterborne diseases. The Dominican Republic scores 60 on Health and 49 on Education.

Deforestation is a serious problem and has been aggravated by tax incentives for the clearing of land for crop production, tourism, and hydroelectric dams. An illegal charcoal and fuel wood market provides a high proportion of urban energy needs. The country also suffers from water shortages and inadequate access to potable water. Less than half of the rural population is served by a safe water supply. The Dominican Republic scores 41 on Environment, below the average for Latin American and the Caribbean.

Democracy and Freedom. Dominican citizens can change their government through democratic means. The 1996 election was generally viewed as fair and avoided the interparty clashes and violence that marked the 1995 election. Fundamental rights are guaranteed in the constitution and generally respected in practice. The judiciary is politicized and is weakened by corruption. Police brutality and arbitrary arrests by security forces raise continued concern among human rights groups. The Dominican Republic receives a score of 50 on Democracy and Freedom, just below the regional average of 52.

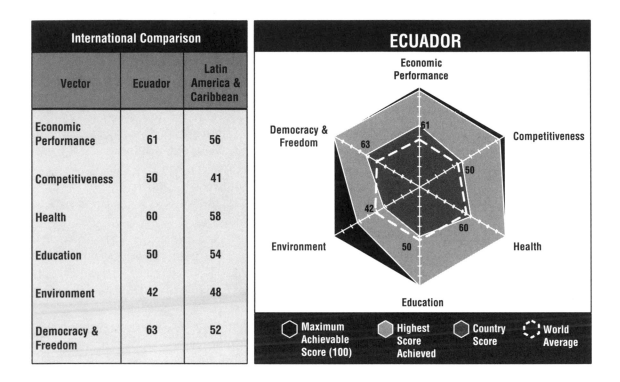

International Comparison		
Vector	Ecuador	Latin America & Caribbean
Economic Performance	61	56
Competitiveness	50	41
Health	60	58
Education	50	54
Environment	42	48
Democracy & Freedom	63	52

ECUADOR

Economic Development. Ecuador's economic performance has been disappointing since the onset of the debt crisis in 1982, when the country suffered a series of shocks, including declining oil prices. Despite several attempts at structural reform and stabilization in the 1980s, the inflation rate rose to 85 percent in 1985, real per capita incomes fell, and Ecuador stopped servicing its debts to commercial creditors. The government that took office in 1992 implemented a series of policy reform measures to modernize the economy and stimulate private sector growth. Prices of petroleum and electricity were allowed to rise to international levels,

expenditures in social services were reduced, and new laws were passed to facilitate privatization and capital markets reform. The stabilization and reform efforts initially yielded important results, including elimination of the public sector deficit and modest growth in GDP, investment, and exports. GDP growth averaged 3.5 percent in 1990–94. Ecuador scores 61 on Economic Performance and 50 on Competitiveness, outperforming the region in both categories.

Social Development and the Environment. Adjustment efforts have reduced the government's resources for the social sector: allocations for education and culture were halved between 1980 and 1991, and public expenditures in health also fell. An estimated 73 percent of the rural population is unable to read and write Spanish. The problem is particularly acute in areas with large concentrations of indigenous peoples with their own language. It is estimated that fewer than half of the children in poverty-stricken areas manage to finish primary school. Overall, social indicators in Ecuador are in line with regional averages. However, a wide disparity remains between child health and mortality rates in urban and rural areas. Government programs tend to be underfunded and fail to reach the poorest. Ecuador scores 50 on Education and 60 on Health, just above the averages for Latin America and the Caribbean.

Deforestation, if it continues unabated, threatens to destroy what remains of Ecuador's natural forests over the next several decades. Rapid population expansion has led to more intensive land use and overgrazing. Other significant environmental problems include inadequate water and sewage facilities in urban areas and contamination caused by improper mining practices. Ecuador scores 42 on Environment, lower than the regional average.

Democracy and Freedom. Ecuadoreans can elect their governments democratically. However, opinion polls and rising voter abstention suggest that the credibility of political institutions has declined significantly in recent years. There is evidence that drug traffickers have penetrated the political system through campaign funding, and the police, the military, and the judiciary through bribery. Ecuador scores 63 on Democracy and Freedom, compared with a regional average of 52.

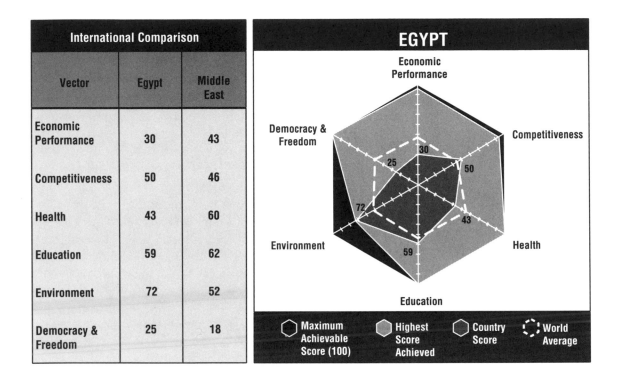

International Comparison		
Vector	Egypt	Middle East
Economic Performance	30	43
Competitiveness	50	46
Health	43	60
Education	59	62
Environment	72	52
Democracy & Freedom	25	18

EGYPT

Economic Development. Egypt has the largest population and the second largest economy in the Arab Middle East. Its government has long pursued a public sector–led, inward-looking development strategy, which emphasizes state ownership and central planning. As a result, public enterprises and economic entities account for one of the largest proportions of output and employment among developing countries. Almost half of the nation's GDP comes from the public sector, including 65 percent of all output in industry and mining. On the international side, Egypt remains heavily dependent on a few key exports (including petroleum and services such as tourism receipts), Suez Canal dues, remittances from Egyptian workers living abroad, and grants from international donors. Merchandise exports remain small and limited.

As a result of the structural adjustment and reform efforts that began in 1990, the Egyptian economy has undergone significant fiscal and monetary contraction, leading to sluggish growth in output, investment, and exports. It scores 30 on Economic Performance, well below the Middle East average of 43. It outperforms the region on Competitiveness, with a score of 50.

Social Development and the Environment. Social conditions in Egypt have improved significantly over the past thirty years. Between 1960 and 1995 life expectancy at birth rose from forty-one to sixty-two. However, indicators for child health, including child mortality and immunization rates, are poor compared with regional averages. The government has initiated three broad goals for social sector development: universal basic services in education and health, an education system providing students with market-relevant skills, and measures to improve the labor market and strengthen the social safety net. Egypt scores 43 on Health, much below the Middle East average of 60. On Education it scores 59, just below the regional average.

For the past two decades, population pressures and urbanization have caused the continued loss of agricultural land in Egypt. Urban areas increasingly suffer from environmental problems related to industrial effluents and inadequate sewage facilities. Egypt scores 72 on Environment.

Democracy and Freedom. In principle Egyptians have the right to change their governments, but the domination of the ruling National Democratic Party in the media, labor unions, and other institutions has diminished citizens' political rights and the opportunities of opposition parties. Terrorism and clashes in upper Egypt between the police and militant Islamic fundamentalist continue, and the security agency has been accused of killing some militants. Women face discrimination in many aspects of society. Egypt scores 25 on Democracy and Freedom. (This score does not reflect Freedom House's ratings in *Freedom in the World 1995– 1996,* which would instead give a score of 0. Adjustments have been made based on the authors' research as well as work experience in over one hundred countries worldwide, which suggest a higher degree of civil liberty in Egypt than in other countries that reccive 0 in this vector.)

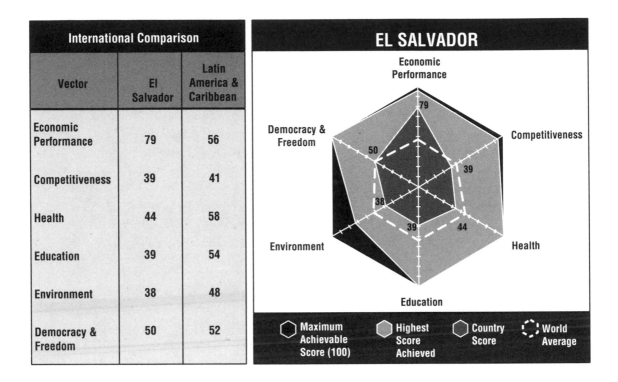

International Comparison		
Vector	El Salvador	Latin America & Caribbean
Economic Performance	79	56
Competitiveness	39	41
Health	44	58
Education	39	54
Environment	38	48
Democracy & Freedom	50	52

EL SALVADOR

Economic Performance

Democracy & Freedom

Competitiveness

Environment

Health

Education

Maximum Achievable Score (100) — Highest Score Achieved — Country Score — World Average

EL SALVADOR

Economic Performance. After more than a decade of civil war, El Salvador is showing strong signs of economic recovery. The National Reconstruction Plan initiated after the 1992 peace accord has been a successful follow-up to the structural adjustment program begun in 1989. GDP grew by an average of 6.2 percent per year over 1990–94, while gross domestic investment rose at a annual rate of 16 percent. In 1995 overall macroeconomic conditions were stable and economic activity continued to expand strongly. Agriculture remains the main source of employment and exports, with coffee accounting for 40 percent of merchandise exports in 1995. El Salvador scores 79 on Economic Performance, ranking third in Latin America and the Caribbean. On Competitiveness it scores 39, just below the regional average.

Social Development and the Environment. Most of El Salvador's social indicators are below the regional averages. Poverty is pervasive in this war-torn country. It is estimated that in 1991–92 two-thirds of rural households lived in poverty, of which over one-third lived in extreme poverty. The illiteracy rate is high, at 29 percent of the population over fifteen years of age, and is much more widespread in rural regions. Sixty-seven percent of maternal deaths occur among rural women. Infant mortality has been declining, partly as a result of the reduction of communicable diseases.

In May 1991 El Salvador endorsed the second phase of the Central American Health Initiative and made a commitment to improving domestic social and health conditions. The government will work jointly with the governments of Guatemala and Honduras to improve access to and quality of health care, boost infant survival and nutrition, control waterborne diseases, and improve drinking water and sanitation. El Salvador scores 44 on Health and 39 on Education, both much below the regional averages.

El Salvador suffers from a host of environmental problems, ranging from deforestation and soil degradation to declining water quality and lack of solid waste treatment. Less than 15 percent of the original forests remain today, and soil loss and damage are accelerating as a result.

Pollution of river water threatens drinking water supplies; only 15 percent of the rural population has access to safe water. There are few controls over the use and disposal of toxic wastes. El Salvador receives a score of 38 on Environment, below the regional average of 48.

Democracy and Freedom. Citizens of El Salvador have the right to change their government through democratic means. However, labor strife, social unrest, police abuses, and the government's failure to fully implement the 1992 peace accords underscore the continued weakness of democratic institutions. While fundamental freedoms are guaranteed in the constitution, they cannot be practiced fully in the light of continuing political violence, repressive police actions, rising crime rates, and the existence of right-wing death squads. An ineffectual judicial system contributes to the climate of insecurity. El Salvador scores 50 on Democracy and Freedom, just below the regional average.

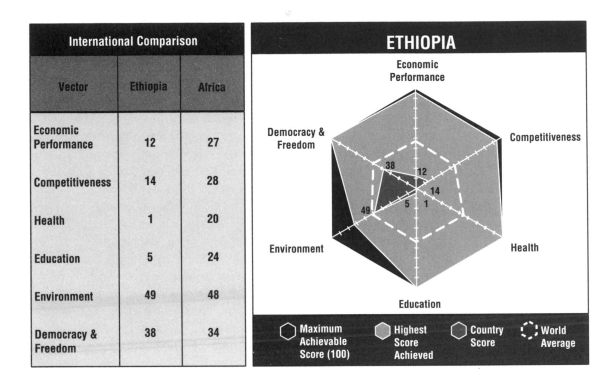

International Comparison		
Vector	**Ethiopia**	**Africa**
Economic Performance	12	27
Competitiveness	14	28
Health	1	20
Education	5	24
Environment	49	48
Democracy & Freedom	38	34

ETHIOPIA

Economic Performance · Competitiveness · Health · Education · Environment · Democracy & Freedom

- **Maximum Achievable Score (100)**
- **Highest Score Achieved**
- **Country Score**
- **World Average**

ETHIOPIA

Economic Performance. A 1995 per capita GDP of U.S. $100 places Ethiopia among the poorest countries in the world. Nearly two decades of civil war, instability, and recurring drought have severely damaged the economic base. The main economic objectives of the transitional government that came to power in 1991 were to reduce macroeconomic imbalances, eliminate structural distortions, improve human capital, and reduce poverty. Overall, the government's reform program has made substantial progress. Real GDP grew an average of 6.6 percent per year over 1993–96, compared with a rate of -2.5 percent during 1990–92.

Agriculture, which accounts for almost 55 percent of national output and 80 percent of employment, remains the major contributor to economic growth.

Exports have risen substantially as Ethiopia's trade regime has been increasingly liberalized, with reduced tariff rates and import exemptions. Coffee remains the dominant export commodity. The government has recently reviewed the legal and regulatory framework to remove impediments to private activities and has established a privatization agency to oversee the upcoming divestiture of state-owned enterprises. It is likely that

GLOBAL Benchmarks

Ethiopia

Ethiopia's score of 12 on Economic Performance is biased downward as a result of the lack of recent economic growth data. Ethiopia scores 14 on Competitiveness, half the average for Africa.

Social Development and the Environment. Ethiopia's social indicators are very poor. In the rural areas there is an acute lack of basic social services, such as health care and safe water supply. Nearly 12 percent of infants die before their first birthday, and one-fifth of all children die before the age of five. Almost 50 percent of children are malnourished. The very high maternal mortality rate of 1,400 per 100,000 live births illustrates the disproportionate vulnerability of women. The national health policy instituted in 1993 emphasizes primary health care, greater reallocation of health resources toward rural regions, and the strengthening of the financial base for health care provision. Ethiopia scores 1 on Health, tied with Congo's as the lowest score in the world.

Two-thirds of Ethiopia's population is illiterate. Education expenditures averaged about U.S. $3 per person per year in 1995. Primary school enrollment actually declined from 38 percent in 1985 to about 27 percent in 1993. Female enrollment in primary schools is only 21 percent. Ethiopia scores 5 on Education, the third lowest in Africa, after Mozambique and Djibouti.

Environmental problems have been aggravated by the civil war, population displacement, and the loss of livelihoods. Recurring droughts have been particularly severe and frequent over the past decade and, along with the war and the cutting and burning of trees for fuel wood, have destroyed vast tracts of forest. An inadequate safe water supply, especially in rural areas, poses serious health risks. Ethiopia receives a score of 49 on Environment.

Democracy and Freedom. In 1995 Ethiopia held its first free and fair election. However, it has been difficult for democratic institutions to take hold, given the continuing unrest caused by armed rebel groups in the countryside, which has led to many casualties and human rights abuses. There is evidence that the government has intimidated, harassed, or imprisoned nonviolent opposition. The state maintains firm control of the broadcast media and has detained a number of journalists for expressing unfavorable opinions. Freedom of religious expression is generally respected. Ethiopia scores 38 on Democracy and Freedom, just above the Africa average.

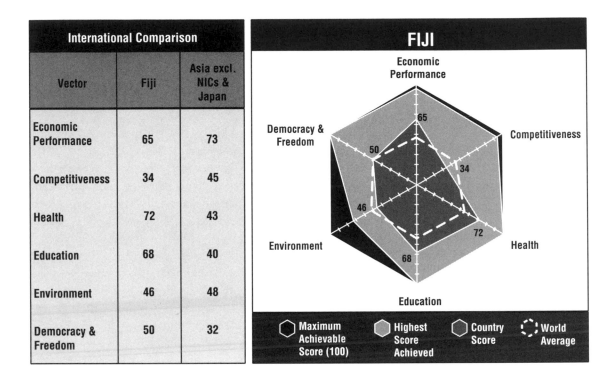

International Comparison		
Vector	Fiji	Asia excl. NICs & Japan
Economic Performance	65	73
Competitiveness	34	45
Health	72	43
Education	68	40
Environment	46	48
Democracy & Freedom	50	32

FIJI

Maximum Achievable Score (100) | Highest Score Achieved | Country Score | World Average

FIJI

Economic Development. With a per capita income of U.S. $2,400 in 1995, Fiji is the largest and most developed country among the Pacific Islands. It is endowed with fertile soils and abundant forestry, mineral, and fishery resources. Although Fiji made moderate income gains in the 1970s, these were quickly eroded as political turmoil in 1987 brought an economic recession. Much of Fiji's growth since 1987 has been in regaining former income levels. Real GDP growth averaged only 2.5 percent over 1991–95, marginally higher than the rate of population growth. Investment activity has remained depressed since 1987.

Private investment fell from around 12 percent of GDP in 1986 to 6 percent in 1989 and has remained stagnant in the 1990s. The investment climate reflects a loss of confidence among Indo-Fijian investors in light of the political and social instability. Fiji scores 65 on Economic Performance, higher than the world average but below the average for Asia. On Competitiveness it scores only 34, well below the regional average.

Social Development and the Environment. Fiji's social indicators are impressive for a country at this income level and are among the best in Asia after the NICs. However, poverty is pervasive and afflicts approximately 25 percent of all households. There is room for improvement in overall income distribution and rural-urban income disparity. Fiji scores 72 on Health and 68 on Education, among the highest scores in Asia after the NICs.

The loss of forests to poorly managed logging and inappropriate farming practices has led to serious problems of soil erosion. Urban areas are affected by toxic wastes, sewage, and air pollution related to development projects, while the widespread use of pesticides, fertilizer runoff, and the salinization of ground water contribute to pollution in rural areas. Fiji scores 46 on Environment, just below the average for Asia.

Democracy and Freedom. Fiji achieved independence from Britain in 1970. It is a multi-ethnic nation with roughly equal numbers of Indians and ethnic Fijians. The constitution promulgated in 1990 ensures ethnic Fijians a parliamentary majority. Ethnic Indians and "other races" (mostly Chinese and Europeans) are entitled to a smaller number of reserved seats in the legislature. While the judiciary is independent, there are questions about its efficiency and impartiality. Police abuse is a persistent problem. The government occasionally pressures the press not to run articles on sensitive topics, such as race relations. Domestic violence, violence against women, and child abuse are serious problems. Fiji scores 50 on Democracy and Freedom.

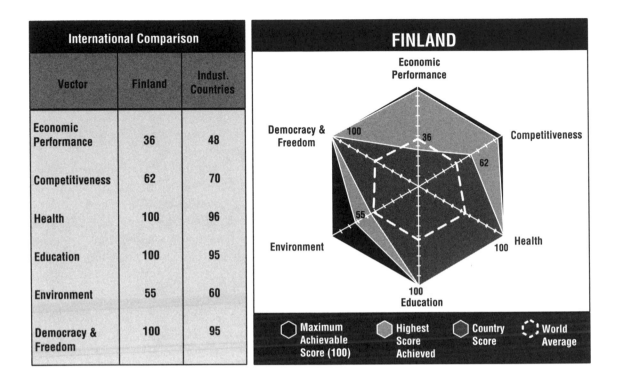

International Comparison		
Vector	Finland	Indust. Countries
Economic Performance	36	48
Competitiveness	62	70
Health	100	96
Education	100	95
Environment	55	60
Democracy & Freedom	100	95

FINLAND

Economic Performance

Democracy & Freedom — 100 — 36 — Competitiveness

62

55

Environment

100 Health

100
Education

○ Maximum Achievable Score (100)　◉ Highest Score Achieved　◎ Country Score　⦚ World Average

FINLAND

Economic Development. Finland is a highly industrialized, largely free-market economy, with a per capita income of U.S. $18,850, close to the OECD average. The main economic driver is the manufacturing sector, principally wood processing, metals, and the engineering industries. Trade is important: exports of goods and nonfactor services represent about 33 percent of GDP. The Finnish economy has undergone a fairly severe recession during the 1990s, with economic growth declining by 2.2 percent per year from 1990 to 1994. Other key indicators, such as gross domestic investment growth, also fell during this period. Unemployment has been a persistent problem, averaging 15 percent during the 1990s. Finland scores 36 on Economic Performance and 62 on Competitiveness, both below the industrial country averages. Its Competitiveness score was hurt by the high fiscal deficit, which averaged 12 percent of GDP during 1991–94.

Social Development and the Environment. Finland has one of the best educational systems in the world, earning a perfect Education score of 100. Public expenditure on education exceeds 7 percent of GDP, a higher level of spending than in most OECD countries. The system is designed to ensure quality and equality and the principle of lifelong learning. Special emphasis is placed on the central role of education in reforming working life and production structures. Schooling is compulsory for nine years, but students normally attend school for ten years.

Finland also has an excellent health care system, which earns a perfect Health score of 100. The government spends over 7 percent of GDP on public health services. The compulsory National Sickness Insurance scheme finances most health care services. Its main disadvantage is the bureaucratic character of central administration.

Manufacturing and power plants cause serious air pollution in Finnish cities. Sulfur emissions from wood pulp plants and other sources have increased soil acidity. However, over 50 percent of the sulfur in Finland's precipitation comes from other countries. Finland scores 55 on Environment, below the average for industrialized countries, mainly because of its high reported level of greenhouse gases present in the air.

Democracy and Freedom. Finland is an established democracy, where fundamental freedoms and rights are guaranteed by law and respected in practice. Legislation enacted in 1992 grants all Finnish citizens rights to their own culture and equal protection under the law. Discrimination on the basis of race, sex, religion, language, and social status is illegal. A recently adopted law prohibits the press from identifying people by race. Finland receives a perfect score of 100 on Democracy and Freedom.

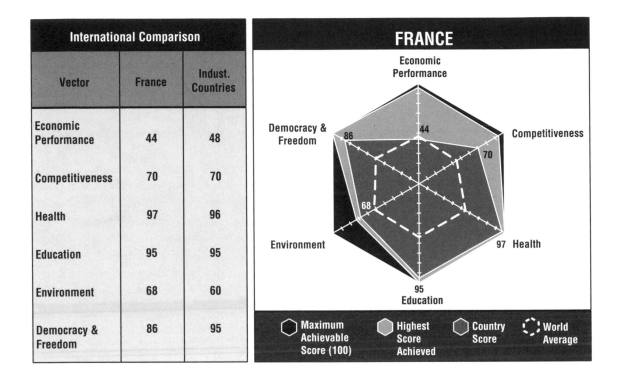

International Comparison		
Vector	France	Indust. Countries
Economic Performance	44	48
Competitiveness	70	70
Health	97	96
Education	95	95
Environment	68	60
Democracy & Freedom	86	95

FRANCE

Economic Development. France is one of the most prosperous countries in the world, with a high standard of living and a well-educated work force. The per capita income level is at the high end of the range for OECD countries. France is still recovering from the economic recession that afflicted most countries in the European Union at the end of the 1980s. The annual economic growth rate over 1990–94 was only 0.8 percent, barely ahead of population growth. Gross domestic investment declined during this period. France's overall score of 44 on Economic Performance is relatively low, below the average for industrialized countries.

However, France scores a much better 70 on Competitiveness, in line with the industrialized country average. It has a sound macroeconomic foundation and boasts high numbers of scientists, engineers, and technicians. It also has reliable and high-quality infrastructure.

Social Development and the Environment. Like most other high-income countries, France has a highly developed education system. Since 1967 education has been compulsory between ages six and sixteen. Despite far-reaching changes introduced in the 1980s, the system continues to be largely controlled by the government, which retains basic powers, such as recruiting and compensating teachers, designing and implementing national curricula, and conferring university diplomas. France scores 95 on Education.

France also receives a high score of 97 on Health, owing to its excellent health indicators. About 75 percent of health care bills are paid by public insurance. The incidence of heart disease is among the lowest in the OECD. However, alcohol consumption per capita is the highest among OECD countries.

Industrial pollution, agricultural activities, and urban waste have polluted many French rivers. The government has launched several major efforts to improve water quality and increase waste treatment capacity. Air pollution remains a problem, especially in major cities, which have high population densities and high levels of vehicular emissions. The government sets annual goals for reducing the main air pol-

lutants, such as sulfur oxides, nitrogen oxides, and carbon. France scores 68 on Environment, a relatively high score among industrialized countries.

Democracy and Freedom. France is an established democracy whose constitution grants the president significant powers, including the authority to rule by decree under certain emergency circumstances and to call a referendum to dissolve a hostile parliament. Fundamental freedoms and rights are protected by law and respected in practice. However, in recent years the threat of terrorism spilling over from Algeria (a former French colony) has led to some restrictions on the freedom of expression. The poor treatment of immigrants is also drawing domestic and international press attention. France scores 86 on Democracy and Freedom, lower than the average of 95 among industrialized countries.

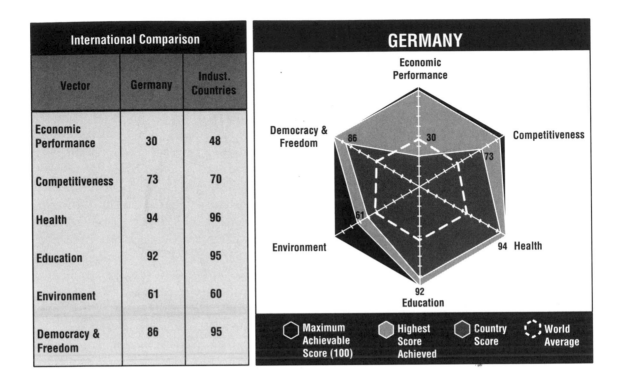

International Comparison		
Vector	Germany	Indust. Countries
Economic Performance	30	48
Competitiveness	73	70
Health	94	96
Education	92	95
Environment	61	60
Democracy & Freedom	86	95

GERMANY

Economic Performance · Competitiveness · Health · Education · Democracy & Freedom · Environment

86 · 30 · 73 · 94 · 92 · 61

Maximum Achievable Score (100) · Highest Score Achieved · Country Score · World Average

GERMANY

Economic Development. With a per capita income of $27,510 in 1995, Germany is one of the wealthiest countries in the world. A great deal of public resources have been put into the process of reunifying the former East and West Germany in an effort to minimize disparities in living standards, incomes, infrastructure, schools, and so forth. The modest GDP growth rate of 1.1 percent over 1990–94 should be viewed in this context. Germans enjoy a high standard of living, abundant leisure time, and comprehensive social benefits. Germany has one of the most highly educated and highly skilled work forces in the world. It has many world-class companies that manufacture technologically advanced products.

Germany scores much higher on Competitiveness (73) than on Economic Performance (30). The factors that lead to the high assessment on Competitiveness include high domestic saving rates; excellent bond ratings; large numbers of scientists, engineers, and technicians; few foreign exchange controls; and outstanding infrastructure. Two of the biggest challenges to Germany's economic position are, paradoxically, by-products of its success: a strong currency, resulting from consistent trade surpluses, and high wage costs, which stem in part from high skill levels and productivity. These constraints could erode German competitiveness as well as slow future growth and investment in manufacturing.

Social Development and the Environment. Germany scores 92 on Education, in line with the industrialized country average. Schooling is compulsory for twelve years, from ages six to eighteen. The majority of educational institutions are public, attendance at which is free. Enrollment in higher education has expanded rapidly since the 1960s. New curricula in higher education have been strongly oriented to practical occupations. Germany also boasts a highly developed system of trade apprenticeships.

Germany has excellent health indicators, earning a Health score of 94. Over 90 percent of health care bills are paid by public insurance. However, the level of alcohol consumption and the incidence of heart disease are among the highest in the European Union.

The major environmental problems are concentrated in eastern Germany. The southern part of eastern Germany has been devastated by air pollution from coal-burning utility plants and industrial plants. Raw sewage and industrial effluents have damaged the rivers in eastern Germany. Germany receives very low scores on indicators measuring emission of greenhouse gases. Overall, Germany scores 61 on Environment, in line with the industrialized country average.

Democracy and Freedom. Since its establishment as a democratic republic at the end of World War II, Germany has become a solid democracy. Citizens have the right to form political parties. However, parties deemed extremist or resembling the Nazi Party in ideology are not allowed. The press and broadcast media are free and independent. Religious freedom is generally respected, except in the case of Scientologists, who are banned from proselytizing in public. Labor, business, and farming groups are free, highly organized, and influential. Germany receives a score of 86 on Democracy and Freedom, below the industrialized country average of 95.

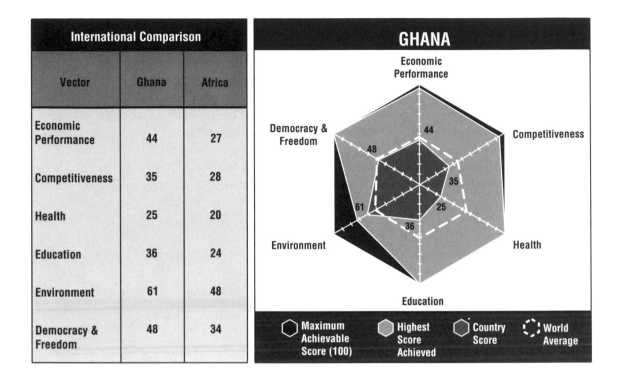

International Comparison		
Vector	**Ghana**	**Africa**
Economic Performance	44	27
Competitiveness	35	28
Health	25	20
Education	36	24
Environment	61	48
Democracy & Freedom	48	34

GHANA

- ⬡ Maximum Achievable Score (100)
- ⬡ Highest Score Achieved
- ⬡ Country Score
- ⬡ World Average

GHANA

Economic Development. Ghana is a low-income country, with per capita GDP of U.S. $410 in 1994. It is endowed with a broad range of natural resources, including arable land, forests, sizable deposits of gold, diamonds, bauxite, and manganese, as well as considerable potential for hydroelectric power. The main economic activities are related to the primary production and export of cocoa and gold. Most of the population is engaged in small-scale agriculture.

Ghana was once among the most prosperous of West African nations. However, decades of inward-looking economic policies and public resource mismanagement, coupled with the deterioration of its external terms of trade, led to substantial declines in income from the 1970s through the 1980s. Since 1983 the government has undertaken a series of stabilization and reform measures to improve macroeconomic conditions and the competitive environment. In 1990–94 Ghana's recovery enjoyed moderate success, with annual GDP growth of 4.3 percent and annual export growth of 7.5 percent. Growth in the 1990s has been driven by public sector investment, whereas private sector investment is lagging. In 1995 Ghana began a three-year structural adjustment program supported by the IMF. The country is currently taking a more outward economic orientation that emphasizes regional cooperation, export growth, and the removal of trade barriers. Ghana's scores on Economic Performance (44) and Competitiveness (35) are both above the averages for Africa.

Social Development and the Environment. Social indicators in Ghana are generally better than those of other countries in sub-Saharan Africa. However, social progress stagnated during a decade of economic decline. In recent years, under the recovery program, economic growth has produced solid improvements in social indicators, including primary school enrollment and poverty trends. The fertility rate of 5.8 children per woman and the very high population growth rate of 3 percent will continue to challenge these improvements in economic opportunities and social conditions. Ghana scores 25 on Health and 36 on Education, both above the average for Africa.

Rapid population growth, overgrazing, and overfarming have led to deforestation, soil degradation, and erosion. Forest loss is estimated at a rate of 278 square miles a year. Ghana faces a serious lack of safe drinking water. Pollution by industrial, commercial, domestic, and community wastes is common. Ghana scores 61 on Environment, a high score compared with both the world average and the Africa average, mainly because of low reported levels of greenhouse gas emissions.

Democracy and Freedom. Ghanaians cannot practice democracy. The 1992 multiparty elections, which gave President Jerry Rawlings a majority of the vote, were deemed neither free nor fair. Continued government interference and inadequate funding have limited the growth of truly independent media. Ghanaians have the right to organize and demonstrate. The judiciary is increasingly independent but is still subject to government influence. Minor legal cases in rural areas are generally handled by traditional courts. Ghana scores 48 on Democracy and Freedom, above the regional average of 34.

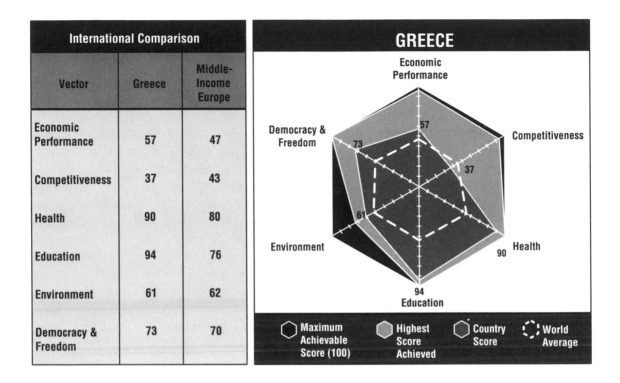

International Comparison		
Vector	Greece	Middle-Income Europe
Economic Performance	57	47
Competitiveness	37	43
Health	90	80
Education	94	76
Environment	61	62
Democracy & Freedom	73	70

GREECE

Economic Performance · Competitiveness · Health · Education · Environment · Democracy & Freedom

Maximum Achievable Score (100) · Highest Score Achieved · Country Score · World Average

GREECE

Economic Development. Greece has one of the lowest income levels in the European Union: in 1994, per capita GNP was U.S. $10,930, measured in purchasing power parity. Tourism is a major economic activity. Growth in GDP during 1990–94 was modest, at 1.4 percent per year. The main economic problems have been high unemployment, inflation (averaging 15 percent per year over 1984–94), and runaway budgetary deficits (averaging 17 percent of GDP over 1989–95). Its Economic Performance score was higher than the world average, at 57.

On Competitiveness Greece receives one of the lowest scores (37) among OECD countries.

The contributing factors include low saving rates, high government budget deficits, a low sovereign debt rating, and relatively few research personnel. Infrastructure in Greece is generally considered adequate.

Social Development and the Environment. Greece scores 90 on Health and 94 on Education, close to the averages for industrialized countries and much above the averages for middle-income Europe. Schooling is compulsory from ages six to fifteen, and the public education system is extensive. About 24 percent of all secondary school graduates enter universities. Public universities are generally more competitive than primary and secondary schools in admissions. The universal public health insurance system covers about 85 percent of all health bills, but many families opt for additional private insurance coverage.

Major Greek cities suffer from severe air pollution; in particular, Athens, where hundreds of people visit hospitals every year for pollution-related respiratory and heart complaints. The main sources of pollutants are industrial plants, power stations, automobiles, and the high-sulphur oil used for central heating. Pollution monitoring stations have been installed throughout greater Athens and in eleven other Greek cities. Greece scores 61 on Environment, in line with the average for middle-income Europe.

Democracy and Freedom. Greece is a democratic country where voting is compulsory. However, restrictions against changes in voting address routinely force hundreds of thousands of citizens to travel long distances in order to vote. The media are generally free and independent. There are some reports of violations of freedom of expression, assembly, and political participation for minorities, as well as religious persecution and police brutality. Religious freedoms remain restricted; those who are not members of the Greek Orthodox community are prohibited from entering certain occupational areas, such as primary school education, the police, and the military. Greece scores 73 on Democracy and Freedom, just above the average of 70 for middle-income Europe.

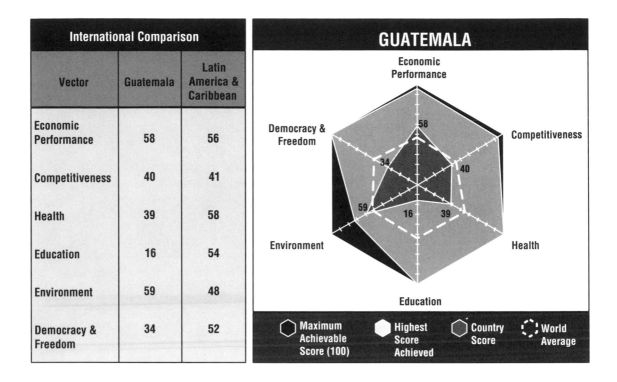

International Comparison		
Vector	Guatemala	Latin America & Caribbean
Economic Performance	58	56
Competitiveness	40	41
Health	39	58
Education	16	54
Environment	59	48
Democracy & Freedom	34	52

GUATEMALA

Economic Development. With per capita GNP of U.S. $1,340 in 1995 and a population of almost 11 million, Guatemala is the largest economy in Central America. It is predominantly agricultural. The country has endured a century of dictatorships, coups d'état, and guerrilla insurgencies. In the early 1980s Guatemala suffered significant economic decline when inward-looking economic policies failed to cope with external shocks or stem declining investor confidence in the face of regional and civil conflict. As the regional and national political situations stabilized, the Guatemalan economy began to recover in the early 1990s.

Between 1990 and 1994, domestic output grew at a rate of 4.1 percent. The improved political and economic climate brought about an investment growth rate of nearly 11 percent. Exports grew more moderately, at 5.2 percent, during this period. Prudent monetary and fiscal policies were instrumental in the economic recovery. Guatemala receives scores of 58 and 40 on Economic Performance and Competitiveness, respectively, both in line with the averages for Latin America and the Caribbean.

Social Development and the Environment. Guatemalan society is sharply segmented, with income and land distribution highly skewed against the rural indigenous population, most of which is of Mayan origin. This imbalance has contributed to the civil strife between successive governments and guerrilla forces based in the highlands since the 1960s. Economic conditions deteriorated throughout the 1980s, and 67 percent of the population was estimated to live in extreme poverty in 1989.

Social indicators are among the worst in the region; those for child health and mortality are particularly poor. An estimated 44 percent of the population is illiterate, and the ratio is particularly skewed toward the indigenous peoples. Guatemala's score of 39 on Health places it just above Bolivia and Haiti in the Latin America and Caribbean region. Its Education score of 16 puts it near the bottom for the region, just above Haiti.

Substantial forests cover more than one-third of the country, but the destruction of natural forest is proceeding at a rapid rate as trees are cut down to provide fuel wood for an estimated three-quarters of all households. In rural areas only 43 percent of the population has access to safe water. Guatemala receives a score of 59 on Environment, higher than the regional average of 48, mainly because of favorable indicators in air quality.

Democracy and Freedom. Citizens can in principle elect their government democratically in Guatemala. However, democratic processes and civilian administration have been undermined by the powerful military and the widespread corruption that has penetrated most public institutions, including the legislature and the judiciary. While fundamental freedoms are guaranteed by the constitution, the exercise of many basic rights has been restricted in a climate of violence, lawlessness, and military repression. The growing crime wave is often attributed to the military and former soldiers. There has been increasing violence against members of rights organizations and civic groups calling for reform and tighter civilian control of the military. Guatemala scores 34 on Democracy and Freedom, well below the regional average of 52.

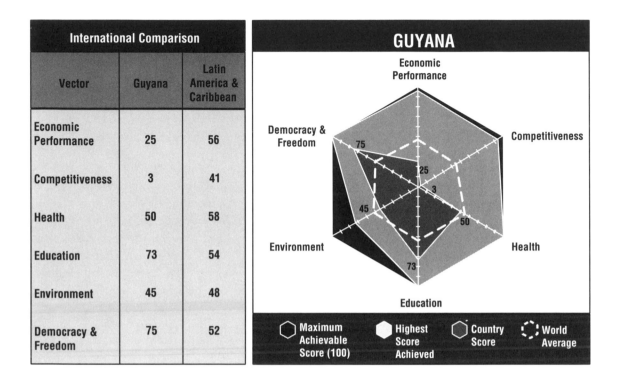

International Comparison		
Vector	Guyana	Latin America & Caribbean
Economic Performance	25	56
Competitiveness	3	41
Health	50	58
Education	73	54
Environment	45	48
Democracy & Freedom	75	52

GUYANA

Economic Performance

Democracy & Freedom

Competitiveness

Environment

Health

Education

| Maximum Achievable Score (100) | Highest Score Achieved | Country Score | World Average |

GUYANA

Economic Development. Guyana is one of the poorest countries in the Western Hemisphere. Its economy is based on commodity exports, including bauxite, sugar, rice, gold, and forestry products. After gaining independence from the United Kingdom in 1966, the government pursued a set of development policies based on extensive state ownership and intervention. Such policies proved inadequate to deal with external shocks in the 1980s. Income stagnated and declined through most of the decade. In 1988 the government reversed course and adopted an economic recovery program supported by the IMF, which included broad

macroeconomic and structural reforms to lead the economy toward a more market-oriented structure. Guyana's economy has responded well to these reform efforts. Annual GDP growth averaged 7 percent over 1992–95, and inflation fell from 83 percent in 1991 to 8 percent in 1995. Guyana's disappointing scores on Economic Performance (25) and Competitiveness (3) are probably biased downward as a result of insufficient data.

Social Development and the Environment. Guyana once had some of the best social indicators in the Caribbean. However, its social infrastructure deteriorated in the wake of the

economic decline, and the country fell behind its neighbors in many indicators. Poverty is pervasive, with an estimated 40 percent of the population living below the poverty line. Guyana's score of 50 on Health is below the average for Latin America and the Caribbean.

Guyana's education indicators remain impressive for a country at this income level. Illiteracy rates are very low, and the country has some of the highest primary enrollment and completion rates in the region. These achievements are reflected in its high Education score of 73.

Sewage and solid waste disposal are serious environmental problems in Guyana. Inadequate and malfunctioning sewage systems and the dumping of solid wastes into drainage canals threaten public health. Parts of the coast lie below sea level, and breaches of its sea defenses occasionally cause latrines and septic tanks to flood, contaminating drinking water. Overall, only 14 percent of the population has access to safe water. Guyana scores 45 on Environment, below the regional average.

Democracy and Freedom. Citizens of Guyana can change their governments democratically. Fundamental rights, such as freedom of expression, religion, and the organization of political parties, civic organizations, and labor unions, are not formally guaranteed in the constitution but are generally respected in practice. The judicial system is independent, although underfunded and understaffed. The police remain vulnerable to corruption, especially in the light of the increasing penetration of the drug trade, particularly from Colombia. Guyana scores 75 on Democracy and Freedom, much above the regional average.

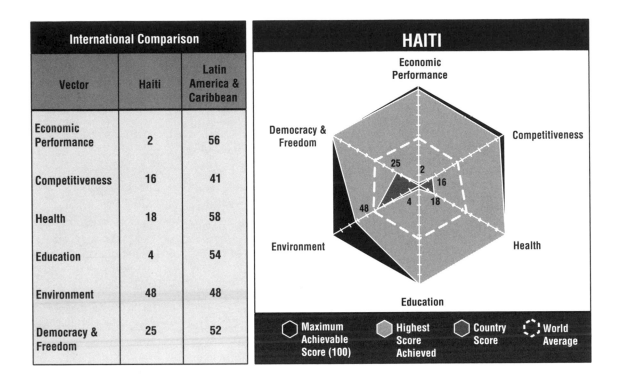

International Comparison		
Vector	Haiti	Latin America & Caribbean
Economic Performance	2	56
Competitiveness	16	41
Health	18	58
Education	4	54
Environment	48	48
Democracy & Freedom	25	52

HAITI

Economic Performance · Competitiveness · Health · Education · Environment · Democracy & Freedom

- Maximum Achievable Score (100)
- Highest Score Achieved
- Country Score
- World Average

HAITI

Economic Development. With an estimated per capita income of U.S. $250 in 1995, Haiti is the poorest nation in the Western Hemisphere. Since it gained its independence from France in 1804, Haiti has endured a history of poverty, violence, instability, and dictatorship. It remains a predominately rural nation. The September 1991 coup that ousted elected President Jean-Bertrand Aristide led to three years of severe economic mismanagement and an international embargo that caused a dramatic decline in living standards. Although President Aristide returned to Haiti in October 1994 and the embargo was lifted, the damage had been done. During fiscal years 1992–94, economic performance deteriorated at an accelerated pace. Real GDP fell by almost 20 percent over 1992–93 and declined further by 10.6 percent in 1994. The economic damage of the embargo was compounded by the destruction of a severe tropical storm in November 1994. Per capita GDP declined at a rate of 5 percent between 1985 and 1994. Bleak economic prospects have accelerated emigration to the neighboring Dominican Republic in the 1990s. Haiti scores 2 on Economic Performance, the lowest in Latin America and the Caribbean. On Competitiveness its score of 16 puts it just above Cuba and Guyana in the region.

Social Development and the Environment. Haiti has some of the poorest social indicators in the world. Social conditions have continued to deteriorate during the 1990s. In 1994 an estimated 50 percent of the population had a caloric intake below 75 percent of requirements (defined by the World Bank), and more than one-fourth of all children suffered from malnutrition. Infant mortality and maternal mortality rates are both alarmingly high. Out of 1,000 live births, 127 are not expected to survive until age five. Over half of adults are illiterate. Haiti scores 18 on Health and 4 on Education, ranking last in the region in both categories.

Extensive cutting of trees and shrubs for firewood and charcoal has devastated Haiti's forests. Less than 2 percent of the country remains forested. This has exacerbated the problems of soil erosion and land degradation.

Safe drinking water is scarce. Sewage systems and sewage treatment are nonexistent. Waterborne diseases are widespread. Haiti receives very low scores in almost all environment variables. Its overall score of 48 in the environment vector is boosted by low reported levels of greenhouse gas emissions.

Democracy and Freedom. The parliamentary election held in 1995 after President Aristide's return was widely considered subject to fraud, calling into question the president's legitimacy. The country has little democratic tradition and extremely weak institutions. Continued economic deterioration and the lack of police discipline have led to steep increases in violent crime and to a climate of lawlessness. While independent media exist, critics of the government are frequently targets of intimidation, including mob attacks. Haiti receives a score of 25 on Democracy and Freedom, well below the regional average of 52.

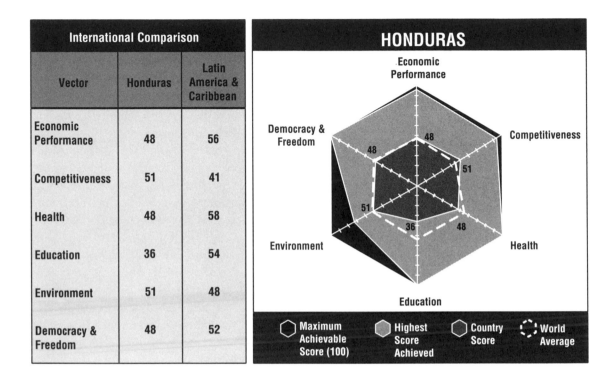

International Comparison		
Vector	Honduras	Latin America & Caribbean
Economic Performance	48	56
Competitiveness	51	41
Health	48	58
Education	36	54
Environment	51	48
Democracy & Freedom	48	52

HONDURAS

Economic Performance · Competitiveness · Health · Education · Environment · Democracy & Freedom

Maximum Achievable Score (100) · Highest Score Achieved · Country Score · World Average

HONDURAS

Economic Development. Honduras ranks among the least developed countries in the Western Hemisphere. Although there has been some economic progress over the past decade, in 1995 per capita income remained low, at U.S. $600, mainly as a result of a severe economic decline followed by stagnation throughout the 1980s. Modest income gains have been made since 1990, as a result of structural reforms that provided the legal framework for expansion and accelerated the implementation of new economic policies. Overall, per capita income grew at only 0.5 percent per year between 1985 and 1994. The new government that took office in 1994 undertook important fiscal measures to reduce the public deficit to 6.9 percent of GDP from over 10 percent during most of the 1980s. Economic growth resumed in 1995, with real GDP increasing by 3.6 percent based on a rapid increase in exports and the elimination of electricity rationing. Honduras scores 48 on Economic Performance, below the regional average of 56. However, it outperforms the region on Competitiveness with a score of 51, mainly because of a high saving rate, a high export-to-GDP ratio, and high levels of foreign direct investment.

Honduras

Social Development and the Environment. Poverty is a pervasive problem in Honduras, particularly in rural areas. One in four adults is illiterate, and almost 19 percent of children under the age of five suffer from moderate to severe malnutrition. Nationally, child and infant mortality rates are found to be closely correlated with inadequate access to a clean water supply. An estimated three-fifths of the population is inadequately housed, which, in turn, leads to other social and health problems. Honduras scores 48 on Health and 36 on Education, both well below the regional averages.

Rapid population growth and urbanization have strained the environment in Honduras. Water pollution by industrial discharges and the lack of abatement threaten the supply of safe drinking water. Less than half of the rural population has access to safe water. Deforestation, resulting from the expansion of subsistence farming and commercial logging, has led to soil degradation and erosion. Honduras scores 51 on Environment, just above the regional average.

Democracy and Freedom. Honduran citizens can elect their government democratically. Constitutional rights regarding free expression, freedom of religion, and the right to form political parties and civic organizations are generally respected in practice. However, democratic institutions are constantly undermined by the military, which maintains a powerful status in economic and social institutions and resorts to threats and violence to preserve its interests. Violence is often linked to economic interests and targeted against business executives, trade unionists, and peasant leaders. The judiciary is weak and plagued by corruption. Moreover, death threats have weakened the resolve of some judges adjudicating human rights cases. Members of the media are also subject to intimidation and threats, especially in covering rights violations and corruption. Honduras scores 48 on Democracy and Freedom, just below the regional average of 52.

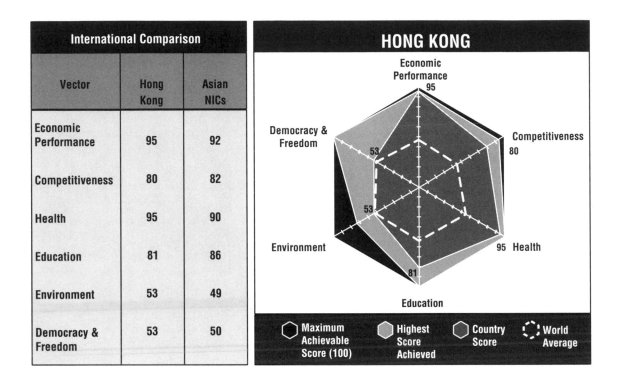

International Comparison		
Vector	Hong Kong	Asian NICs
Economic Performance	95	92
Competitiveness	80	82
Health	95	90
Education	81	86
Environment	53	49
Democracy & Freedom	53	50

HONG KONG

Economic Development. After several decades of rapid economic growth, Hong Kong enjoys a per capita income of U.S. $21,650, higher than that of the United Kingdom, Australia, and Canada. Hong Kong is a free-market economy, with few tariffs and nontariff barriers, low levels of taxation, and high levels of economic freedom for firms and individuals. A densely populated island territory, Hong Kong is a model of economic efficiency and prosperity. Shortages of labor and land have put upward pressure on prices, making Hong Kong one of the most expensive business locations in the world. In recent years economic ties with mainland China have been intensified as Hong Kong firms have made substantial direct and portfolio investments in manufacturing operations in China. Formerly a British colony, Hong Kong was politically reunited with mainland China in July 1997. Hong Kong receives very high scores on both Economic Performance (95) and Competitiveness (80). On Economic Performance it ties with Singapore as second worldwide. This score is due to strong economic growth rates, high levels of per capita income, and the depth of financial markets. Its Competitiveness score is based on a high saving rate, significant levels of exports, and relatively good infrastructure.

Hong Kong

Social Development and the Environment. Hong Kong's social indicators are in line with its high-income, developed status. Its health indicators are comparable to those of OECD countries, earning it a high Health score of 95. Free health services are provided through a network of public hospitals and clinics, although many citizens opt for private care. On Education Hong Kong scores 81, compared with an Asian NIC average of 86, mainly because of lower primary, secondary, and tertiary enrollment rates. Education is compulsory until grade nine and is provided free or at very low cost through a network of public and government-subsidized schools. Higher education opportunities have been expanded in recent years but remain inadequate. Tertiary students abroad represent 50 percent of those at home.

Hong Kong's environmental problems are manifestations of urbanization, rapid development, and congestion. As an economic entity, Hong Kong has one of the highest population densities among the world's countries. Emissions from vehicles, industrial activities, and energy generation are the major source of pollutants. Hong Kong does not participate in any major global environmental conventions, and few registered environmental nongovernment organizations (NGOs) operate there. Hong Kong scores 53 on Environment, above the Asia average and the highest among the Asian NICs.

Democracy and Freedom. Citizens of Hong Kong cannot change their government freely. Hong Kong was governed as a British colony for nearly 150 years. Following its return to China, the Hong Kong Special Administrative Region is governed by its own laws, based on British common law. The chief executive officer of the region is appointed by China, and the current legislature comprises members elected partly by general elections and partly by an electoral college, from a list of candidates approved by China.

Under British rule, freedoms of expression, of religion, and of organizing labor unions were generally respected in practice. The judiciary, which is independent of the executive and recognizes due process, is to remain unchanged under the new administration. Freedom of assembly and demonstration has so far been respected. However, both printed and broadcast media practice self-censorship to avoid antagonizing China. Hong Kong receives a score of 53 on Democracy and Freedom. (Note that Freedom House does not rate Hong Kong. Our rating is based on the current political climate and the civil liberties observed.)

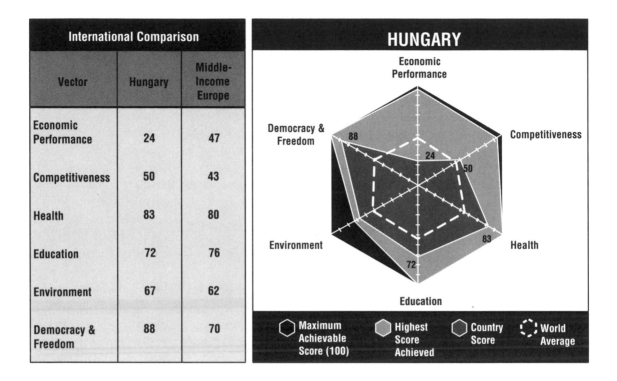

International Comparison		
Vector	Hungary	Middle-Income Europe
Economic Performance	24	47
Competitiveness	50	43
Health	83	80
Education	72	76
Environment	67	62
Democracy & Freedom	88	70

HUNGARY

Economic Development. With an estimated per capita income of U.S. $3,840 in 1995, Hungary is one of the most economically advanced countries in eastern Europe. It led its socialist neighbors in experimenting with market-type reforms. The New Economic Mechanism, introduced in the late 1960s and accelerated through the 1980s, was a major step forward in establishing the basic legal and institutional framework for a market economy. However, despite its head start, Hungary's reform efforts stalled in the 1990s. The drastic reorientation of trade after the collapse of the Soviet bloc also contributed to its disappointing economic performance in the first half of the 1990s. GDP actually declined at a rate of 2 percent between 1990 and 1994, while exports shrank by 6 percent per year. Hungary receives a low score of 24 on Economic Performance.

In March 1995 the Socialist-Liberal coalition government adopted an emergency stabilization program, which has generally produced positive results. Hungary led the former socialist countries in privatization, by selling substantial stakes in the gas, electricity, and oil industries to foreign investors. It scores 50 on Competitiveness, above the world average, mainly because of high levels of foreign direct investment and a relatively small average budget deficit in 1988–91.

Social Development and the Environment. As a former socialist country, Hungary has a very equitable income distribution. The income share of the lowest 40 percent of households is about 26 percent, compared with 18 percent in Canada and 22 percent in Japan. Its health indicators are impressive for a country at this level of per capita income. Life expectancy at birth is seventy years, and maternal, infant, and child mortality rates are low. Hungary scores 83 on Health, compared with an average of 80 for middle-income Europe. Its Education score of 72 is earned by moderately high scores in the primary school enrollment and completion indicators.

While air is considered cleaner in Hungary than in some neighboring countries, air pollution is still a significant problem in many urban and industrial areas. An increasing number of children in Hungary's industrial cities are developing chronic respiratory diseases. About 41 percent of the population is exposed to high levels of sulfur and nitrogen dioxide. Sewage facilities exist for just over half of the population. Hungary receives a score of 67 on Environment, a relatively high score, because of the high percentage of the population with access to a safe water supply.

Democracy and Freedom. Hungary is a multiparty democracy. The 1994 elections were free and fair. Fundamental freedoms are protected by law and respected in practice. The judiciary is independent, as demonstrated by several cases in which the Constitutional Court nullified aspects of the government's economic austerity program in 1995. The print media are generally free and independent. The state owns two television stations but has plans to privatize them. Hungary scores 88 in Democracy and Freedom.

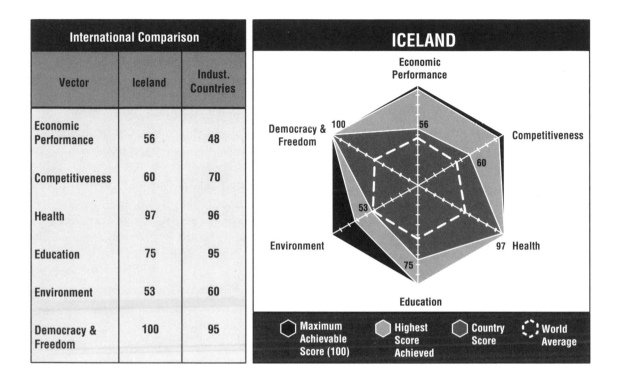

International Comparison		
Vector	Iceland	Indust. Countries
Economic Performance	56	48
Competitiveness	60	70
Health	97	96
Education	75	95
Environment	53	60
Democracy & Freedom	100	95

ICELAND

Economic Development. Iceland is a small, island economy with a very high standard of living. GNP per capita was U.S. $19,210 in 1994. The country has a prosperous, Scandinavian-style economy, which is basically market oriented but provides an extensive social safety net. It enjoys low unemployment rates of around 5 percent as well as a relatively even distribution of wealth. The economy is heavily dependent on the fishing industry, which provides 75 percent of export earnings. Iceland's Economic Performance score is 56, just above the world average. Its score of 60 on Competitiveness is somewhat higher but is below the average among industrialized countries. Iceland receives high scores on Competitiveness indicators such as sovereign bond rating; numbers of scientists, engineers, and technicians; and ease of foreign exchange conversion. However, its score on budget deficits is low, as deficits averaged 4 percent of GDP per year from 1989 to 1994.

Social Development and the Environment. Iceland has very good social indicators and scores 97 on Health. Life expectancy at birth is seventy-nine years, the highest in the world, while the infant mortality rate is among the lowest. The Health Service Act of 1978 guarantees all citizens access

Iceland

to the best health service available. Iceland receives a relatively low score of 75 on Education, mainly because illiteracy rates are not available. The Education score is also biased downward by a low rate of enrollment in higher education.

Some environmental sources rank Iceland among the world's heaviest users of artificial fertilizers. Nitrates and phosphates washing off farmlands are polluting ground and surface water supplies. Iceland scores 53 on Environment, lower than the industrialized country average, mainly because of high levels of greenhouse gas emissions.

Democracy and Freedom. Icelanders can change their governments democratically. Fundamental freedoms and rights are guaranteed by the constitution. The judiciary is independent. Over 95 percent of eligible workers belong to free labor unions, and all workers enjoy the right to strike. Censorship is banned under the constitution. and the media openly offer pluralistic views. Despite its highly homogeneous population, the country has outlawed any form of discrimination based on race, language, social class, or gender. Iceland receives a perfect score of 100 on Democracy and Freedom.

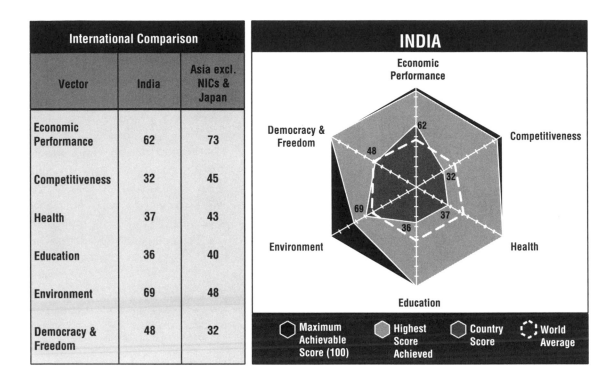

International Comparison		
Vector	India	Asia excl. NICs & Japan
Economic Performance	62	73
Competitiveness	32	45
Health	37	43
Education	36	40
Environment	69	48
Democracy & Freedom	48	32

INDIA

Economic Performance
62
Competitiveness
48
Democracy & Freedom
32
69
37
36
Environment
Health
Education

Maximum Achievable Score (100) · Highest Score Achieved · Country Score · World Average

INDIA

Economic Development. India is the second most populated nation in the world and one of the poorest. Per capita income is estimated at U.S. $350 in 1995. Since independence from Britain in 1947, India has pursued a planned approach to development, characterized by heavy state involvement in the economy. The state has traditionally maintained extensive regulation and ownership in key sectors, such as banking, basic industries, utilities, and infrastructure. India's growth rates have remained modest over the past decade. Per capita GDP increased at a rate of 2.9 percent from 1985 to 1994, which was insufficient to bring the majority of the population out of poverty.

In June 1991 the new government launched a major structural adjustment effort and shifted to a more market-oriented development strategy. Key reforms include the liberalization of trade, investment, capital and money markets, banking, and the tax system. The economy has responded well to these changes, yielding a growth rate of over 6 percent in both 1994 and 1995. India scores 62 on Economic Performance, below the overall average for Asia (excluding the NICs and Japan). Its low score of 32 on Competitiveness reflects its persistently high government budget deficit, low overall levels of foreign direct investment, and a low ratio of exports to GDP. India's sovereign bond rating is also weak.

Social Development and the Environment. Poverty is widespread in India and particularly afflicts rural areas. India's social indicators are among the poorest in Asia. Maternal, infant, and child mortality rates are all very high. Close to half of the adult population is illiterate. Fewer than two-thirds of school children complete grade five, and secondary and tertiary education enrollment rates are low. India scores 37 on Health and 36 on Education, well below the averages for Asia.

The major environmental problems are related to population growth, industrial development, and urbanization. Urban pollution is serious, with sulfur dioxide levels in nine of the ten major cities exceeding national standards. Untreated sewage, industrial effluents, and excessive use of pesticides and fertilizers pollute both surface and ground water. Less than half of the urban population has access to sanitation. India scores 69 on Environment, the highest score in Asia, despite the problems described above. This score is boosted by India's active participation in major global environmental conventions, and the high number of environmental NGOs operating in India.

Democracy and Freedom. India is a democratic country in which citizens can change their governments in multiparty elections. However, overall, the rule of law is weak. Corruption undermines many levels of government. Sporadic violence instigated by religious or ethnic groups is often met with excessive force by the police and security forces. The judiciary is independent but seriously backlogged. Judges are also prone to bribery, which tilts the judiciary system in favor of the rich. Police torture of suspects and abuse of prisoners is widespread. Violence against women is common in India, particularly in relation to dowry disputes. Forced prostitution, street children, child prostitution, and child labor are serious problems. Religious freedom is guaranteed by law. Members of lower castes are often subject to discrimination and sometimes to random violence. India scores 48 in Democracy and Freedom, higher than the overall average for Asia (excluding the NICs and Japan).

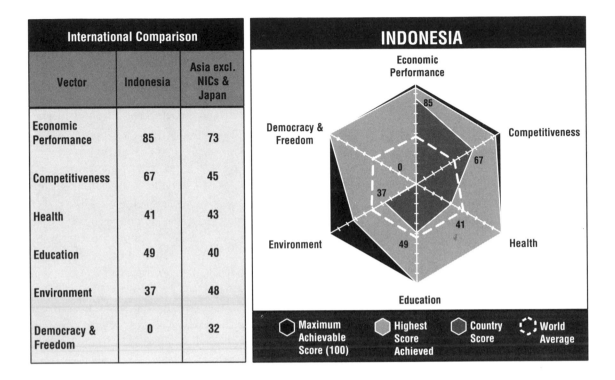

International Comparison		
Vector	Indonesia	Asia excl. NICs & Japan
Economic Performance	85	73
Competitiveness	67	45
Health	41	43
Education	49	40
Environment	37	48
Democracy & Freedom	0	32

INDONESIA

Economic Development. With a per capita GDP of U.S. $880 in 1994, Indonesia ranks among the lower-middle-income countries worldwide. It is endowed with abundant and diverse natural resources, including oil, mineral deposits, and timber. Over the past three decades, Indonesia has enjoyed rapid and consistent economic growth, with GDP rising at a rate of 6.7 percent annually since 1965. The nation's economy has become less dependent on oil, more diversified and industrialized, and increasingly open and driven by the private sector. Indonesia's development strategy is based on maintaining macroeconomic stability through appropriate fiscal and monetary policy, careful debt management, and stronger domestic saving and investment. Indonesia earns a very high score of 85 on Economic Performance and 67 on Competitiveness.

Social Development and the Environment. Indonesia's poor have benefited substantially from the booming economy. Central to the country's development strategy is the enhancement of human resources through improved efficiency, quality, and delivery of health and education. The government is also working to reduce poverty by increasing the access of the urban poor to basic education and health services and targeting programs for the very poor. The incidence of poverty declined from around 60 percent in the early 1970s to about 14 percent in 1996. Universal primary education has been achieved and illiteracy has fallen by almost two-thirds. Enrollment in secondary and tertiary educational institutions has risen sharply. Indonesia's Education score of 49 is above the average for Asia. However, Indonesia's Health score of 41 is low compared with the regional average, reflecting slow progress in health indicators such as infant and maternal mortality rates.

Selective logging to support the wood and pulp industries has done tremendous damage to Indonesia's indigenous rainforest. The remaining forests and mangroves are threatened by population pressure and inland migration. Industrial wastes and sewage pollute rivers in port cities, presenting a serious risk to urban residents dependent on these rivers for drinking water and fish. Only one-third of Indonesians have access to safe water. Indonesia scores 37 on Environment, the second lowest in Asia.

Democracy and Freedom. Indonesians have not been able to exercise their rights to change their governments as a result of institutional barriers, the power of the military, and several decades of President Suharto's authoritarian rule. Military personnel hold many legislative seats and key administrative posts. The army and police violate civilian rights with impunity. Official corruption is rampant. Self-censorship among journalists is widespread. Freedom of association is limited; the police must be notified of all political meetings. Citizens of Chinese descent face significant restrictions and discrimination and are often targets of violence during periods of economic downturn. Indonesia receives 0 on Democracy and Freedom.

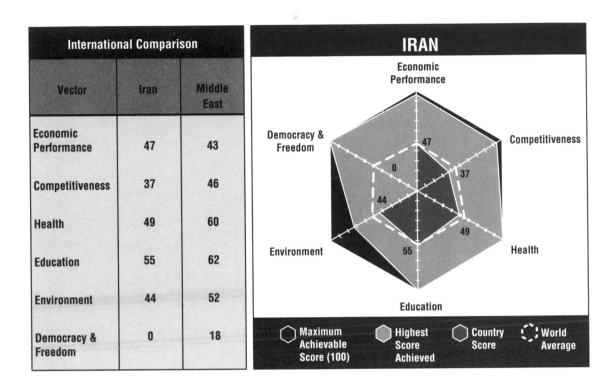

International Comparison		
Vector	Iran	Middle East
Economic Performance	47	43
Competitiveness	37	46
Health	49	60
Education	55	62
Environment	44	52
Democracy & Freedom	0	18

IRAN

Economic Performance

Democracy & Freedom

Competitiveness

47

0

37

44

49

Environment

55

Health

Education

Maximum Achievable Score (100)   Highest Score Achieved   Country Score   World Average

IRAN

Economic Development. Before the 1979 revolution and the 1980–88 war with Iraq, Iran was one of the most advanced economies in Middle East. Following the Islamic revolution, Iran's new leaders established an economic system that discouraged private enterprise and favored management by the state. The petroleum industry, banking system, transportation, and utilities were nationalized. The change of government in 1989 brought some economic reforms. However, a reportedly corrupt and intransigent bureaucracy, coupled with hardline militants in the parliament, have constrained these reform efforts.

With a per capita GDP of about U.S. $1,019 in 1994, Iran ranks among the middle-income developing countries. Oil remains the principal export. Recent economic performance has been mixed. GDP growth has been high, averaging 5.2 percent over 1990–94. However, domestic investment growth has been negative over the same period. Iran scores 47 on Economic Performance, which is the world average but above the Middle East average. The country's Competitiveness score is relatively low, at 37, owing to low levels of foreign direct investment, high inflation (averaging 23 percent in 1984–94), and a very low number of scientists and engineers.

GLOBAL Benchmarks

Iran

Social Development and the Environment. Iran's social indicators are generally lower than those of its smaller, oil-rich neighbors in the Arab Middle East. However, it has made great progress in improving child survival and nutrition rates over the past three decades. Life expectancy at birth is now sixty-eight years, compared with fifty in 1960. High fertility and population growth rates will continue to challenge the improvement of social conditions and economic opportunities. Over a quarter of the adult population is illiterate, and the differential between male and female illiteracy is nearly 20 percent, indicating the disadvantaged social position of women. Overall enrollment rates for female students at all educational levels are 10 percent lower than those for the male population. Iran scores 49 on Health and 55 on Education, both below the Middle East averages.

Iran suffers from serious water pollution in the Persian Gulf, mostly related to oil tanker accidents, downed airplanes, and black rain and toxic fumes from burning oil wells in Kuwait. Drought and inefficient use of water have led to shortages of drinking water. Iran's air is polluted, especially in the urban areas, by emissions from cars, refinery operations, and industry. Iran scores 44 on Environment, below the Middle East average.

Democracy and Freedom. Iran does not have a democratic political system. While there are direct elections, in effect the country is run mainly by the Shiite clerical elite, which must approve all candidates who run for office. The few political parties that do exist are barred from participating in elections. The state silences political dissent through extreme measures, such as threats of arbitrary detention, torture, summary trials, and execution. The government executes several hundred people every year for political reasons.

There is no independent judiciary in Iran. Judges must meet strict political and religious qualifications, and they can serve simultaneously as prosecutors during trials. The broadcast media are state owned and serve to disseminate government propaganda. The Baha'i and Kurdish minorities are often persecuted. Iran receives a score of 0 on Democracy and Freedom.

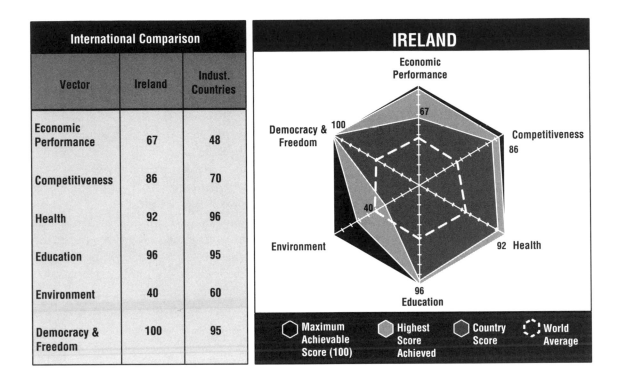

International Comparison		
Vector	Ireland	Indust. Countries
Economic Performance	67	48
Competitiveness	86	70
Health	92	96
Education	96	95
Environment	40	60
Democracy & Freedom	100	95

IRELAND

Economic Development. Ireland is a small, open economy on the periphery of Europe. Before joining the European Union in 1973, Ireland relied on trade barriers to protect local industry. The government gradually dismantled these barriers in the mid-1970s, leading to a radical restructuring of the economy. By the mid-1980s, Irish unemployment had reached 20 percent and it stood at 12 percent in 1995, one of the highest rates in the European Union. As many as 30,000 people emigrated from Ireland annually throughout the 1990s.

The degree to which it has embraced foreign trade is evidenced by the fact that exports accounted for about 75 percent of GDP and imports accounted for some 60 percent of GDP in 1995. During the 1990s Ireland has had one of the most successful economic performances in all of Europe. From 1990 to 1994 GDP grew at a 4.5 percent rate, and exports of goods and non-factor services grew by 10 percent per year. The software, electronics, and tourism industries have been the main engines of growth. Software and electronics growth has been stimulated by attractive incentives for foreign investors, access to the European market, and special training programs that strengthen work force skills in technical areas, such as computer science, software engineering, mathematics, and information technology. Ireland scores 67 on Economic Performance and 86 on Competitiveness, ranking second among industrialized countries.

Social Development and the Environment. Social indicators in Ireland are about average for the European Union. Its Health score of 92 is slightly below average for industrialized countries, mainly as a result of relatively low immunization rates. Indicators for the prevalence of AIDS and rate of increase in HIV infections are both below the average for the European Union. Public expenditure on health is below the European Union average. About 90 percent of all health care bills are paid by public insurance.

Ireland has very low illiteracy rates and scores 96 on Education, above the industrialized country average. Although the government supplies more than 90 percent of funds for education, Irish schools are not state owned but run by community and religious groups. Almost 92 percent of the population is Roman Catholic, and the church plays a predominant role in education. Schooling is compulsory from age six to age fifteen. Enrollments in tertiary education have increased steadily, with nearly five times as many students enrolled in some form of higher education in 1995 as in 1965.

Ireland suffers from increasing problems of solid waste and air pollution, particularly in urban areas. Emission levels of carbon dioxide and other greenhouse gases are high. Rapid urbanization has led to a net loss of forest and woodland over the past decade. Ireland receives a score of 40 on Environment, the lowest among industrialized countries.

Democracy and Freedom. Irish citizens can change their government democratically. Basic freedoms and fundamental rights are protected. The press is independent and generally free. The judiciary is independent. The Roman Catholic church is strong, but other faiths and religious practices are respected in practice. Ireland receives a perfect score of 100 on Democracy and Freedom.

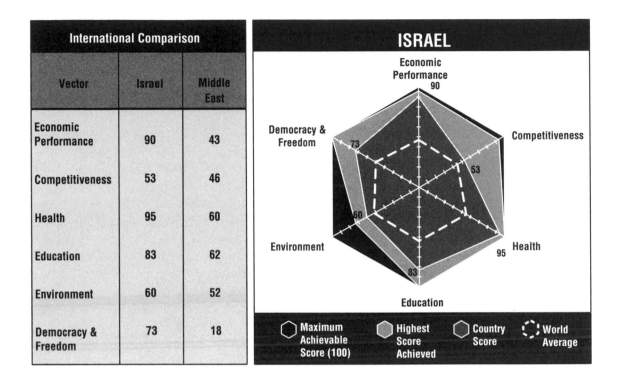

International Comparison		
Vector	Israel	Middle East
Economic Performance	90	43
Competitiveness	53	46
Health	95	60
Education	83	62
Environment	60	52
Democracy & Freedom	73	18

ISRAEL

Economic Performance 90

Democracy & Freedom 73

Competitiveness 53

Environment 60

Health 95

Education 83

Maximum Achievable Score (100)   Highest Score Achieved   Country Score   World Average

ISRAEL

Economic Development. Israel is a small, high-income country where the government partici-pates extensively in the economy, from owner-ship and operation of key sectors to heavy regulation. The country is dependent on imports of many essential commodities, includ-ing crude oil, grain and other foodstuffs, and many industrial raw materials. Diamonds, high-technology machinery and electronic equipment, and agricultural commodities (including fruits and vegetables) are the main exports.

On Economic Performance, Israel receives a very high score of 90. This score is driven by strong GDP growth of 6.2 percent a year from 1990 to 1994. Investment and exports have also registered high growth rates during the 1990s. On Competitiveness Israel's score is 53, just above the world average. Its score is boosted by the high number of scientists and engineers in the population, a good sovereign risk rating, and high-quality infrastructure but is reduced by relatively low scores in indicators such as budget deficit, average inflation rate, and for-eign exchange controls.

Social Development and the Environment. In Israel a disproportionate level of public resources and foreign aid (mainly from the United States)

is devoted to defense and the military. Military expenditures amounted to 9.5 percent of GDP in 1994. Israel's health indicators are comparable to those in the industrialized countries, which is reflected in its high Health score of 95. The nation's life expectancy of 77 is among the highest in the world. A lower Education score of 83 is mainly due to the relatively low gross enrollment ratios at the primary and secondary levels compared with those in the industrialized countries.

Israel's environmental problems are mainly related to water scarcity and pollution. Groundwater pollution caused by industrial and domestic waste, chemical fertilizers, pesticides, and seawater intrusion threatens the country's already limited resources. Population pressure and industrialization have also caused air pollu-

tion and degradation of marine resources. Israel scores 60 on Environment, higher than the Middle East average.

Democracy and Freedom. Israeli citizens elect their government democratically. Both Arab-based parties and far-right Jewish groups are represented in the parliament. The judiciary is independent, and due process rights are respected. A 1979 law provides for administrative detention without charge for renewable six-month periods. The security agency, Shin Bet, has been accused of torturing Palestinian detainees. The print media are privately owned and independent. Religious freedom is respected, and each community has jurisdiction over its members regarding issues of marriage and divorce. Israel scores 73 on Democracy and Freedom, well above the Middle East average of 18.

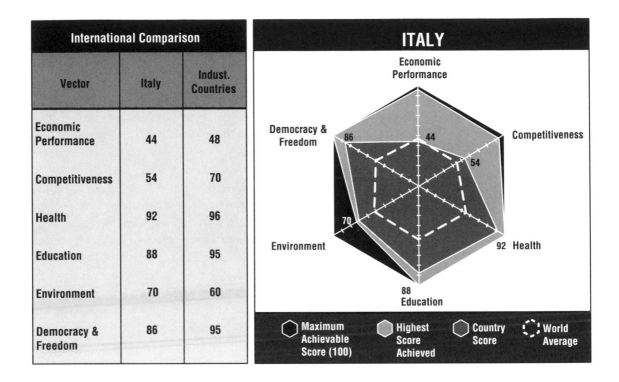

International Comparison		
Vector	Italy	Indust. Countries
Economic Performance	44	48
Competitiveness	54	70
Health	92	96
Education	88	95
Environment	70	60
Democracy & Freedom	86	95

ITALY

Economic Performance • Democracy & Freedom 86 • 44 • Competitiveness 54 • Environment 70 • 92 Health • 88 Education

○ Maximum Achievable Score (100) ⬡ Highest Score Achieved ⬡ Country Score ⬡ World Average

ITALY

Economic Development. Italy, the fifth largest industrial economy in the world, is a member of the Group of Seven advanced industrialized nations. The country is still divided into a developed industrialized north and an underdeveloped agricultural south, which is dominated by state-owned companies. Services account for about 66 percent of the economy, industry 31 percent, and agriculture 3 percent.

Italy's score on Economic Performance is quite low at 44. The economy grew only 0.7 percent a year from 1990 to 1994, while domestic investment growth declined. On Competitiveness Italy's score of 54 is slightly higher, just above the global average but much lower than the industrialized country average. Italy earns points for the high number of scientists and engineers in the population as well as its high-quality infrastructure. However, Italy mostly underperforms the industrialized countries as a group in indicators including exports as a share of GDP, foreign direct investment, and government deficits.

Social Development and the Environment. Education is free and compulsory for children aged six to fourteen years in Italy. State schools enroll over 90 percent of all students. About one-third of the adult population has an upper-secondary

GLOBAL Benchmarks

or tertiary education degree. Initiatives are currently under way to increase participation rates in upper-secondary and postsecondary courses, particularly in the vocational sector. Italy's below-average Education score of 88 is due mainly to lower enrollment ratios at all levels than in other industrialized countries.

Italy's health indicators are mostly comparable to those of other European Union countries. Universal, comprehensive, and in some cases free health services are provided to citizens through the National Health Services. The system is financed by payroll taxes, contributions from the self-employed, and general tax revenues, but Italy also has a small but growing private health sector. Italy's Health score (92) is hurt by low immunization rates and a rapid increase in HIV infections.

Italy has a great variety of environmental laws, but implementation and enforcement have been uneven. The major environmental issues are air and water pollution. There have

been some improvements in recent years with the installation of new waste treatment plants and increased environmental awareness among its citizens. Sulfur dioxide emissions have declined since the 1970s. Italy scores 70 on Environment, among the highest in the industrialized country category.

Democracy and Freedom. Italians can change their government through democratic means. However, corruption at many levels of the government has undermined democratic institutions. Other than reorganizing the prewar Fascist Party, Italian citizens can freely form political parties. The judiciary is independent but often considered inefficient and prone to corruption. In 1996 there was reportedly a backlog of some 2.8 million unheard cases. The press is generally free and independent, and fundamental freedoms guaranteed in the constitution are respected in practice. Italy receives a score of 86 on Democracy and Freedom, lower than the industrialized country average.

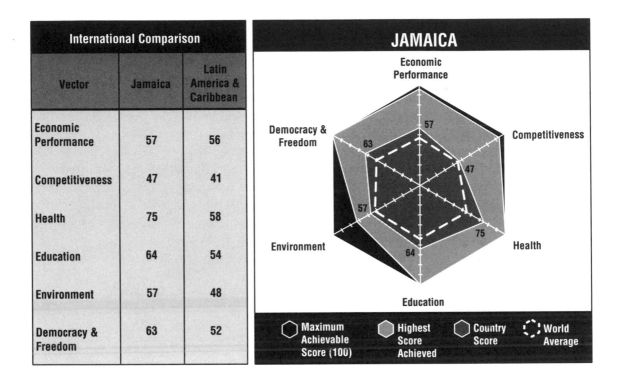

International Comparison		
Vector	Jamaica	Latin America & Caribbean
Economic Performance	57	56
Competitiveness	47	41
Health	75	58
Education	64	54
Environment	57	48
Democracy & Freedom	63	52

JAMAICA

Economic Performance · Competitiveness · Health · Education · Environment · Democracy & Freedom

Maximum Achievable Score (100) · Highest Score Achieved · Country Score · World Average

JAMAICA

Economic Development. The Caribbean island nation of Jamaica is endowed with rich natural resources and has a relatively well educated and skilled labor force. During the decade following independence in 1962, Jamaica experienced strong economic growth. Since 1973, however, the Jamaican economy has faltered, as high inflation and macroeconomic instability have recurred. A comprehensive reform program initiated in 1989 aimed to lower inflation, enhance international competitiveness, improve public finances, and increase per capita income levels. GDP growth between 1990 and 1994 was 3.9 percent a year. However, exports declined at a 1 percent rate during the same period. Tourism is the nation's principal foreign exchange earner.

Jamaica's Economic Performance score of 57 is above the regional average. Its moderate Competitiveness score (47) results from high levels of foreign direct investment and a high ratio of exports to GDP, but the score is hurt by high inflation rates, a low sovereign risk rating, and the small proportion of scientists, engineers, and technicians in the economy.

Social Development and the Environment. The government's strong commitment to social development is reflected in its Social and Economic Support Program and the 1987 Human

GLOBAL Benchmarks

Resources Development Program. Jamaica's social indicators have improved significantly over the past three decades. Life expectancy at birth is now 74, and infant mortality has dramatically improved. Jamaica's Health score of 75 is much higher than the average in Latin America and the Caribbean.

While enrollment in primary and secondary education is almost universal, at least 15 percent of Jamaica's adult population is illiterate. Despite concerns about declining equality, the country's Education score (64) shows that Jamaica's education indicators are better than the regional average.

Estimates are that 32 percent of the population lives below the poverty line. Unemployment is high, at 16 percent of the labor force. Urban poverty and unemployment aggravate the country's serious and rising crime problem. Housing shortages in urban areas have led to overcrowded squatter settlements and inadequate basic services.

Deforestation, caused by excessive grazing, subsistence crop cultivation in marginal lands, and the conversion of forests into plantations, is a major environmental problem in Jamaica. In the Kingston metropolitan area, the discharge of sewage and industrial effluent has contaminated groundwater. Less than half of the country's rural residents have access to safe water. Jamaica scores 57 on Environment.

Democracy and Freedom. Jamaican citizens have been able to change their government democratically since the country's independence from the United Kingdom in 1962. However, democratic processes are weakened by prevalent fraud, police intimidation, and bribery during elections. Although most fundamental freedoms and rights are guaranteed in the constitution, criminal violence fueled by poverty and drugs, as well as police violations of rights, has heightened a sense of insecurity among citizens. The judiciary is independent, but it is slow and lacks resources, especially in addressing police abuses. The press is independent and free of government control. Jamaica scores 63 on Democracy and Freedom, higher than the average of 52 for Latin America and the Caribbean.

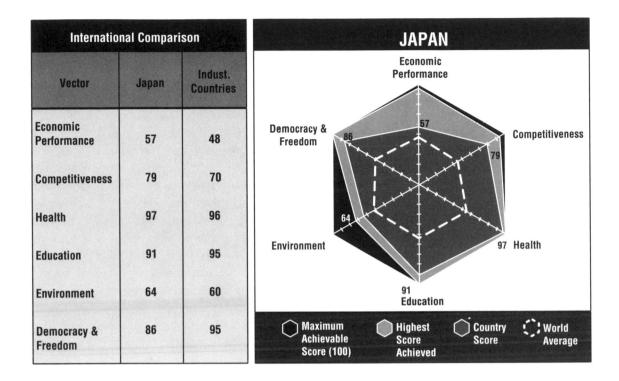

International Comparison		
Vector	Japan	Indust. Countries
Economic Performance	57	48
Competitiveness	79	70
Health	97	96
Education	91	95
Environment	64	60
Democracy & Freedom	86	95

JAPAN

Economic Development. Although Japan has few natural resources, it has risen from its post–World War II ruin to become the world's second largest economy in just several decades. Government-industry cooperation, a strong work ethic, and a comparatively small budget allocation for defense have helped contribute to this very strong "export machine." The industrial sector is a key sector, contributing 40 percent of the country's GDP and a vast majority of its exports.

Japan is still recovering from a deep recession that began in 1992, subjecting the country to five years of low growth and high unemploy-ment by historical standards. Japan's Economic Performance score (57) is above the average for the world and for the industrialized countries. Growth in gross domestic investment declined between 1990 and 1994. In the competitive-ness vector, Japan's score is high at 79. This score is earned by a high sovereign bond rating, the government budget surplus, high gross domestic saving, the large number of scientists and engineers in the population, and the high quality of Japan's infrastructure as well as its low inflation rates.

Social Development and the Environment. As one of the richest countries in the world, Japan

enjoys very high standards of living and excellent social indicators. Elementary and lower-secondary education is compulsory and provided free of charge. There are national and local, public and private institutions at all levels of education, and the national, prefectural, and municipal governments all contribute to financing the nation's public education system. Japan's Education score (91) is below the industrialized country average because of its relatively low level of gross tertiary enrollment.

The health status of the Japanese population is among the best in the world. Life expectancy at birth is seventy-nine years, the world's highest, while the nation's infant mortality rate is among the world's lowest. The Japanese system stresses preventive health care, including health education, consultations, checkups, and immunization. Coverage is universal for all citizens and is collectively financed through public medicare and insurance schemes, while medical care is provided largely by private institutions.

Urban areas such as Tokyo, Osaka, and Yokohama suffer from considerable air pollu-tion. Acid rain remains a serious problem in many parts of the country. Overall, Japan has tightened its air quality regulations and has substantially reduced emissions of sulfur dioxide and nitrogen oxides from its power plants. Japan scores 64 on Environment, just above the average for industrialized countries.

Democracy and Freedom. Japanese citizens can change their government democratically. All fundamental freedoms are guaranteed and protected. The judiciary is independent. A continuing civil liberties concern involves the 700,000 residents of Korean descent who are denied Japanese citizenship at birth even after several generations have lived in Japan and who face discrimination in housing, education, and employment opportunities. Although freedom of expression is guaranteed, the education ministry continues to censor passages in history textbooks describing Japan's military aggression during the 1930s and 1940s. Journalists often practice self-restraint regarding politically or socially sensitive subjects. Japan scores 86 on Democracy and Freedom, below the average for industrialized countries.

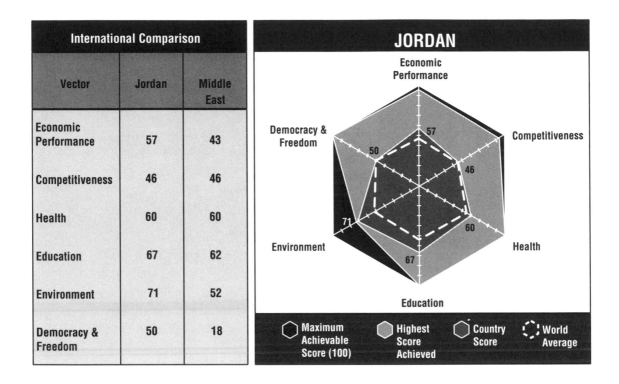

International Comparison		
Vector	Jordan	Middle East
Economic Performance	57	43
Competitiveness	46	46
Health	60	60
Education	67	62
Environment	71	52
Democracy & Freedom	50	18

JORDAN

Economic Development. Without the oil reserves enjoyed by its Arab Middle East neighbors, Jordan has relied on skilled Jordanian workers employed in other Gulf countries for foreign exchange earnings. For a decade after 1973, Jordan enjoyed an economic boom, benefiting from high levels of official grants and concessional loans. However, the boom ended in 1982, when oil prices fell, remittances from Jordanian expatriate workers declined, and foreign grants were significantly reduced. The Palestinian-Israeli peace accord created unprecedented opportunities for Jordan to expand linkages in banking, tourism, transport,

and exports with Israel and the increasingly independent Palestinian West Bank and Gaza.

Jordan's Economic Performance score (57) is above average in the Middle East and the world, owing to its high GDP growth rate (8.2 percent) and domestic investment growth rate (6.5 percent) in the 1990–94 period. Its Competitiveness score of 46 is in line with both the Middle East and world averages. In the competitiveness vector, the strongest indicator for Jordan is its government budget surplus. However, Jordan's Competitiveness score is hurt by such indicators as low levels of domestic saving and foreign direct investment.

Jordan

Social Development and the Environment. Jordan has made significant progress in its social indicators. Life expectancy now stands at seventy years, while infant mortality has decreased 75 percent since 1960. It scores 60 on Health and 67 on Education, both of which are in line with Middle East averages. On Health Jordan's score is strengthened by its good child survival and health indicators and a slow rate of growth in HIV infections but hurt by high fertility and population growth rates. In the education vector, Jordan is strong in primary school completion rates but weak in secondary and tertiary enrollment ratios.

The main environmental problems in Jordan are related to its population and industrial growth. Water is a scarce commodity, and conservation efforts are lacking. The arable land area is rapidly decreasing, mainly as a result of urban expansion and desertification. Jordan scores 71 on Environment, the second highest score in the Middle East.

Democracy and Freedom. Jordan is ruled by King Hussein. Although parliamentary elections are held in Jordan, citizens cannot change their government democratically. The king appoints the prime minister and can dissolve the legislature. The authorities are aggressive in dealing with suspected Islamic fundamentalists, often resorting to arbitrary arrests, torture, and other abuses. The judiciary is subject to government influence. Censorship is in place for subjects including the royal family, the armed forces, and monetary policy. Islam is the state religion. Residents of the Baha'i faith face some discrimination, and the religion is prohibited from running schools. Jordan scores 50 on Democracy and Freedom, well above the Middle East average of 18.

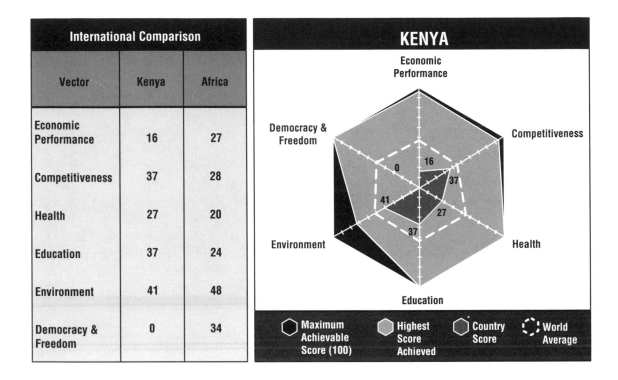

International Comparison		
Vector	Kenya	Africa
Economic Performance	16	27
Competitiveness	37	28
Health	27	20
Education	37	24
Environment	41	48
Democracy & Freedom	0	34

KENYA

Economic Performance

Democracy & Freedom

Competitiveness

Environment

Health

Education

0   16

41   37

27

37

- Maximum Achievable Score (100)
- Highest Score Achieved
- Country Score
- World Average

KENYA

Economic Development. Kenya's economy is heavily dependent on agriculture, which employs about 70 percent of the labor force and contributes about one quarter of GDP. The industrial sector is relatively developed and diversified. Tourism remains Kenya's principal source of foreign exchange, providing 22 percent of export earnings, while coffee and tea production together account for an additional 24 percent.

The early 1990s were marked by a sharp decline in all major macroeconomic performance indicators. Between 1990 and 1994, GDP grew less than 1 percent a year, while gross domestic investment declined. Per capita income stagnated between 1985 and 1994. A series of structural reforms have occurred since that time. In 1996 the government was able to reach an agreement with the IMF and the World Bank on a new set of policy reforms aimed at accelerating the reform progress made since 1993. The new program emphasizes the strengthening of public expenditure management, the establishment of a national social security fund, and continued privatization in important economic sectors.

Kenya scores poorly on Economic Performance (16), owing to its poor indicators in eco-

nomic growth in recent years. Its Competitiveness score of 37 is higher than the Africa average. In Competitiveness Kenya is relatively strong in the saving rate and the ratio of exports to GDP, but is hurt by low levels of foreign direct investment, a poor sovereign risk rating, high inflation rates, and persistent government deficits.

Social Development and the Environment. Poverty is a pervasive problem in Kenya; 45 percent of the rural population and 30 percent of the urban population are estimated to live below the poverty line. Kenya's social indicators are slightly better than the averages in Africa, as shown by scores of 27 on Health and 37 on Education. Despite improvement in recent years, fertility and population growth rates remain very high. Maternal mortality averaged 650 per 100,000 live births in 1993, and child survival and child health indicators are poor. An estimated 22 percent of the adult population is illiterate. Only three-quarters of schoolchildren complete grade five, and the nation's gross secondary ratio is only 25 percent.

The country's dependence on tourism has given the Kenyan government a keen interest in environmentally sustainable development. Nearly 6 percent of Kenya's land area is protected, much of it in its game reserves. An aggressive antipoaching program has reduced the threat to endangered species. The country's main environmental problems are soil erosion, desertification, and deforestation. Water pollution from urban and industrial sources is increasingly serious around major urban areas, and the increased use of fertilizer and pesticides is diminishing water quality. Only half of the population has access to safe water. Kenya receives 41 in Environment, below the Africa average.

Democracy and Freedom. The citizens of Kenya cannot choose their government. In recent years the Moi regime has used police powers, executive decrees, and a cooperating judiciary to suppress the opposition. The regime and the ruling party have complete control over the broadcast media. The government has threatened to expel foreign correspondents for negative reporting on the country. Lawlessness and corruption have plunged the government into a crisis of credibility. The legal right of workers to strike has been suspended by a decree. Kenya receives 0 in Democracy and Freedom.

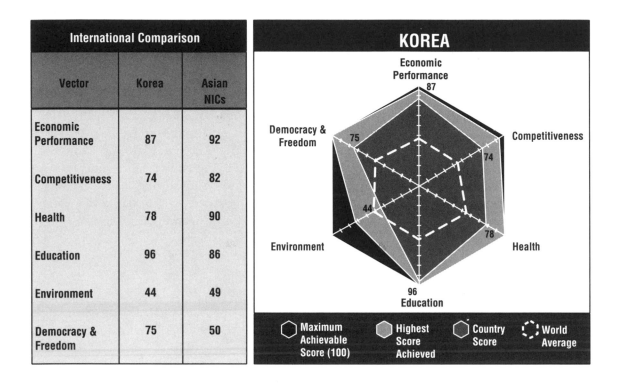

International Comparison		
Vector	Korea	Asian NICs
Economic Performance	87	92
Competitiveness	74	82
Health	78	90
Education	96	86
Environment	44	49
Democracy & Freedom	75	50

KOREA

Economic Performance
87

Democracy & Freedom   75   Competitiveness   74

44   78

Environment   96   Health
Education

Maximum Achievable Score (100) — Highest Score Achieved — Country Score — World Average

KOREA

Economic Development. The Republic of Korea (South Korea) has been one of the world's fastest-growing economies over the past four decades. The driving force behind the economy's dynamic growth has been the planned development of an export-oriented economy in a vigorously entrepreneurial society. In its recent economic history, the country has gone through four distinct phases: war and reconstruction (1950–60), export takeoff (1961–73), heavy industry (1973–79), and finally overall liberalization since 1980. Korean industries are now highly competitive in the export of high value-added products, such as electronics components, automobiles, and chemicals.

Korea receives one of the world's highest scores on Economic Performance (87), boosted by a 7 percent GDP growth rate and a 11 percent export growth rate in 1990–94. Its per capita GDP of U.S. $9,700 in 1995 ranks it below the other Asian NICs (Hong Kong, Singapore, and Taiwan) and places it in the category of upper-middle-income countries. Korea also receives very high scores in the competitiveness vector (74) as a result of high gross domestic saving, a good ratio of exports to GDP, a government budget surplus, and the high number of scientists and engineers in the population.

Social Development and the Environment. Korea has some of the world's best education indicators, which is particularly impressive for a country at its per capita income level. Illiteracy has been practically eradicated. Primary and secondary enrollment is universal, while tertiary enrollment is nearly 55 percent, among the world's highest. Korea scores 96 on Education, ranking first among the Asian NICs. Korea's health indicators are weaker: it scores 78 on the Health vector, compared with the Asian NIC average of 90. Indicators are particularly weak in the areas of maternal health, child survival, and child health.

Korea suffers from urban environmental problems typical of rapidly developing countries. Rapid urbanization and industrialization have brought severe air pollution, traffic congestion, and solid waste disposal problems to major urban areas. Despite improvements in sewage systems and industrial pollution con-

trols, untreated discharges still contaminate many water supplies. Over a quarter of the population in the rural areas does not have access to safe water. Korea scores 44 on the Environment vector, below the Asia average and the lowest among the Asian NICs.

Democracy and Freedom. Since 1992 and after several decades of military rule, South Koreans can change their government democratically. The 1988 constitution limits the president to a single five-year term and revokes the executive's power to dissolve the legislature. A free and independent judiciary is currently prosecuting several former presidents for corruption and human rights abuses. The state-funded broadcast media offer pluralistic views, and the print media practice some self-censorship. Women face discrimination in many aspects of society, and domestic violence against women remains a widespread problem. Korea receives a score of 75 on Democracy and Freedom, well above the average of 36 in Asia and higher than the Asian NIC average of 50.

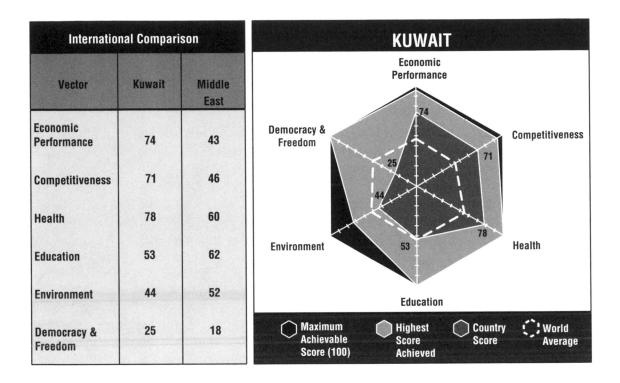

International Comparison		
Vector	Kuwait	Middle East
Economic Performance	74	43
Competitiveness	71	46
Health	78	60
Education	53	62
Environment	44	52
Democracy & Freedom	25	18

KUWAIT

Economic Performance

Democracy & Freedom

74

25

44

Competitiveness

71

78

53

Environment

Health

Education

Maximum Achievable Score (100)   Highest Score Achieved   Country Score   World Average

KUWAIT

Economic Development. Kuwait, with a per capita income estimated at U.S. $24,730 in 1994, is one of the wealthiest countries in world. The oil sector strongly dominates the economy. Kuwait has the third largest oil reserves in the world, trailing only Saudi Arabia and Iraq. Earnings from oil generate over 90 percent of both export and government revenues. Most of the nonoil sector has been dependent on oil-derived government revenues for support. Iraq destroyed or seriously damaged 80 percent of Kuwait's 950 operating oil wells during the Gulf War, devastating Kuwait's economy. It took three years to restore Kuwait's oil production after the war.

Kuwait's economic performance during the 1990s has been strong, earning it a score of 74 in the economic performance vector, owing in large part to the economic recovery from the wartime destruction. The country's Competitiveness score, at 71, is also high, as a result of strong indicators that include gross domestic saving, exports as a percentage of GDP, and high-quality infrastructure. However, Kuwait is weak in the number of scientists, engineers, and technicians in the population.

Social Development and the Environment. Kuwait's social indicators are weak for a country with such a high income level. Over one-fifth of the adult population is illiterate, and the fraction is higher among women. Primary and secondary enrollment rates are low for the country's level of development. Kuwait receives only 53 points in the education vector. The country is stronger on Health, scoring 78. Its score is hurt by high population growth as well as maternal and child health indicators that are only average.

The 1991 Gulf War brought environmental disaster to Kuwait. The destruction and burning of oil wells resulted in massive air and soil pollution. Millions of barrels of oil spilled into the Gulf continue to threaten marine life and other wildlife. Troop movements also damaged the fragile desert soils. The extraordinary harm done to Kuwait's environment during the Gulf War cannot not be entirely captured by the indicators in the development web. Kuwait receives a score of 44 on Environment, below the Middle East average.

Democracy and Freedom. Ruled by an emir from the al-Sabah family, which has ruled the state since 1756, Kuwait is a kingdom whose citizens do not have the right to change their government. Broad executive power is vested in the emir. He appoints the executive branch and can dissolve the legislature and suspend articles of the constitution at will. Most key government positions are occupied by members of the al-Sabah family. The judiciary is not free from government influence. Many fundamental freedoms, such as freedom of expression and association, are not respected if they involve criticism of the emir or the al-Sabah family.

The government severely restricts and tightly controls the organization of trade unions. Kuwait scores 25 on Democracy and Freedom, very low compared with the world average but higher than the Middle East average.

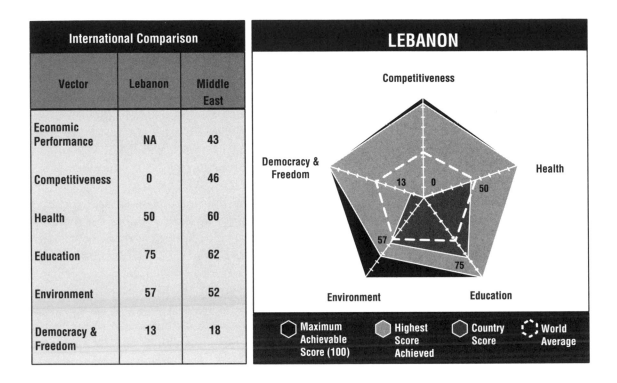

International Comparison		
Vector	Lebanon	Middle East
Economic Performance	NA	43
Competitiveness	0	46
Health	50	60
Education	75	62
Environment	57	52
Democracy & Freedom	13	18

LEBANON

Competitiveness

Democracy & Freedom

Health

13 0 50

57

75

Environment

Education

○ Maximum Achievable Score (100)   ● Highest Score Achieved   ⬡ Country Score   ⬡ World Average

LEBANON

Economic Development. A prosperous, upper-middle-income nation until the mid-1970s, Lebanon was devastated by a decade and a half of violent civil war and military occupation. Rebuilding the nation's economy has been a huge task requiring a massive mobilization of resources, capital financing, and restoration of institutions over an extended period of time. Since the cessation of the conflict in 1990, the Lebanese government has attempted to normalize economic conditions and begin economic recovery by controlling inflation and rapid currency depreciation. GDP growth was 8.0 percent in 1994 and 6.5 percent in 1995.

The lack of economic data prevents the assignment of a score for Lebanon in the economic performance vector. Its Competitiveness score of 0 is based on only one available indicator and is most likely biased downward.

Social Development and the Environment. The civil conflict had a severe impact on social conditions in Lebanon. Nearly one-quarter of the population—close to a million people—were displaced and live in unhealthy conditions. Urban poverty problems are particularly acute in Beirut. War damage has severely diminished the capacity of public health facilities. Public and social services are either nonexistent or of poor quality. Most health services are provided by nongovernment organizations associated with the war situation. Power plants are operating at only one-third capacity, and water treatment and sewage are virtually absent. During the civil war, most schools were damaged and school enrollment dropped. Lebanon's Health score of 50 is worse than the scores of Jordan and Tunisia, which have much lower income levels. Lebanon's relatively high score of 75 on Education reflects its prewar status as a highly educated society.

The principal environmental issues in Lebanon are related to land degradation and water pollution resulting from rapid urbanization and industrial development. Chronic political instability and open military conflicts between Lebanon and its neighbors have also adversely affected its environment. After the 1982 invasion by Israel, the Ministry of the Environment ceased most of its work. Lebanon scores 57 on Environment, just above the Middle East average.

Democracy and Freedom. Lebanese citizens cannot change their government democratically. Syria's heavy military presence and political influence have made it difficult for democratic institutions and procedures to take hold and function. In addition, Israel occupies and maintains a "security zone" in southern Lebanon, and fighting and armed conflict occasionally break out between Israeli troops and Hezbollah guerillas there. The Lebanese security forces are often accused of human rights violation. The judiciary is not independent, and corruption is common. The state-owned Lebanon Television has a legal monopoly on television until 2012. Under intimidation, journalists generally practice self-censorship. Lebanon receives a score of 13 on Democracy and Freedom, just below the Middle East average of 18.

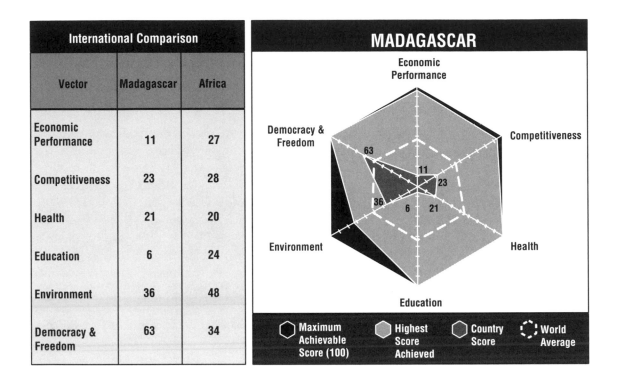

International Comparison		
Vector	**Madagascar**	**Africa**
Economic Performance	11	27
Competitiveness	23	28
Health	21	20
Education	6	24
Environment	36	48
Democracy & Freedom	63	34

MADAGASCAR

Economic Performance

Democracy & Freedom

63

11

23

36   6   21

Competitiveness

Environment

Health

Education

Maximum Achievable Score (100) Highest Score Achieved Country Score World Average

MADAGASCAR

Economic Development. Madagascar, which occupies the world's fourth-largest island, is endowed with abundant, diverse natural resources and a large pool of low-cost labor. However, its per capita income of U.S. $230 in 1995 ranks it as one of the least developed countries in the world. The national economy is predominantly agricultural, with 80 percent of the population living in rural areas. The agricultural sector is dominated by small-scale farms producing both food and export crops. Madagascar's chief exports are vanilla, coffee, and shellfish.

Political transition to a multiparty democracy and the disruption of the adjustment process significantly affected Madagascar's economic and financial performance over 1991–95. During that period, real per capita income declined 10 percent, domestic investment fell at a rate of over 7 percent a year, the fiscal situation deteriorated, the competitiveness of the economy declined, and poverty increased. Madagascar receives a very low score of 11 on Economic Performance. On Competitiveness, its score, 23, is hurt by a low saving rate, a persistent government deficit, and a high average inflation rate.

Social Development and the Environment. Poverty is widespread in this underdeveloped

Madagascar

country. Most of Madagascar's social indicators are below sub-Saharan Africa standards. Life expectancy is only fifty-two years, and 164 children of 1,000 live births are not expected to live beyond the age of five. Malaria is a major health problem, and tuberculosis and other communicable diseases are increasing. Chronic malnutrition is as high as 40 percent in certain areas. Population growth (3.2 percent) and fertility rates (6 births per woman) are very high. Illiteracy is a serious problem. Already low, school enrollment rates are falling rapidly, and just over a quarter of all students complete grade five. The nation's public health and education systems are underfunded and inefficient. Madagascar scores 21 on Health, just above the Africa average. Its Education score (6) is one of the lowest in Africa.

The major environmental problem in Madagascar is deforestation. Three-quarters of the country's forested lands are already destroyed. The traditional slash-and-burn technique of farming has exacerbated the degradation of the land. Only 10 percent of the population in rural areas has access to safe drinking water. Surface water is heavily contaminated with untreated sewage and other organic wastes. Madagascar scores 36 in the environment vector, among the lowest scores in Africa.

Democracy and Freedom. Citizens of Madagascar can change their government democratically. However, truly democratic institutions have yet to take hold. Political opponents are often subject to intimidation and in some cases arrest for being "threats to security." The judiciary is generally free and independent. Women are well represented in government and urban managerial occupations, especially compared with the situation in mainland African countries. The press is generally free, but the broadcast media are state owned and usually present the government's views. Madagascar scores 63 on Democracy and Freedom, much higher than the Africa average of 36.

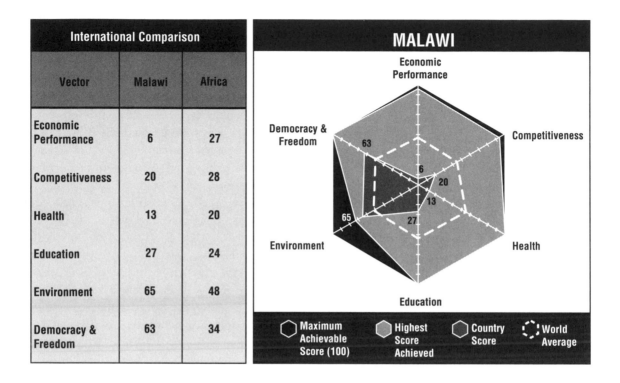

International Comparison		
Vector	**Malawi**	**Africa**
Economic Performance	6	27
Competitiveness	20	28
Health	13	20
Education	27	24
Environment	65	48
Democracy & Freedom	63	34

MALAWI

- ⬡ Maximum Achievable Score (100)
- ⬡ Highest Score Achieved
- ⬡ Country Score
- ⬡ World Average

MALAWI

Economic Development. With a per capita income of U.S. $160 in 1995, Malawi remains one of the poorest countries in the world. Geography poses daunting challenges to the nation's economic development. It is small and land-locked, lacks mineral resources, and is among the most densely populated sub-Saharan nations. The economy is extremely undiversified, with 85 percent of the labor force employed in agriculture. Maize and burley tobacco production accounts for 40 percent of GDP.

Major droughts in 1992 and 1994 and falling tobacco prices led to losses of more than one-quarter of GDP. These shocks were com-pounded by the suspension of external assistance as donors expressed displeasure over poor economic management by the government. In 1994 a full-blown macroeconomic crisis developed in the face of runaway government expenditures, steep depreciation in the exchange rate, and deterioration in government budget management.

A very low Economic Performance score of 6 reflects declining GDP and negative growth in gross domestic investment between 1990 and 1994. Malawi showed strong signs of recovery in 1995. On Competitiveness Malawi scores 20, hurt by its negative domestic saving ratio, low levels of foreign direct investment, and a persistently high inflation rate, which averaged 19 percent between 1984 and 1994.

Social Development and the Environment. Poverty is pervasive and deeply rooted in this nation, with an estimated 30 percent of the population having incomes inadequate to purchase basic nutritional needs. Malawi's social indicators are among the worst in the world. Life expectancy is a very low forty-four years. Out of 1,000 live births, 221 children do not survive past the age of five. Fertility averages 7 children per woman. Malawi also has one of the highest prevalences of HIV infection and AIDS in Africa, and infection is increasing at alarming rates. Water and sanitation are severely inadequate. Adult illiteracy is at about 44 percent, and the primary enrollment ratio is low. Fewer than half of all students reach grade five. Malawi scores 13 on Health and 27 on Education.

Contributing to Malawi's environmental problems are population density and growth rates that are among the highest in Africa. Deforestation has been exacerbated by the influx of refugees from neighboring Mozambique. Malawi scores 65 on Environment, higher than the Africa average of 48.

Democracy and Freedom. In 1994 the citizens of Malawi for the first time elected their government in a multiparty election. To minimize the political influence of the army, military personnel were barred from voting. The judiciary is not wholly independent, as shown by the questionable charges brought by the government against its key political and media opponents in 1994. Charges that the government interfered with state broadcasting and intimidated journalists tarnished Malawi's reputation for having some of the most freely operated media in Africa. Freedoms of expression, of assembly, and of religion are generally respected. Malawi receives a score of 63 on Democracy and Freedom, much higher than the Africa average.

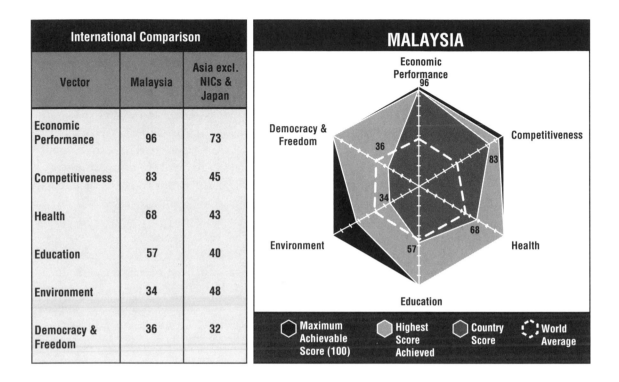

International Comparison		
Vector	Malaysia	Asia excl. NICs & Japan
Economic Performance	96	73
Competitiveness	83	45
Health	68	43
Education	57	40
Environment	34	48
Democracy & Freedom	36	32

MALAYSIA

Economic Performance 96

Democracy & Freedom — 36

Competitiveness — 83

Environment — 34

Health — 68

Education — 57

Maximum Achievable Score (100) · Highest Score Achieved · Country Score · World Average

MALAYSIA

Economic Development. Like many of its Southeast Asian neighbors, Malaysia has achieved remarkable economic success, sustaining one of the world's highest growth rates. Per capita GDP grew at an average annual rate of 5.6 percent between 1985 and 1994, led by strong expansion in the manufacturing sector, particularly in export-oriented industries such as electronics and electrical machinery. Growth remained strong in the 1990s, with investment and exports increasing 15 percent and 13 percent respectively in 1990–94. Malaysia's stunning growth rates earn it the highest Economic Performance score (96) among the countries assessed by the web model.

Throughout the period of growth, Malaysia has kept inflation and the balance of payments under control. Its good economic foundation is reflected in its high Competitiveness score of 83. Indicators in which Malaysia is particularly strong include domestic saving rate, ratio of exports to GDP, level of foreign direct investment level, government budget surplus, and low average inflation rate of 3.1 percent between 1984 and 1994.

Social Development and the Environment. One of Malaysia's most outstanding social achievements is its poverty alleviation program. In 1970 almost half the population was counted among the absolute poor. By 1995, the level had fallen below 10 percent. The government's programs to educate and to redistribute wealth toward the Malay population, whose income lagged far behind that of the Chinese and Indian populations, have reduced income discrepancies. Such programs have played a major role in maintaining social stability in the multiethnic country.

Malaysia's social indicators are higher than the averages in Asia. Life expectancy at birth is seventy-one years, and maternal and child health and survival indicators have greatly improved. Malaysia's success in bringing basic education to the majority of the population is reflected in its high primary enrollment ratio and completion rate for grade five. The government spends about one-third of its total expenditure on education. Malaysia scores 68 in the health vector and 57 in the education vector.

Malaysia suffers from serious deforestation as a result of large-scale commercial logging in tropical rain forests. Industrial discharges and runoff from tin mines have also polluted an estimated 40 percent of the rivers in the peninsular area of the country. Air pollution is increasingly a problem due to rapid industrial development. About one-third of the rural population has no access to safe water. Malaysia receives a score of 34 on Environment, the lowest in Asia.

Democracy and Freedom. The freedom of Malaysians to change their government democratically is limited. The government maintains considerable control over the media, bans outdoor rallies, and uses its security laws against dissidents. Official policy discriminates against Chinese, Indians, and other non-Malays in education, employment, and business affairs. Freedom of speech is restricted, and the discussion of certain sensitive issues is prohibited. Media freedom in limited in Malaysia, and coverage is heavily biased in favor of the ruling party. The government maintains censorship and has the power to close down newspapers. Malaysia scores 36 on Democracy and Freedom, slightly higher than the average score for the region.

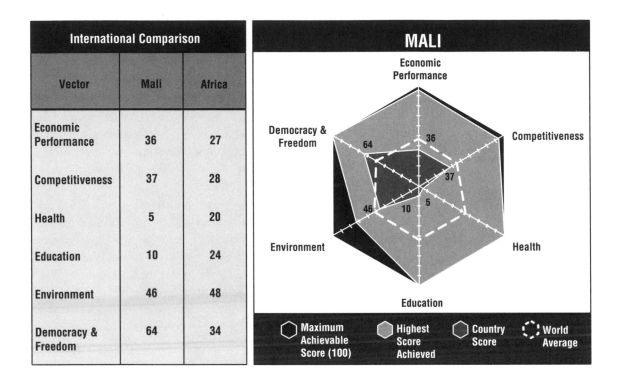

International Comparison		
Vector	Mali	Africa
Economic Performance	36	27
Competitiveness	37	28
Health	5	20
Education	10	24
Environment	46	48
Democracy & Freedom	64	34

MALI (chart)

Economic Performance — 36
Competitiveness — 37
Health — 5
Education — 10
Environment — 46
Democracy & Freedom — 64

Maximum Achievable Score (100) | Highest Score Achieved | Country Score | World Average

MALI

Economic Development. Mali is one of the least developed countries in the world, with a per capita income of $250 in 1995. The mainstays of the traditional economy are millet, rice and other cereals, and nomadic cattle raising. Exports are dominated by traditional commodities such as cotton and livestock. The modern sector includes cotton processing, gold mining, and some light manufacturing. Per capita income grew at a slow rate of 1 percent between 1985 and 1994. Mali scores 36 on Economic Performance, higher than the Africa average.

Since 1988 the government of Mali has implemented a wide range of economic and sec-toral policy reforms under its structural adjustment program. The underlying objective of the reform program was to improve the competitiveness of the economy and lay the foundation for sustained, long-term growth. Structural adjustment efforts have helped move Mali from a closed, heavily controlled system to one of the more open and liberal economies in the African currency zone. Its improved economic environment is reflected in a Competitiveness score of 37, higher than the regional average. Inflation remained in check between 1984 and 1994, averaging 3.4 percent. However, the saving ratio and levels of foreign direct investment are low.

Mali

Social Development and the Environment. As one of the poorest countries in the world, Mali has some of the worst social indicators. Adult illiteracy, at 69 percent, is among the world's highest. Primary education enrollment rates are very low, at about 32 percent, and of those enrolled only three-quarters complete grade five. Basic health services are not widely available. Maternal mortality is estimated at 1,200 per 100,000 live births, and over 214 of 1,000 children do not survive until the age of five, bringing life expectancy down to forty-nine years. Mali's Health score of 5 and Education score of 10 are among the lowest in Africa and the world.

In 1994 the government initiated a program to reduce poverty and improve standards of living through sustained economic growth, expanded access to basic health and primary education, and targeted interventions to address the needs of vulnerable groups. It was followed in 1995 by a program that placed specific emphasis on improving both access to and quality of education.

Water scarcity is the dominant environmental issue in Mali, which is threatened by severe, recurring drought. The destruction of trees and of firewood, overcultivation, and overgrazing in wet years have all led to land degradation and soil erosion. Drought, poaching, and loss of natural habitat also threaten to decimate much of Mali's wildlife. Mali scores 46 on Environment, just below the Africa average.

Democracy and Freedom. After three decades of military rule and dictatorship, Mali's citizens can change their government democratically. The current government was elected in 1992 by universal suffrage in free and fair elections. However, outbreaks of sporadic violence and military conflict between the government and armed rebel groups continue to threaten this newly created democracy. An entrenched bureaucracy riddled with corruption undermines the government's ability to promote economic development. Minority and religious rights are mostly respected. The media are among the most open in Africa. Mali receives a score of 64 on Democracy and Freedom, much higher than the regional average score of 34.

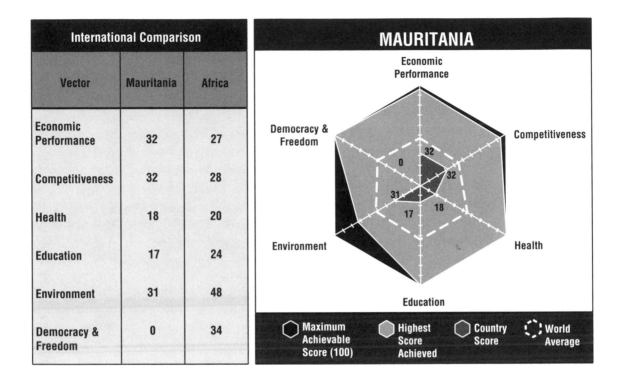

International Comparison		
Vector	**Mauritania**	**Africa**
Economic Performance	32	27
Competitiveness	32	28
Health	18	20
Education	17	24
Environment	31	48
Democracy & Freedom	0	34

MAURITANIA

Maximum Achievable Score (100) · Highest Score Achieved · Country Score · World Average

MAURITANIA

Economic Development. Although the country covers a vast area, Mauritania is inhabited by only 2 million people. Most of the country's land is desert and provides a very limited natural resource base. Per capita income in Mauritania was U.S. $460 in 1995. Between 1989 and 1992, Mauritania suffered a series of internal and external shocks that severely affected its economic and financial performance, disrupted economic activity, and slowed adjustment. Since 1992 Mauritania has intensified its adjustment and structural reform efforts and has achieved encouraging results. Structural reforms have been implemented in such key areas as trade, foreign exchange, pricing, the tax system, public enterprises, public expenditure, civil service, and social sector policies.

Mauritania scores 32 on Economic Performance and 32 on Competitiveness, both of which are higher than the Africa averages. The Economic Performance score is hurt by declining exports in the early 1990s and stagnation of per capita GDP between 1985 and 1994. In Competitiveness Mauritania earns points for its exports-to-GDP ratio and for a relatively low inflation rate, averaging 7 percent over the 1984–94 period.

Social Development and the Environment. Mauritania's social indicators mostly reflect its status as a low-income country. It receives a score of 18 on Health and 17 on Education, both of which are below the regional averages. Life expectancy at birth is low at fifty-one years. Fertility, maternal mortality, and child mortality rates are very high. An estimated 65 percent of the adult population is illiterate. Fewer than three-quarters of children attend primary school.

Alleviating Mauritania's high degree of poverty has been difficult because of lagging long-term economic growth, given its high population growth rate. The government has made serious efforts to help the poor cope with the difficult conditions brought by economic downturn and adjustment. Despite budgetary constraints, the government has protected basic social services such as education and health.

Close to 80 percent of the country lies in the Sahara Desert. Drought and overgrazing have contributed to the gradual encroachment of the desert on marginal land. The major environmental problems are deforestation, desertification, and the scarcity of water. Mauritania receives a score of 31 on Environment, one of the lowest in Africa.

Democracy and Freedom. Mauritanians cannot change their government democratically. The 1992 presidential polls were widely considered fraudulent, while the legislative poll was boycotted by opposition parties. The ruling Social Democratic Republican Party is supported by the military. Censorship and state ownership severely restrict media freedom. "Promoting disharmony" and "insulting the president" are punishable offenses. There is no freedom of religion in the country; all Mauritanians are Sunni Muslims by statute and are not allowed to possess other religious texts. The legal system is influenced by the *shari'a* law and discriminates against women. Mauritania receives a score of 0 on Democracy and Freedom.

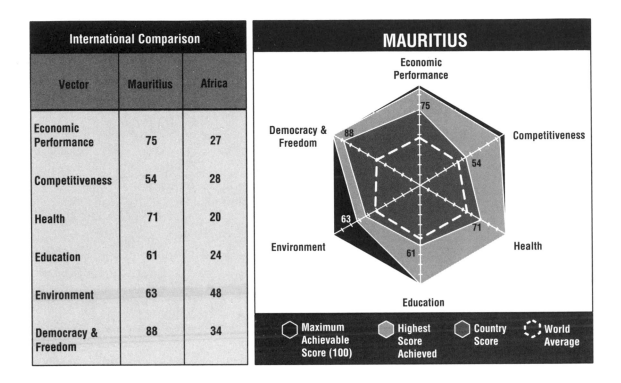

International Comparison		
Vector	Mauritius	Africa
Economic Performance	75	27
Competitiveness	54	28
Health	71	20
Education	61	24
Environment	63	48
Democracy & Freedom	88	34

MAURITIUS

Economic Performance · Competitiveness · Health · Education · Environment · Democracy & Freedom

Maximum Achievable Score (100) · Highest Score Achieved · Country Score · World Average

MAURITIUS

Economic Development. Since 1970, when GNP per capita was about U.S. $300, Mauritius, which consists of three islands in the Indian Ocean, has evolved from a low-income, agriculture-based economy to a dynamic and diversified economy with a 1995 per capita income of U.S. $3,280. Measured in purchasing-power parity, Mauritius's per capita income was estimated at over U.S. $13,000 in 1995. Growth in the 1970s was spurred by sugar production, which provided almost one-fifth of GDP and over half of export earnings. Diversification into manufacturing and tourism reduced the role of the sugar sector to 6 percent

of GDP and only one-fifth of export earnings in 1994. Export-processing zones now account for over half of gross export earnings.

With the exception of a relatively short period of sluggish growth in 1979–81, Mauritius' record is one of solid growth and prudent financial management. Per capita income rose rapidly at a rate of nearly 6 percent between 1985 and 1994. Investment and export growth remained brisk in the early 1990s. This strong performance has been made possible by a liberal economic environment, including an open exchange and trade regime, incentives for foreign private investment, strong resource mobilization, conservative public expenditure policies, prudent credit expansion, and good governance. Mauritius scores 75 in the economic performance vector, and its solid economic foundation earns it a Competitiveness score of 54, both among the highest in Africa.

Since 1988, however, the economy has faced increasing cost pressures as the country approaches full employment. Mauritius is in a critical juncture in its development as it aspires to enter the ranks of newly industrializing economies.

Social Development and the Environment. Standards of nutrition, health care, and general education in Mauritius exceed those of most neighboring countries and are impressive for a country at its development level. The benefits of the rapid increase in per capita income and full employment have reached the vast majority of Mauritians. Life expectancy at birth is now seventy years, compared with fifty-nine years in 1960. Maternal and child mortality indicators are all better than the averages for Africa. Primary enrollment is nearly universal. However, higher education opportunities are limited in this small country. Mauritius scores 71 on Health and 61 on Education, the highest scores in Africa.

Over the past decade and a half, the government has put into place extensive social safety mechanisms. Mauritians now face the challenge of adapting their welfare system to a more efficient mechanism of social support while ensuring services to those with the greatest need.

Land degradation, an environmental issue, is primarily caused by the overuse of pesticides and fertilizers. Other environmental problems include water pollution by industrial wastes and conservation of rare species. Both rural and urban populations have good access to safe water by Africa standards. Mauritius scores 63 on Environment, among the highest in Africa.

Democracy and Freedom. Citizens of Mauritius can change their government through free, fair, and competitive elections. Ethnic and religious minorities are guaranteed representation in the legislature. The largely independent judiciary system is based on both British and French precedents. Freedom of religion is respected. The press is independent and rigorous, and freedoms of assembly and association are protected. Mauritius scores 88 on Democracy and Freedom, one of the highest scores in Africa.

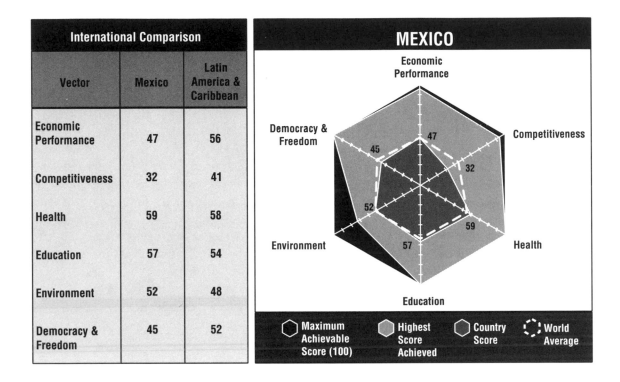

International Comparison		
Vector	Mexico	Latin America & Caribbean
Economic Performance	47	56
Competitiveness	32	41
Health	59	58
Education	57	54
Environment	52	48
Democracy & Freedom	45	52

MEXICO

Economic Performance

Democracy & Freedom

Competitiveness

Environment

Health

Education

- Maximum Achievable Score (100)
- Highest Score Achieved
- Country Score
- World Average

MEXICO

GLOBAL Benchmarks

Economic Development. For a short period after the signing of the North America Free Trade Agreement in December 1992, Mexico saw bright prospects for accelerating investment and economic growth through closer ties with its more prosperous North American trade partners. However, its growth potential was abruptly halted by the unfolding of a major financial crisis in 1994. Following mounting pressure on Mexico's exchange rate and a near-depletion of its foreign exchange reserves, the Mexican government was forced to allow the peso to depreciate dramatically in the free market in December 1994. The collapse of the peso plunged Mexico into its deepest recession in six decades.

In 1995 the government initiated a reform program aimed at stabilizing the economy and restoring international confidence. Mexico has made substantial progress on adjustment, especially in increasing discipline in its fiscal and monetary policies. Although investment has begun to trickle back into the country, millions of poor and middle-class Mexicans are still suffering from the distressed economy.

Mexico scores 47 on Economic Performance, below the regional average as a result of its modest GDP growth rate between 1990 and

1994 and the stagnation of per capita income over 1985–94. Its Competitiveness score, 32, is also below the regional average and is hurt by a very high government deficit, averaging close to 10 percent, and a low sovereign bond rating.

Social Development and the Environment. Mexico's social indicators are generally in line with those in Latin America and the Caribbean. Life expectancy at birth was seventy-one years in 1995, compared with fifty-seven in 1960, while infant mortality had declined almost two-thirds. Mexico has achieved universal enrollment in primary school, but secondary and tertiary enrollment ratios remain low. Mexico receives 59 in Health and 57 in Education, both of which are just above the regional averages.

Air, water, and land pollution is severe around urban and industrial areas, especially Mexico City. To combat air pollution, the government has established controls on auto emissions in recent years. Inadequate treatment of sewage and industrial effluents has led to heav-

ily polluted rivers. Mexico scores 52 in the environment vector, just above the average for Latin America and the Caribbean.

Democracy and Freedom. While Mexican citizens in principle can change their government democratically, the domination of the Institutional Revolutionary Party (PRI) in financial, institutional, and media resources has brought the fairness of the elections into question. Signs are that opposition parties may seriously challenge the PRI in the presidential election in 2000. Both the judiciary and the police force are politicized and prone to corruption. Overall, the rule of law is weak. The media, while mostly private, rely on the government for a large portion of their advertising revenue and operating costs. The military has been accused of human rights violations, especially in the suppression of the ongoing Chiapas rebellion. Mexico scores 45 on Democracy and Freedom, lower than the average for Latin America and the Caribbean.

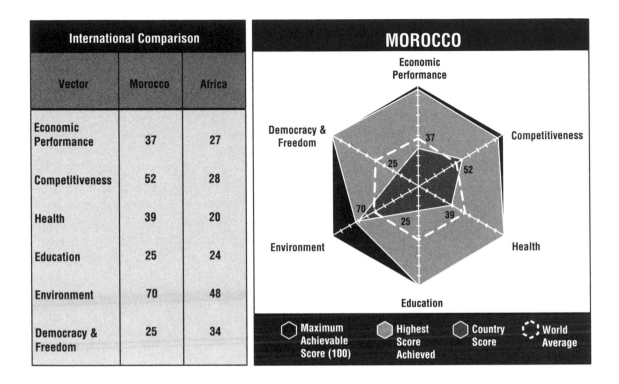

International Comparison		
Vector	**Morocco**	**Africa**
Economic Performance	37	27
Competitiveness	52	28
Health	39	20
Education	25	24
Environment	70	48
Democracy & Freedom	25	34

MOROCCO

Economic Performance

Democracy & Freedom

Competitiveness

Environment

Health

Education

37 · 25 · 52 · 70 · 25 · 39

Maximum Achievable Score (100)	Highest Score Achieved	Country Score	World Average

MOROCCO

Economic Development. With a per capita income of U.S. $1,130 in 1995, Morocco ranks among the low- to middle-income developing countries. The country has made great progress in stabilizing and managing its economy over the past decade, particularly in reorienting its economy from heavy state control to a primary reliance on market mechanisms. Morocco's Economic Performance score (37) is higher than the Africa average but below the world average, as a result of declining growth in gross domestic investment and slow GDP and export growth in 1990–94. The country performs much better in the competitiveness vector, scoring 52 owing to a high level of foreign direct investment, low inflation rates, and a relatively small government budget deficit. Morocco will need sustained and rapid growth to reduce its 16 percent unemployment rate, especially given the population's high rate of growth.

Social Development and the Environment. Morocco's social indicators continue to lag those in countries with similar income levels. The disparity between urban and rural areas is serious, particularly regarding poverty levels and indicators of literacy and health. Public expenditure on health amounted to under 1 percent of GDP in 1995, below the norm for countries at similar development levels. Funds have been concentrated on large urban hospitals rather than on small rural dispensaries. Infant mortality and maternal mortality are high and life expectancy is low relative to other low- to middle-income nations. Over half of the adult population is illiterate. Morocco scores 39 on Health and 25 on Education.

Soil erosion, a major problem in Morocco, has resulted from the expansion of farmland into marginal areas, overgrazing, the destruction of vegetation for firewood, and the conversion of forests to farmland. Untreated sewage is the primary cause of water contamination in some areas. Only 18 percent of the rural population has access to potable water. Morocco scores 70 in the environment vector, the highest score in Africa, primarily because of high scores on several indicators, including greenhouse gas emissions, participation in major global environmental conventions, and the number of environmental NGOs registered.

Democracy and Freedom. Moroccans are ruled by a king and cannot change their government democratically. The king wields enormous executive and legislative powers. Governance is neither transparent nor accountable. The constitutional guarantee of free expression is not upheld in practice, especially if it involves criticism of the king, his family or the institution of monarchy. The broadcast media are controlled by the government. Freedom of assembly is restricted by several decrees. The judiciary is highly subject to government influence. Women are often discriminated by the use of the *shari'a* law, which governs matters of family law. Morocco scores 25 on Democracy and Freedom, lower than the average for Africa.

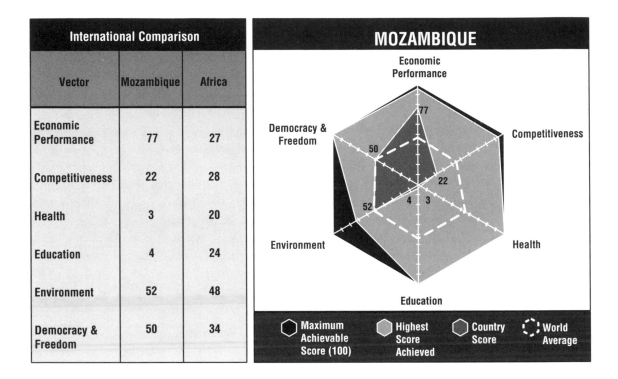

International Comparison		
Vector	Mozambique	Africa
Economic Performance	77	27
Competitiveness	22	28
Health	3	20
Education	4	24
Environment	52	48
Democracy & Freedom	50	34

MOZAMBIQUE

Economic Performance

Democracy & Freedom

Competitiveness

Environment

Health

Education

77   50   22   52   4   3

Maximum Achievable Score (100) — Highest Score Achieved — Country Score — World Average

MOZAMBIQUE

Economic Development. Mozambique endured nearly fifteen years of civil war, which ended in 1992. The end of hostilities and favorable weather spurred growth of 19 percent in 1993 and allowed more modest growth of 5 percent in 1994, earning Mozambique a very high Economic Performance score of 77. The score is also boosted by a brisk domestic investment and export growth rate between 1990 and 1994. However, that growth was built on a low base, and Mozambique remains one of the poorest countries in the world, with a per capita income of U.S. $80 in 1995.

Mozambique has made steady albeit slow progress in implementing the reform agenda begun in 1987. However, macroeconomic stabilization is still elusive, and structural reform is far from complete. Progress in banking reform has been slow. The weakness of the country's economic foundation is reflected in its low Competitiveness score of 22. Competitiveness indicators that are particularly weak are the low national saving rate and runaway budget deficit.

Social Development and the Environment. Social indicators in Mozambique are among the worst in the world. The nation's social service infrastructure has been decimated by the civil war.

Mozambique

Close to two-thirds of the population lacks access to health services. Life expectancy at birth is forty-six years. The country's fertility rate (6.4 children per woman), maternal mortality rate (1,500 deaths per 100,000 live births), and child mortality rate (277 per 1,000 live births die before the age of five) are among the world's highest. Chronic malnutrition is estimated to affect 30 to 40 percent of the nation's children. HIV infections are increasing at alarming rates. Close to two-thirds of the adult population is illiterate, a rate much higher than the sub-Saharan Africa average. Mozambique scores 3 on Health and 4 on Education.

The struggle for independence and the ensuing civil war in Mozambique led to widespread displacement of its population, devastation of livelihoods, and extensive environmental problems. Population pressures in areas affected by refugees from the war have made the environment more vulnerable. Two-thirds of the population lacks access to safe water. Mozambique scores 52 on Environment, just above the Africa average.

Democracy and Freedom. In 1994 the citizens of Mozambique chose their government in the country's first open, free, and fair election. However, institutions of democracy are still weak after the two preceding decades of military conflict and repressive rule. While media freedom is protected in the constitution, the state continues to monopolize reporting in the media through ownership and other influences. The judiciary system lacks resources and is prone to political influences. Religious freedom is generally respected. Mozambique receives a score of 50 on Democracy and Freedom, higher than the Africa average.

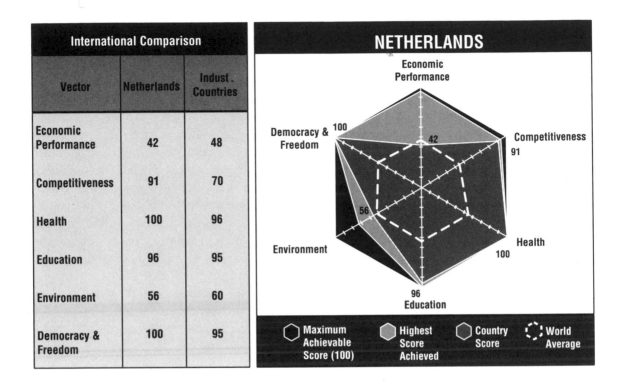

International Comparison		
Vector	Netherlands	Indust. Countries
Economic Performance	42	48
Competitiveness	91	70
Health	100	96
Education	96	95
Environment	56	60
Democracy & Freedom	100	95

NETHERLANDS

- Maximum Achievable Score (100)
- Highest Score Achieved
- Country Score
- World Average

THE NETHERLANDS

Economic Development. The Netherlands is one of the most developed and affluent economies in the world. The government historically has played a very active role in the economy. In 1994 total government expenditure represented 52 percent of GNP. The government makes its presence felt in many ways, including regulations, permit requirements, welfare programs, and programs affecting most types of economic activity.

On Economic Performance the Netherlands receives a less than stellar score of 42. Economic growth in the early 1990s was slow, gross domestic investment growth was negative, and export growth was only moderate. In the competitiveness vector, however, the country receives a very strong score of 91—one of the highest in the world. The country earns high scores in nearly all Competitiveness categories. The export to GDP ratio is over 50 percent, the saving rate is high at 24 percent of GDP, and inflation rates are low, averaging 1.6 percent from 1984 to 1994.

Social Development and the Environment. Social indicators in the Netherlands are among the best in the world. The country scores 96 on Education and a perfect score of 100 on Health. Access to education is a constitutional right, obliging the government to fund public and private schools on an equal basis. The Compulsory Education Act requires all students to attend school full-time until the age of sixteen and at least part-time until the age of eighteen. More than half of the labor force holds at least a qualification at the upper secondary level. The government spends about 10 percent of its total expenditure on health and pays about 70 percent of all health costs. Life expectancy at birth is seventy-eight, one of the highest in the world.

The Netherlands is the most densely populated country and one of the most polluted countries in Europe. About half of the pollution comes from other countries. The nation suffers from severe surface water pollution, smog, and acid rain. The degree of air pollution from vehicles and industrial activities is high enough to cause concern for human health, crops, and forests. The Netherlands scores 56 on Environment, below the average for industrialized countries average.

Democracy and Freedom. The Netherlands is a constitutional monarchy in which citizens can change their government democratically. Fundamental freedoms and rights are protected and respected. A series of constitutional amendments incorporate welfare state provisions and democratic reform. The judiciary is independent and generally efficient. The Netherlands receives a perfect score of 100 on Democracy and Freedom.

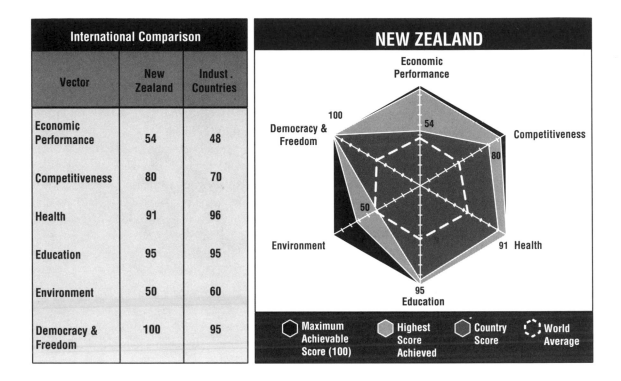

International Comparison		
Vector	New Zealand	Indust. Countries
Economic Performance	54	48
Competitiveness	80	70
Health	91	96
Education	95	95
Environment	50	60
Democracy & Freedom	100	95

NEW ZEALAND

Economic Development. Since 1984 the government of New Zealand has been reorienting the country's economy from a slow-growing, primarily agricultural one to an open, free-market system that can compete globally. Starting in 1984, the government embarked on what the OECD labeled as the most comprehensive economic liberalization program ever undertaken by a developed country. The results of the program generally have been positive. Inflation has declined from double-digit levels to 3 percent a year in the 1990s, and economic growth has risen from 2 percent per year during the 1980s to 3 percent a year during the 1990s.

On Economic Performance New Zealand's score of 54 is just above the world average. While GDP growth is strong, other indicators, such as the ratio of M2 to GDP and the level of international reserves, are below the world averages. On Competitiveness New Zealand scores much higher at 80. The country receives favorable scores because of a high saving rate, a small government deficit, a high bond rating, low inflation, and freedom of foreign exchange.

Social Development and the Environment. Illiteracy is practically nonexistent in this affluent country. Attendance at primary and most of secondary school is compulsory. However, only half of the students who begin secondary education complete all five years. Education accounted for 16 percent of total government expenditure and 7 percent of GDP in 1992. New Zealand scores 95 on Education, the industrialized country average.

Universal access to tax-financed health care has been in place in New Zealand since 1938. In the 1980s the need to contain costs led to health care reform, which is shifting the health system toward regional service delivery, independent providers, and private health insurance. New Zealand's health indicators are generally in line with the OECD average. Its low Health score (relative to OECD countries), 91, mainly reflects relatively low child immunization rates and a slightly higher maternal mortality rate.

As a result of extensive clearing for pasture land, only one-third of New Zealand's indigenous forest remains, although commercial forest stocks are growing. New Zealand completed major revisions of its natural resource management laws in 1991, aiming to achieve sustainable use of its resources. New Zealand scores 50 in the environment vector, lower than the industrialized country average, as a result of high levels of solid wastes in urban centers and of emissions of greenhouse gases.

Democracy and Freedom. New Zealanders can change their government democratically. New Zealand has no written constitution, but all fundamental freedoms are respected in practice. Four parliamentary seats are reserved for representatives of the indigenous Maori minority. The judiciary is independent, and due process rights are protected. The press is vigorous, and the broadcast media express pluralistic views. New Zealand receives a score of 100 on Democracy and Freedom.

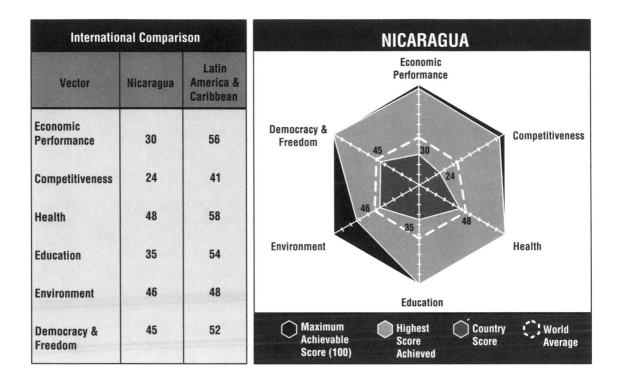

International Comparison		
Vector	Nicaragua	Latin America & Caribbean
Economic Performance	30	56
Competitiveness	24	41
Health	48	58
Education	35	54
Environment	46	48
Democracy & Freedom	45	52

NICARAGUA

Economic Development. Nicaragua, with a per capita GNP of U.S. $390 in 1995, is one of the poorest countries in Latin America. Its economy is predominantly agricultural. Coffee, cotton, sugar, beef, and bananas account for nearly 70 percent of exports.

When civilian rule resumed in 1991 after ten years of military conflict, the government initiated a comprehensive stabilization and adjustment plan in an effort to bring about recovery and growth. Stabilization measures reduced inflation from hyperinflationary levels to single digits by 1992. Nicaragua's Economic Performance score of 30 is among the lowest in

Latin America and the Caribbean. The score is hurt by declines in per capita income of 6 percent a year between 1985 and 1994 as well as a low level of foreign exchange reserves.

In the second half of 1995 the government began a structural reform program that included measures to strengthen fiscal performance, tighten central bank credit to the state banks, privatize, and reform the public sector. Nicaragua's weak economic foundation is reflected in its Competitiveness score of 24, which is one of the lowest in the region.

Social Development and the Environment. Although social indicators in Nicaragua have improved over the past twenty years, they remain very low. Half of the population is estimated to live below the poverty line. The infant mortality rate is 51 per 1,000 live births, and over 12 percent of children under five suffer from some form of malnutrition. Fertility and population growth rates are high and will continue to challenge efforts to improve social conditions. Nicaragua suffers from an acute lack of clean water and sanitation and a severe deterioration of primary health care facilities. Nicaragua's Health score of 48 is well below the regional average.

Over a third of all adults are illiterate. Schooling among Nicaraguan adults averages 4.0 years and only 1.6 years for the extremely poor. There is a lack of qualified teachers, and school facilities are deteriorating, particularly in rural areas. While primary enrollment is relatively high, dropout rates are also high—over half of primary school students drop out by grade five. Nicaragua's Education score of 35 is higher only than Haiti's and Guatemala's among countries in Latin America and the Caribbean.

No undisturbed natural forests remain in western Nicaragua because of intense logging, clearing, and the use of wood and charcoal for fuel. Consequently, soil erosion is rampant throughout most of western Nicaragua. A dramatic rise in the use of pesticides has contaminated the water supply in much of the country. Only roughly 20 percent of the rural population has access to safe water. Nicaragua scores 46 on Environment.

Democracy and Freedom. Nicaraguans can change the government through democratic means. However, the elected government's authority has been undermined by the Sandinistas' continued control of the military as well as by the military's independence from civilian rule. Intermittent political violence, corruption, and an escalating, drug-related crime wave have constrained the development of civic activities. The court system has been overwhelmed by the rising number of criminal cases. Military and police abuses are reportedly widespread. The press and the broadcast media are mostly politicized and partisan. Nicaragua scores 45 on Democracy and Freedom, lower than the regional average.

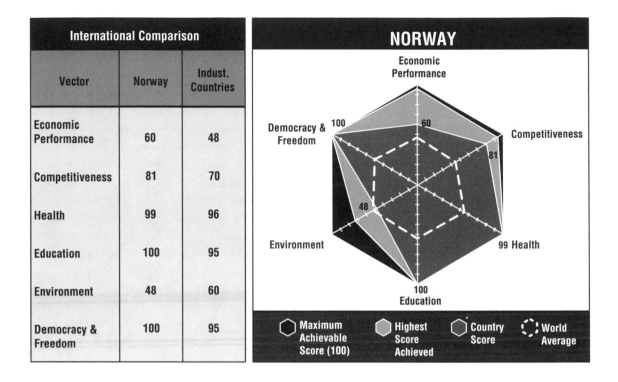

International Comparison		
Vector	Norway	Indust. Countries
Economic Performance	60	48
Competitiveness	81	70
Health	99	96
Education	100	95
Environment	48	60
Democracy & Freedom	100	95

NORWAY chart with legend: Maximum Achievable Score (100); Highest Score Achieved; Country Score; World Average

NORWAY

Economic Development. Norway is a prosperous country with abundant natural resources. Since 1975 the exploitation of large crude oil and natural gas reserves has helped to maintain high growth. Petroleum and natural gas represent about 40 percent of Norwegian exports. The country has an extensive set of welfare programs, which are largely funded by revenues from the petroleum and gas industries. Norway's purchasing-power parity estimate of GNP per capita was U.S. $20,210 in 1994, making it one of the world's wealthiest countries.

In the economic performance vector, Norway receives a score of 60, which ranks it fourth among industrialized countries. The country scores well on economic growth, per capita income, export growth, ratio of M2 to GDP, and level of international reserves. Norway scores 81 on Competitiveness, boosted by its high saving rate, a high proportion of scientists, engineers, and technicians in the population, freedom of foreign exchange, and high-quality infrastructure.

Social Development and the Environment. As one of the world's richest nations, Norway has very good social indicators. Illiteracy is practically nonexistent. In the 1997–98 school year, compulsory education, starting at the age of six, increased

from nine to ten years. About 54 percent of the population enrolls in tertiary education. Norway has few private schools and no private school tradition. The total public expenditure on education constitutes 7.6 percent of GNP. Norway's Education score is a perfect 100.

As in other Nordic countries, health services are the responsibility of the public sector. From 1970 to 1991, the share of health expenditures as a percentage of GDP rose from 5.0 percent to 7.6 percent, and the total expenditure on health care per capita more than doubled. Norway's slightly less than perfect Health score of 99 reflects immunization rates that are slightly lower than the OECD average.

Industrial development has brought environmental problems to this highly developed nation. Norway suffers from problems of air pollution and acid rain, especially in cities and industrial areas. Pollution originating outside Norway—especially from the more heavily industrialized regions of central Europe and the United Kingdom—is a serious problem. Protected natural areas constitute 15 percent of the country's area. Norway scores 48 on Environment, the second lowest among industrialized countries, mainly because of high levels of greenhouse gas emission.

Democracy and Freedom. In Norway, a strong and established democracy, all fundamental freedoms and rights are protected and respected. The judiciary is independent. One notable aspect of the Norwegian society is the equality afforded to female citizens. Women constitute roughly 45 percent of the labor force and hold more than one-third of the seats in the national legislature. Discrimination on the basis of race, gender, language, and class is prohibited by law. Norway scores a perfect 100 on Democracy and Freedom.

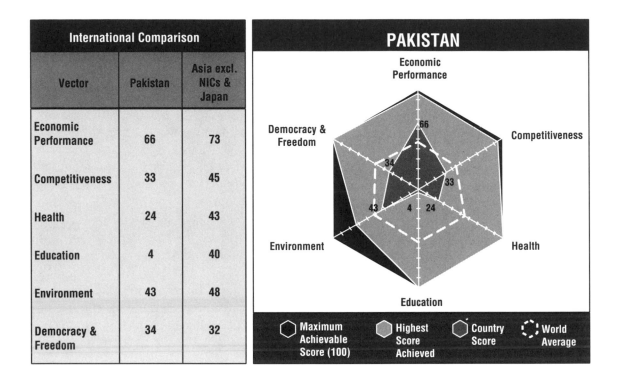

International Comparison		
Vector	Pakistan	Asia excl. NICs & Japan
Economic Performance	66	73
Competitiveness	33	45
Health	24	43
Education	4	40
Environment	43	48
Democracy & Freedom	34	32

PAKISTAN

Economic Performance · Competitiveness · Health · Education · Environment · Democracy & Freedom

Maximum Achievable Score (100) · Highest Score Achieved · Country Score · World Average

PAKISTAN

Economic Development. With a 1995 per capita income of U.S. $460, Pakistan is a low-income developing nation. The country faces serious development challenges, as a high rate of population growth could double the number of citizens to 250 million in two decades. Rapid and sustained economic growth is a critical factor in improving living standards in the face of the pressure of population growth. Between 1985 and 1994 per capita income rose only 1.3 percent a year. Pakistan earns a score of 66 on Economic Performance, below the peer group average of 73. One of its strongest indicators is export growth, which averaged 11 percent over the 1990–94 period.

In 1988 Pakistan began to overhaul its economic and social policies in order to strengthen public finances, stimulate private sector investment and growth, and improve social conditions. The government that took office in 1993 expanded the economic reform program to improve macroeconomic management, broaden the privatization effort, and accelerate trade policy reform. Pakistan's weak economic foundation is reflected in its low Competitiveness score of 33, which is hurt by a persistent government deficit averaging 8 percent of GDP, a weak sovereign bond rating, and a low ratio of exports to GDP.

Pakistan

Social Development and the Environment. Pakistan's social indicators are among the poorest in Asia, reflecting years of inadequate attention to basic social services. Rapid population growth is increasing the burden on the social service infrastructure. Fertility rates are high, and maternal mortality and other women's health indicators are poor. Pakistan scores 24 on Health, higher only than Bhutan, Cambodia, and Papua New Guinea in Asia.

Close to two-thirds of Pakistan's adult population is illiterate, and just over 25 percent of children attend secondary school. The gender disparity in education is particularly serious—women are more than twice as likely to be illiterate and half as likely to attend primary and secondary school. Ethnic and regional rivalries have contributed to political instability and delayed efforts to reach a consensus on development policies and programs. Pakistan receives a score of 4 on Education, the lowest in Asia.

In Pakistan rapid population growth and urbanization have aggravated air pollution, congestion, shortages of safe drinking water and housing, and the proliferation of squatter settle-ments. Barely half of the population has access to safe water, and 80 percent of illnesses are estimated to be caused by waterborne diseases. Only two cities have sewage treatment plants. Pakistan scores 43 on Environment, lower than the Asia average.

Democracy and Freedom. Pakistanis in principle can change their government through free elections. However, corruption and the concentration of power in the hands of the landowning elite have weakened democratic institutions. In the face of widespread civil unrest, the government has resorted to arbitrary arrests and detention of activists and political opponents. Security officials often use excessive force and are accused of abusing detainees. The judiciary is vulnerable to pressure from the government and other powerful individuals. Media freedom has deteriorated in recent years as the government has moved to suppress the views of the opposition and any criticism of the government and the judiciary. Violence against women and their lack of legal recourse are a persistent problem. Pakistan scores 34 on Democracy and Freedom, just below the regional average.

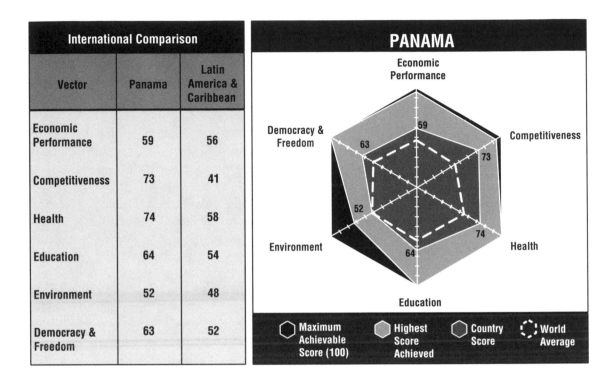

International Comparison		
Vector	Panama	Latin America & Caribbean
Economic Performance	59	56
Competitiveness	73	41
Health	74	58
Education	64	54
Environment	52	48
Democracy & Freedom	63	52

PANAMA

Economic Performance — 59

Competitiveness — 73

Health — 74

Education — 64

Environment — 52

Democracy & Freedom — 63

- Maximum Achievable Score (100)
- Highest Score Achieved
- Country Score
- World Average

PANAMA

Economic Development. The Panamanian economy is among the most prosperous and stable in Latin America. Its 1995 per capita income is estimated at U.S. $2,270. However, Panama's economy is highly segmented between its dynamic, internationally oriented service sector and a more rigid and inefficient, domestically oriented sector. The inability of the domestic sector to respond to external shocks led to poor economic performance throughout the 1980s and into the early 1990s. Per capita income declined at a rate of over 1 percent between 1985 and 1994. Unemployment remained around 14 percent.

Over 1990–95 Panama made great progress in reforming its economy and reducing structural imbalances. Inflation was brought down to below international levels, foreign exchange reserves were increased, and public finance accounts were balanced. The government that took office in September 1994 accelerated the reform process, focusing on maintaining fiscal and external balance and redressing the pervasive price distortions in the economy.

Between 1990 and 1994 GDP grew at a brisk 7 percent while gross domestic investment increased 20 percent annually. Overall, Panama scores 59 on Economic Performance, just above the regional average. On Competitiveness Panama scores 73, the highest in Latin America and the Caribbean. Its strong score is earned by a continuing budget surplus (averaging 5 percent in 1990–93), a low average inflation rate, and a high ratio of exports to GDP.

Social Development and the Environment. Over a decade of poor economic performance impeded job creation and aggravated already pervasive poverty and income inequality in Panama. Income declines during the period of external shocks and economic adjustment disproportionately affected the poorest segment of the population. While Panama's social indicators are generally better than the Latin America averages, they do not mask the lack of progress, especially in the health area. During the 1980s, immunization rates declined 13 percent, the incidence of growth retardation among children rose 25 percent, the number of tuberculosis cases doubled, and the number of malaria cases climbed tenfold. Panama receives 74 in Health and 64 in Education, both higher than the regional averages.

During the 1980s Panama lost about 139 square miles of tropical rainforests a year to government-sponsored colonization projects. The widespread loss of forest cover is depleting vast tracks of land of topsoil, leading to vicious cycles of soil degradation. Only two-thirds of Panama's rural population has access to safe water. Panama receives a score of 52 on Environment, just above the regional average.

Democracy and Freedom. Citizens of Panama can change their government through democratic means, and the constitution guarantees most fundamental freedoms. However, there is an increasing tendency in the government to restrict the media and suppress nonviolent opposition. The judicial system is inefficient, politicized, and prone to corruption. There were 18,000 court cases pending in 1995, mainly as a result of the drug-fueled crime wave. Panama receives a score of 63 on Democracy and Freedom, higher than the regional average of 52.

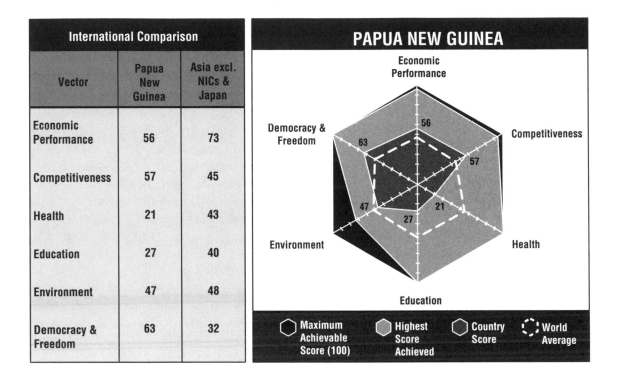

International Comparison		
Vector	Papua New Guinea	Asia excl. NICs & Japan
Economic Performance	56	73
Competitiveness	57	45
Health	21	43
Education	27	40
Environment	47	48
Democracy & Freedom	63	32

PAPUA NEW GUINEA

Economic Development. Papua New Guinea is endowed with a rich natural resource base, including major gold and copper deposits, large oil and natural gas reserves, vast expanses of agricultural land, and extensive forests and maritime fisheries. While 85 percent of the population is engaged in subsistence agriculture, the mineral sector dominates the economy. Economic development in Papua New Guinea has been constrained by its geographical and cultural fragmentation. More than 700 distinct languages are spoken in the country, and most population centers are separated from others by rugged terrain on the mainland or large distances between the islands.

Poor economic management plunged the country into a severe macroeconomic crisis in 1993–94, featuring a widening fiscal deficit, declining international reserves, and pressure to devalue the exchange rate. The government undertook major budget revisions in March 1994 and began a structural reform program in 1995. Papua New Guinea scores 56 on Economic Performance, the second lowest score in Asia, after the Philippines. Its score is hurt by a dangerously low foreign reserve ratio and declining growth in domestic investment over 1990–94. On Competitiveness the country scores 57, just higher than the average in Asia.

Papua New Guinea

Social Development and the Environment. Although the nation's per capita GNP in 1994 was estimated at U.S. $1,160, over 80 percent of the population had an average per capita income of only U.S. $350 because of a highly skewed distribution of wealth. Thus Papua New Guinea's average social indicators tend to be worse than those for countries at similar development levels. Rapid population growth is leading to a general decline in welfare. Since the mid-1980s the country has also experienced deterioration of basic public services.

Fertility in Papua New Guinea is among the highest in the world, while health and maternal indicators are very poor. Women face particular difficulties in the male-dominated society, having limited access to educational opportunities and health services. Adult illiteracy is measured at 28 percent, and just over two-thirds of primary school children complete grade five. Gender disparity in literacy is especially wide: the literacy levels of the male and female adult populations differ by 20 percent. Papua New Guinea receives a very low score of 21 on Health, just above the scores of Bhutan and Cambodia. A score of 27 on Education places Papua New Guinea just above Pakistan, Bhutan, Bangladesh, and Cambodia.

Unsustainable logging has destroyed many of Papua New Guinea's tropical forests and areas rich in biodiversity. Poor management, inadequate government oversight, corruption, and inefficiency aggravate deforestation. Open-pit mining has caused serious pollution and environmental damage in many areas. In rural areas only 20 percent of the population has access to safe water supplies. Papua New Guinea scores 47 on Environment, just below the average in Asia.

Democracy and Freedom. Citizens of Papua New Guinea can change their government democratically, although elections are often characterized by violence and fraud. The judiciary is generally independent. In recent years the restriction of journalists' access to cover the secessionist insurgency in Bougainville Island has violated the media's freedom. The military and the security forces have been accused of rights abuses against civilians on Bougainville. Official corruption is reportedly widespread. Tribal fighting in the highlands, criminal violence in the urban areas, and violence against women are serious problems. Papua New Guinea receives 63 for Democracy and Freedom, higher than the Asia average.

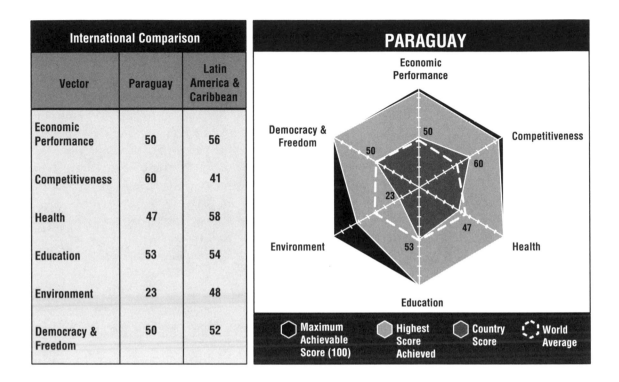

International Comparison		
Vector	Paraguay	Latin America & Caribbean
Economic Performance	50	56
Competitiveness	60	41
Health	47	58
Education	53	54
Environment	23	48
Democracy & Freedom	50	52

PARAGUAY

Economic Performance · Democracy & Freedom · Competitiveness · Environment · Health · Education

Maximum Achievable Score (100) · Highest Score Achieved · Country Score · World Average

PARAGUAY

Economic Development. Paraguay's economy is primarily agriculture based and thus highly dependent on weather conditions and developments in the international commodity market. Agriculture accounts for 25 percent of GDP and 40 percent of employment. While Paraguay's official per capita income is estimated at U.S. $1,650 in 1995, this figure does not correctly reflect living standards, as a large share of the economic activity occurs in the informal economy. This sector includes unregistered border trade with Argentina, Bolivia, and Brazil, the volume of which may exceed the official GDP.

The government that came to power in 1989 substantially improved macroeconomic policy management through important reforms, including the unification of multiple exchange rates and the liberalization of the exchange market and the capital account. The public sector deficit was reduced, and financial management of public enterprises was tightened. The government also passed a new tariff code in 1992 that lowered and simplified tariff rates.

Paraguay scores 50 on Economic Performance, compared with a regional average of 56. The score that is hurt by a weak per capita income growth rate of 1 percent in 1985–94. Its score of 60 on Competitiveness represents a tie with Costa Rica for third in Latin America and the Caribbean. That score is boosted by a high level of foreign direct investment level and an average budget surplus in 1990–93.

Social Development and the Environment. Paraguay's social indicators are generally slightly below those in Latin America and the Caribbean owing to a lower level of development. However, relative to other countries in the region, Paraguay has a more even income distribution and lower levels of poverty. Primary education is nearly universal, although 26 percent of primary schoolchildren do not complete grade five. Community participation in social service delivery is strong. Paraguay's Health score of 47 is below the average in Latin America and the Caribbean. Its Education score of 53 is in line with the regional average.

Because a severe recession in 1982–83 prevented the full implementation of a national reforestation program, large areas of forest were lost in the 1980s as a result of land clearing for agriculture. Water pollution and solid waste collection are also serious problems, especially in the cities. Less than two-thirds of the urban population and less than 10 percent of the rural population in Paraguay have access to a safe water supply. Paraguay scores 23 on Environment, the lowest score in the world.

Democracy and Freedom. The citizens of Paraguay cannot have free and fair elections because of military interference, irregularities, and fraud. The government's resort to repression and the weak rule of law undermine constitutionally guaranteed political rights and civil liberties. The judiciary is often influenced by the ruling party and the military and is prone to corruption. In recent years Colombian narcotics traffickers have reportedly infiltrated different levels of the government to facilitate their expanded operations in Paraguay. The media are generally independent, but journalists covering certain sensitive subjects may be targeted by security forces for abuse and threats. Paraguay scores 50 on Democracy and Freedom, just below the regional average.

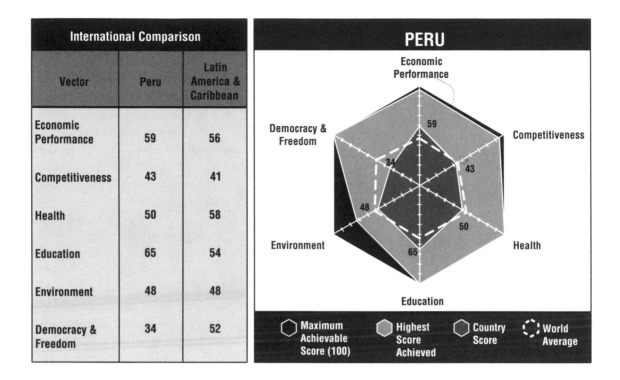

International Comparison		
Vector	Peru	Latin America & Caribbean
Economic Performance	59	56
Competitiveness	43	41
Health	50	58
Education	65	54
Environment	48	48
Democracy & Freedom	34	52

PERU

Economic Performance · Competitiveness · Health · Education · Environment · Democracy & Freedom

59 · 43 · 50 · 65 · 48 · 34

Maximum Achievable Score (100) · Highest Score Achieved · Country Score · World Average

PERU

Economic Development. Despite its considerable natural resource endowments, Peru's economy has declined over the last three decades. Its 1995 per capita income of U.S. $2,320 was below the average in Latin America and the Caribbean. Thirty years of misguided policies, economic mismanagement, and rampant and escalating political violence took a serious toll on the economy, leading to its virtual collapse by 1990. Public finance was in shambles, and tax collections were less than 5 percent of GDP. Hyperinflation escalated prices by a factor of 27 million over three decades.

Since 1990 the government has pursued bold economic reforms, liberalizing interest and exchange rates and international capital flows and establishing the independence of the central bank. Public monopolies and price controls have been eliminated, and labor market efficiency and inflation have improved.

Peru scores 59 on Economic Performance, just above the regional average. The country receives high scores for gross domestic investment and GDP growth in 1990–94. However, per capita GDP in 1995 remained below the 1985 level. On Competitiveness Peru's score, 43, is also above the average in Latin America and the Caribbean, boosted by its government budget surplus.

Social Development and the Environment. Peru has made significant progress in improving its social conditions. Life expectancy at birth is now sixty-six years, compared with forty-eight years in 1960. Although infant mortality is now less than half the level in 1960, the decline has not been as rapid as in the rest of the developing world. Peru's Health score of 50 is below the regional average. Primary education is nearly universal, and secondary enrollment is relatively high. Tertiary enrollment, at 31 percent, is particularly impressive for a country at Peru's level of development. Peru's Education score, 65, outperforms the regional average by over 10 points. Rapid economic growth between 1993 and 1995 helped reduce poverty.

Recent logging activities and centuries of grazing have degraded much of Peru's land, threatening soil productivity and increasing erosion. As a result of economic decline in the late 1980s, much of the country's infrastructure has become dysfunctional. Less than 40 percent of the country's population has access to safe water. In 1990 cholera broke out in Peru and spread by means of poor-quality water. Sewage treatment facilities are inadequate. Peru scores 48 on Environment, the average for the region. Its score is boosted by low levels of greenhouse gas emissions.

Democracy and Freedom. While Peruvians in principle can change their government democratically, in reality they are ruled by a presidential-military regime under President Alberto Fujimori. The 1995 election was essentially a state-controlled plebiscite in which massive government resources financed Fujimori's campaign. Fujimori dissolved Congress in 1992 and has ruled by decree since then. The independence of the judiciary was seriously undermined when it was made an arm of the executive in 1992. In 1995 the government implemented an amnesty law that absolves those who are implicated in human rights violations during the counterinsurgency against the Shining Path, essentially stripping victims and their families of legal recourse. The media are largely private, but most journalists practice self-censorship. Peru scores 34 on Democracy and Freedom, lower than the regional average of 52.

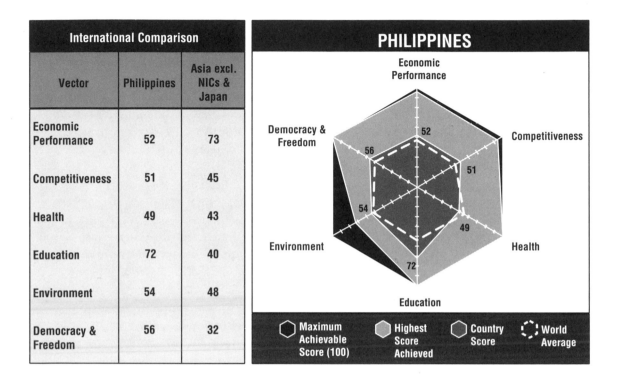

International Comparison		
Vector	Philippines	Asia excl. NICs & Japan
Economic Performance	52	73
Competitiveness	51	45
Health	49	43
Education	72	40
Environment	54	48
Democracy & Freedom	56	32

PHILIPPINES

Economic Performance

Democracy & Freedom

Competitiveness

52

56

51

54

49

Environment

Health

72

Education

Maximum Achievable Score (100) Highest Score Achieved Country Score World Average

PHILIPPINES

Economic Development. During the 1980s economic progress in the Philippines generally lagged behind that in its dynamic Southeast and East Asian neighbors. Two decades of economic mismanagement and political excesses left the country vulnerable to external shocks in the 1980s. The government that took office in 1986 vigorously pursued structural reforms while ensuring increased democracy and participation in economic recovery. The Philippines is now in the midst of an economic recovery that holds more promise of sustained growth than at any time since the debt crisis of the early 1980s. Recent agreements to liberalize trade

through free-trade agreements involving the World Trade Organization and the Association of Southeast Asian Nations have improved prospects for manufactured exports. Reforms begun in 1994 have accelerated economic growth, which was led by robust expansion of exports and investment.

The Economic Performance score of the Philippines, 52, is the lowest in Asia, reflecting its slow growth from the mid-1980s through 1994. GDP growth was slow at 1.6 percent from 1990 to 1994. Growth rates were much higher in 1994 and 1995, averaging more than 5 percent a year. The Philippines scores 51 on

Competitiveness, higher than its peer group average.

Social Development and the Environment. Social indicators are generally good in the Philippines compared with those in countries at its level of development. Progress, especially in health, however, has been slower than in most other developing countries. Income disparities are large, and poverty remains pervasive, afflicting 35 to 40 percent of the population. The Philippines scores 49 in Health, slightly higher than the regional average.

Educational achievements are impressive in the Philippines. Adult illiteracy is estimated at 5 percent. Primary school attendance is nearly universal, and secondary enrollment is high. Tertiary enrollment is especially high at 27 percent. The Philippines receives a score of 72 on Education, the highest in Asia after the Asian NICs.

Rapid population growth, urbanization, and the growth of industry have put pressure on the nation's environment. Air and soil pollution poses increasing health hazards, particularly in urban areas. Disposal of industrial and other toxic wastes has polluted many rivers. Illegal logging and deforestation have destroyed two-thirds of the indigenous forests in the Philippines. The Philippines scores 54 in the environment vector, just higher than the average in Asia.

Democracy and Freedom. Citizens of the Philippines can change their government democratically, although elections are often marred by violence and fraud. The rule of law is weak, and a wide income disparity has allowed the economic elite to wield significant political power. Corruption also weakens governance. The judiciary is independent, but the judicial system is heavily backlogged and favors politically connected and wealthy individuals. Kidnaping, bank robberies, the trafficking of Filipino women, and child prostitution are serious problems. Freedom of religion is respected, and workers are free to join unions. The Philippines receives a score of 56 on Democracy and Freedom, much higher than the regional average of 32.

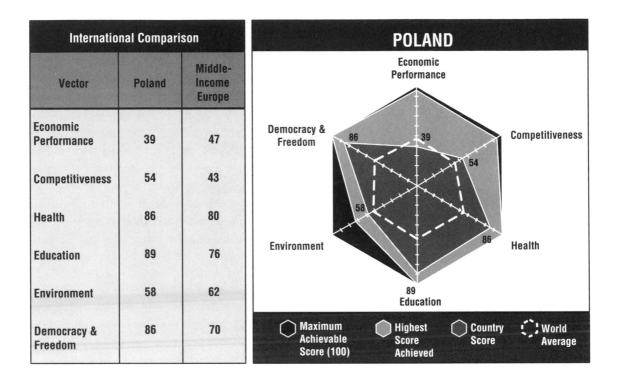

International Comparison		
Vector	Poland	Middle-Income Europe
Economic Performance	39	47
Competitiveness	54	43
Health	86	80
Education	89	76
Environment	58	62
Democracy & Freedom	86	70

POLAND

Economic Performance · 39 · Competitiveness · 54 · Health · 86 · Education · 89 · Environment · 58 · Democracy & Freedom · 86

Maximum Achievable Score (100) · Highest Score Achieved · Country Score · World Average

POLAND

Economic Development. Poland has a diversified economy in which industry accounts for 44 percent and agriculture accounts for 7 percent of GDP. Per capita income was estimated at U.S. $2,800 in 1995. In 1990 Poland was the first eastern European nation to embrace bold market-oriented reform when it embarked on a comprehensive economic restructuring and privatization program in the midst of a recession. While output growth averaged only 1.6 percent between 1990 and 1994, a 7 percent GDP growth was registered for 1995. Prospects for sustained increases in economic output and per capita income are good, given the increased

dynamism and diversity in the economy and confidence on the part of investors. Tight fiscal management and sound macroeconomic policies are providing a healthy foundation for growth.

Poland's Economic Performance score of 39 reflects stagnated growth in incomes and investment during 1990–94. Poland scores 54 on Competitiveness, above the world average.

Social Development and the Environment. Poland's social development is very advanced for a country at its per capita income level. Infant and child mortality rates are higher than levels in OECD countries, but other health indicators approach those of Poland's more prosperous western neighbors. Enrollment in primary and secondary schools is nearly universal. Tertiary enrollment is 23 percent. Poland receives 86 in Health and 89 in Education.

Poland suffers from severe air pollution, which is a primary cause of respiratory ailments. About three-quarters of the nation's forests show some damage from air pollution. Water pollution from industrial and municipal wastes has increased dramatically over the past few decades. Much of the industry-generated hazardous waste is not properly disposed of. Poland receives a score of 58 on Environment, the second lowest in middle-income Europe.

Democracy and Freedom. Polish citizens have the right to change their government democratically. Recent parliamentary and presidential elections were considered free and fair. Poland has a vigorous and independent press. Most of the media are private; however, foreign ownership of newspapers and magazines is limited by law. Most fundamental freedoms are respected, including freedom of expression, of assembly, of association, and of religion. Anti-Semitism is a continuing problem. The judiciary is not totally independent, being prone to political pressure and influences. Free and independent labor union constitute a strong political force in the country. Poland scores 86 on Democracy and Freedom, well above the average score of 70 in middle-income Europe.

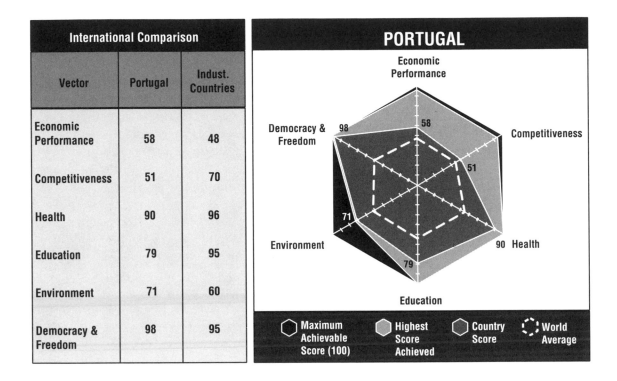

International Comparison		
Vector	Portugal	Indust. Countries
Economic Performance	58	48
Competitiveness	51	70
Health	90	96
Education	79	95
Environment	71	60
Democracy & Freedom	98	95

PORTUGAL

Economic Performance

98 Democracy & Freedom   58   Competitiveness

71 Environment   51

90 Health

79 Education

Maximum Achievable Score (100) — Highest Score Achieved — Country Score — World Average

PORTUGAL

Economic Development. With a per capita GDP of U.S. $9,320 in 1994, Portugal lags behind most European Union members in economic development. The economy is based on the principles of free enterprise and private ownership. Since 1986 the country has undergone a period of economic transformation and rapid expansion. The state has reprivatized many of the enterprises seized in the aftermath of the 1974 revolution. Portugal experienced a rapid real GDP growth of 4 percent a year during the second half of the 1980s, but economic growth in the 1990s slowed as a result of the recession that afflicted much of Europe.

Portugal's score of 58 in Economic Performance is higher than the industrialized country average, boosted by a high rate of growth in per capita GDP from 1985 to 1994 and strong foreign exchange reserves (nearly nine months of import coverage). Its Competitiveness score, 51, is the lowest among industrialized countries. The score is hurt by a persistent and high government deficit and a relatively high inflation rate from 1985 to 1995.

Social Development and the Environment. Social indicators in Portugal are slightly below those in more prosperous industrialized countries. In the health area, maternal and child mortality rates are relatively high. As many as 10 percent of all births are not attended by trained health personnel. Portugal receives a Health score of 90, below the industrialized country average of 96.

Basic education is universal, free, and compulsory for nine years. Secondary education is not compulsory, and the enrollment ratio is low relative to that in other European nations. Higher education enrollment is only 20 percent. As many as 13 percent of all adults were deemed illiterate in 1995. Expenditures on education are estimated at about 5.6 percent of GDP and about 21 percent of the state budget. Portugal receives an Education score of 79, much lower than the industrialized country average.

Portugal's air pollution problems are caused mainly by a heavy concentration of traffic and industry. The most serious pollution problems are in urban areas and areas close to power stations and cement plants. Most water pollution occurs in coastal areas. Portugal scores 71 in the environment vector, higher than the average in industrialized countries.

Democracy and Freedom. The Portuguese can change their government through democratic means. Portuguese living at home and abroad can participate in direct, competitive elections. Freedom of association is guaranteed, with the exception of fascist organizations, which are prohibited by law. All other fundamental freedoms are protected by law and respected in practice. The print media are generally free and independent. Workers have the right to strike and are represented by competing communist and noncommunist organizations. Portugal receives a score of 98 on Democracy and Freedom, higher than the industrialized country average of 95.

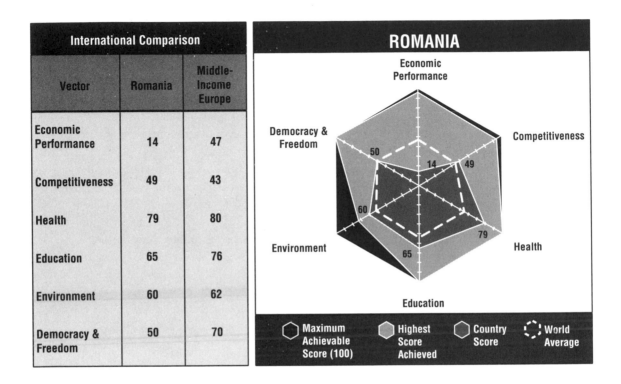

International Comparison		
Vector	Romania	Middle-Income Europe
Economic Performance	14	47
Competitiveness	49	43
Health	79	80
Education	65	76
Environment	60	62
Democracy & Freedom	50	70

ROMANIA

Maximum Achievable Score (100) · Highest Score Achieved · Country Score · World Average

ROMANIA

Economic Development. With a per capita income of U.S. $1,270 in 1994, Romania is one of the least developed countries in Europe. Unlike some of its eastern European neighbors, Romania was poorly positioned to face the challenges of transition from a command-style economy into a market-based system, being fundamentally inward looking, uncompetitive, and overindustrialized and having an aging capital stock in many industries. Between 1985 and 1994 per capita income fell at a rate of 4.5 percent a year. In 1992 the economy approached a crisis as output declined by almost one-third, inflation reached 750 per-cent, and the current account turned negative. Since 1991 the government has implemented a number of macroeconomic stabilization programs and pursued gradual and systematic structural reforms.

Romania scores 14 on Economic Performance, mainly as a result of declining GDP and negative investment growth from the mid-1980s through 1993. GDP grew modestly in both 1994 and 1995. Romania receives a higher score of 49 on Competitiveness. Its performance is hurt by a high inflation rate, which averaged 62 percent between 1984 and 1994, and a poor sovereign bond rating. Indicators in which Romania are strong compared with other middle-income European countries include high domestic saving, a small government deficit, and a large proportion of scientists and engineers in its population.

Social Development and the Environment. Income distribution in Romania is more even than in most middle-income developing countries, which accounts for its good social indicators relative to its income level. However, poverty increased substantially during the period of economic downturn and the initial transition to a market economy. Romania scores 79 on Health. Among Health indicators, the country is weak in maternal mortality rate and contraceptive prevalence among women. Romania scores 65 on Education, below the average in middle-income Europe. Primary and secondary enrollment rates are moderate, while the tertiary enrollment level is low, at 13 percent. The adult literacy rate for Romania is not available.

Like many of its east European neighbors,

Romania neglected the environment during decades of Soviet-style development that focused on the development of heavy industries. Some of Romania's industrial areas are considered to be among the most polluted places in Europe. Romania scores 60 in the environment vector, just below the average for middle-income Europe.

Democracy and Freedom. Romanians in principle have the right to elect their government. However, there are signs that the dominant political party—the Party of Social Democracy in Romania—and the government are seeking to monopolize power. Many elected local and regional officials from opposition parties were suspended or forced to resign after the 1992 elections. Libel and slander laws limit the freedom of the press. The judiciary is not fully independent; the parliament can overturn Constitutional Court decisions with a two-thirds majority. Religious freedom is generally respected. Romania scores 50 on Democracy and Freedom.

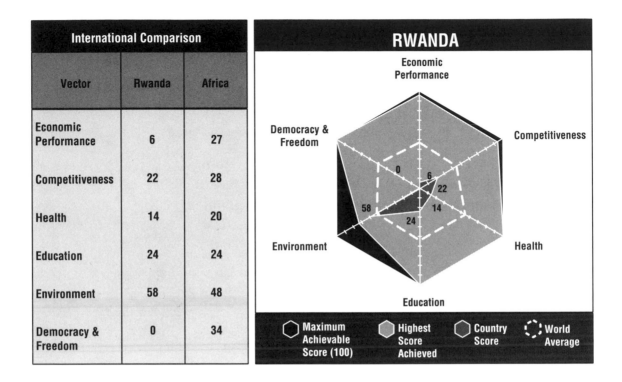

International Comparison		
Vector	Rwanda	Africa
Economic Performance	6	27
Competitiveness	22	28
Health	14	20
Education	24	24
Environment	58	48
Democracy & Freedom	0	34

RWANDA

Economic Performance

Democracy & Freedom

Competitiveness

Environment

Health

Education

○ Maximum Achievable Score (100)   ◑ Highest Score Achieved   ⬡ Country Score   ⸬ World Average

RWANDA

Economic Development. Rwanda, with a GNP per capita of U.S. $210 in 1993, is one of the poorest nations in the world. The country is landlocked, resource poor, and primarily rural. Over 90 percent of the population derives a livelihood from agriculture, including the cultivation of coffee and tea, which account for 80 percent of Rwanda's export earnings. Since 1990 Rwanda has been torn by a full-scale civil war, sporadic ethnic violence, and the 1994 genocide directed against the Tutsi minority and moderate Hutus, which have brought massive economic and social dislocation to its population. Real GDP declined 50 percent in 1994 and only partially recovered in 1995. Rwanda's economic conditions stabilized after 1994 with the help of substantial inflows of external aid, much of which has been directed at humanitarian efforts.

Rwanda receives a very low score of 6 on Economic Performance because of declining incomes and investment associated with the 1994 ethnic conflict. It scores 22 on Competitiveness, below the average for Africa. Its score is hurt by a negative saving ratio (–69 percent), a runaway budget deficit, and low levels of exports and foreign investment.

Social Development and the Environment. Rwanda's social indicators, which used to be above average for sub-Saharan Africa, deteriorated in the late 1980s and worsened in 1994 with the escalation of ethnic violence. Life expectancy is only forty-nine years. The infant mortality rate is high, and 139 out of 1,000 children die before the age of five. Maternal mortality is among the highest in the world. Rwanda suffers from the world's worst AIDS epidemic, with an estimated one-fifth of the population testing HIV positive. HIV infection is growing at a 7 percent annual rate. The incidence of malaria, caused by deteriorating health conditions, is high. More than 40 percent of the adult population is illiterate. Primary and secondary enrollment ratios are low, and dropout rates are high. Rwanda scores 14 on Health and 24 on Education.

Environmental problems in Rwanda have been exacerbated by the 1994 civil war and the displacement of populations and refugees. Political instability and civil strife have aggravated pervasive problems of deforestation, land degradation, cultivation of marginal lands, and limited accessibility to safe water. Rwanda scores 58 in the environment vector, a high score relative to the extent of environmental destruction caused by the war, mainly because of low reported levels of greenhouse gases associated with low levels of economic activity.

Democracy and Freedom. The Rwandan government was not elected democratically. The current Tutsi-led government took power by force in 1994. Although political parties exist, two Hutu-dominated parties closely identified with the 1994 massacres have been banned. Many parts of the country, particularly areas affected by incursions from Hutu extremists based in Congo, are still very insecure. Hundreds of thousands of Hutu refugees continue to languish along the county's border.

Television and radio are state controlled, while independent newspapers practice restraint when reporting on the government. Rwandans are struggling to identify the proper role of the media. During the genocide, journalists were both the targets of attacks and important instigators of anti-Tutsi violence. Rwanda scores 0 on Democracy and Freedom.

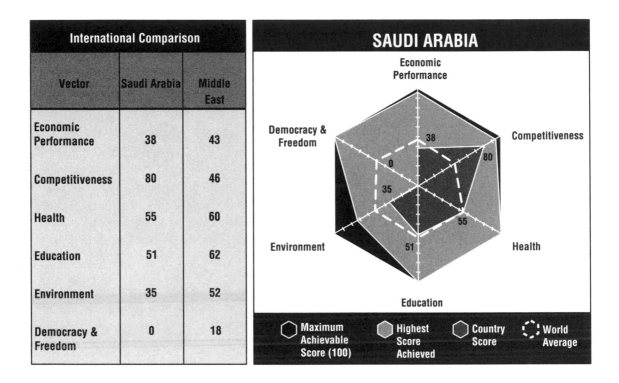

International Comparison		
Vector	Saudi Arabia	Middle East
Economic Performance	38	43
Competitiveness	80	46
Health	55	60
Education	51	62
Environment	35	52
Democracy & Freedom	0	18

SAUDI ARABIA

Economic Development. Saudi Arabia is an upper-middle-income country with an estimated per capita GNP of U.S. $7,050 in 1994. The oil sector strongly dominates the economy. Saudi Arabia has the richest oil reserves in the world and is one of the largest exporters of petroleum. Earnings from hydrocarbons generate over 90 percent of export revenues, 70 percent of government revenues, and 40 percent of GDP. Most of the nonoil sector has been dependent on oil-derived government revenues for support.

In the economic performance vector, Saudi Arabia has a comparatively low score of 38

because of a decline in real per capita income from the mid-1980s to the early 1990s. GDP growth was slow, 1.9 percent, over the 1990–94 period. On Competitiveness Saudi Arabia receives a much higher score of 80, owing to its high saving rate, low inflation, high ratio of exports to GDP, and high-quality infrastructure.

Social Development and the Environment. Overall, social indicators in Saudi Arabia are worse than those in countries at comparable income levels. Maternal and infant mortality rates are relatively high. The fertility rate is high at 6.2 children per woman. An estimated 37 percent of all adults are illiterate, a level more often seen in less developed countries. Primary, secondary, and tertiary enrollment levels are all low. Gender disparity in education is particularly serious. School enrollment for females is significantly lower than that for males, and almost half of adult females are illiterate. Saudi Arabia scores 55 on Health and 51 on Education, both of which are below the Middle East averages.

The major environmental problems in Saudi Arabia are air pollution in the urban areas, coastal pollution, water depletion, and desertification. Heavy oil tanker traffic in the Persian Gulf and spillage from a large number of coastal refineries have resulted in many oil slicks. Water is pumped from aquifers at rates faster than it can be replenished. More than a quarter of the rural population has no access to safe water. Saudi Arabia scores 35 in the environment vector, the lowest score in the Middle East.

Democracy and Freedom. The Saudi government is not democratically elected. Political parties are illegal, and there are no elections for any government positions. The country's policies are set by King Fahd, who issues executive decrees and wields power over the judicial system. Radio and TV are state controlled, and independent newspapers are highly controlled by the government and practice self-censorship. Citizens cannot criticize the royal family, the government, or Islam. The country's legal system is in strict accordance with Islamic law. Discrimination on the basis of sex is widely practiced. Women cannot be with unrelated men at work, in schools, or in other public places. Morals police enforce a strict dress and behavioral code, particularly for women. Authorities continue to crack down on a largely nonviolent but radical Islamic fundamentalist opposition. Saudi Arabia scores 0 on Democracy and Freedom.

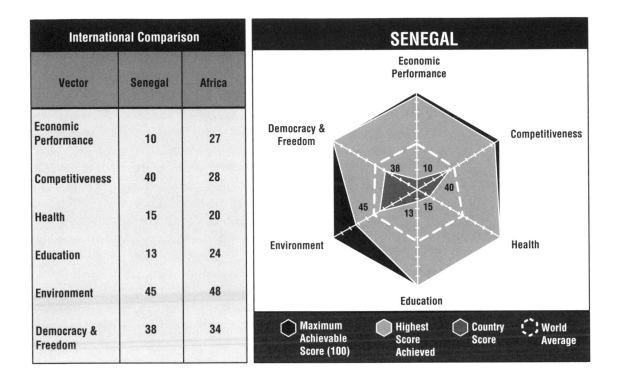

International Comparison		
Vector	Senegal	Africa
Economic Performance	10	27
Competitiveness	40	28
Health	15	20
Education	13	24
Environment	45	48
Democracy & Freedom	38	34

SENEGAL

Economic Performance

Democracy & Freedom

Competitiveness

Environment

Health

Education

Maximum Achievable Score (100) · Highest Score Achieved · Country Score · World Average

SENEGAL

Economic Development. Senegal's economy is predominantly rural and highly vulnerable to climatic variations and commodity price fluctuations. Its per capita income in 1995 was estimated at U.S. $570. About 40 percent of the cultivated land in Senegal is used to grow peanuts, an important export crop. Mining is dominated by the extraction of phosphate, but production has faltered in recent years as a result of the worldwide decline in demand for fertilizers. The modern sector includes industrial fishing, chemical industries, manufacturing, and tourism.

Misguided economic policies, poor public resource management, and inefficient indus-tries all contributed to the country's economic downturn and balance-of-payment difficulties in the early 1990s. The government has since undertaken a series of economic reform and structural adjustment efforts.

Senegal receives a low score of 10 on Economic Performance as a result of declining per capita income from its level in the mid-1980s, lack of economic growth, and negative investment growth from 1990 to 1994. Senegal did better in the competitiveness vector, scoring 40. Its score is boosted by a high ratio of exports to GDP and a low average inflation rate of 3 percent between 1984 and 1994.

Senegal

Social Development and the Environment. Senegal's social indicators are generally below the average in sub-Saharan Africa. Life expectancy is low at fifty years. Maternal mortality exceeds 1 percent, and over 10 percent of all children do not survive past age five. The fertility rate is high, averaging 5.9 children per woman. In recent years health care resources have shifted from urban-based hospitals to rural health centers. Close to two-thirds of all adults are illiterate. Primary enrollment in 1992 was about 60 percent. Secondary enrollment was very low at 16 percent. Senegal scores 15 on Health and 13 on Education, both of which are below the regional averages.

Senegal's main environmental problems are deforestation and soil degradation, much of which is attributed to the excessive harvesting of wood for fuel, overgrazing, and cultivation of marginal land. Poaching and overharvesting of birds and game are also rampant. Access to safe water is inadequate, especially in rural areas. Senegal receives a score of 45 in the environment vector, just below the Africa regional average of 48.

Democracy and Freedom. The Socialist Party, which has been in power for the past three decades, has impeded the formation of a true opposition force in Senegal, though elections are regularly held. The press is independent, and freedom of expression is respected. Permit requirements have restricted freedom of assembly, and public marches have been under serious government control since riots broke out in February 1994. Low pay and short terms for judges make the technically independent judiciary sensitive to pressure. A lack of resources has seriously affected the administration of justice. Senegal scores 38 on Democracy and Freedom, just above the Africa average of 34.

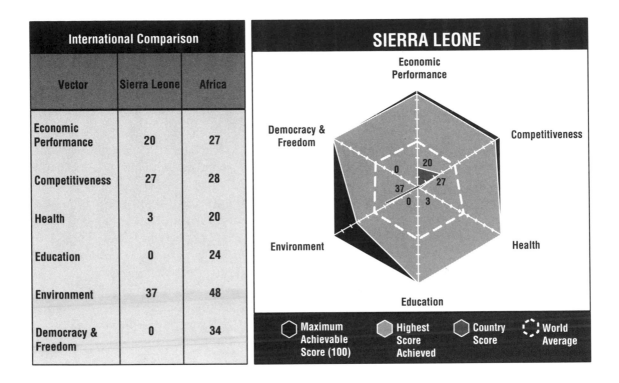

International Comparison		
Vector	Sierra Leone	Africa
Economic Performance	20	27
Competitiveness	27	28
Health	3	20
Education	0	24
Environment	37	48
Democracy & Freedom	0	34

SIERRA LEONE

Economic Performance · Democracy & Freedom · Competitiveness · Environment · Health · Education

Maximum Achievable Score (100) · Highest Score Achieved · Country Score · World Average

SIERRA LEONE

Economic Development. Despite its vast natural endowments—minerals, fertile and varied soil, and rich fisheries—Sierra Leone remains one of the poorest countries in the world, with a per capita GDP of U.S. $150 in 1994. Its economy is predominantly agricultural, and farming is mostly labor intensive. Coffee and cocoa are the traditional agricultural exports. The mining sector accounts for nearly 20 percent of GDP and is the most important source of foreign exchange earnings.

Two decades of mismanagement left the economy unprepared for external shocks and deteriorating terms of trade in the 1980s. In 1989 the government embarked on an economic recovery program that combined strict fiscal discipline with structural reform. However, widespread economic disruption caused by attacks from rebel forces since 1991 reforms have prevented the desired growth and recovery. An estimated 2 million people have been displaced by the civil war.

Sierra Leone receives an Economic Performance score of 20 and a Competitiveness score of 27, both of which are below average in Africa. The poor scores reflect declining per capita incomes and high inflation rates between 1984 and 1994 and low rates of investment and export growth.

Sierra Leone

Social Development and the Environment. Social indicators in Sierra Leone are among the worst in the world. Over two-thirds of the population lives in absolute poverty. Mortality rates for infants, children under five, and mothers are the highest in the world, and life expectancy at birth (forty years) and primary school enrollment are among the lowest. Adult illiteracy is estimated at 69 percent for the adult population and 90 percent for female adults. Secondary enrollment is very low at 17 percent. Sierra Leone scores 3 on Health and 0 on Education, among the lowest in Africa.

Deforestation is an increasing problem in Sierra Leone. Little of its forest land is protected. Sierra Leone has lost about 85 percent of its wildlife habitats, threatening some species with extinction. Only 20 percent of its rural population has access to a safe water supply. Sierra Leone scores 37 on Environment, lower than the regional average of 48.

Democracy and Freedom. Citizens of Sierra Leone do not have the right to choose their government freely. For several years the country has been ravaged by war between the military-dominated government and the rebel Revolutionary United Front, resulting in starvation, disease, and massive human rights violations against its citizens. Amnesty International reported that the conflict has developed into a campaign of terror aimed at unarmed civilians, who have been captured, tortured, and deliberately and arbitrarily killed (Kaplan, 1996, p. 415). Sierra Leone receives 0 for Democracy and Freedom, compared with the Africa average of 34.

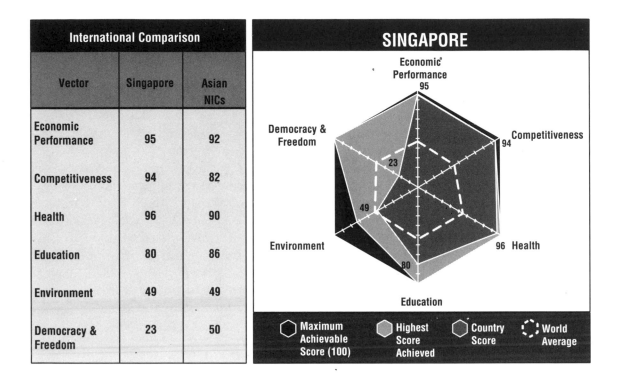

International Comparison		
Vector	Singapore	Asian NICs
Economic Performance	95	92
Competitiveness	94	82
Health	96	90
Education	80	86
Environment	49	49
Democracy & Freedom	23	50

SINGAPORE

Economic
Performance
95

Democracy & Freedom

Competitiveness
94

23

49

Environment

96 Health

80

Education

Maximum Achievable Score (100) — Highest Score Achieved — Country Score — World Average

SINGAPORE

Economic Development. Singapore is one of the world's most prosperous and competitive economies. With a per capita GNP of U.S. $22,500 in 1994, it has one of the world's highest standards of living. It has an open, entrepreneurial economy with strong service and manufacturing sectors and excellent support infrastructure and trading links derived from its entrepôt history. Singapore attracts substantial inflows of foreign direct investment in the chemicals, plastics, petrochemical, electronics, and information technology industries.

Singapore's Economic Performance score (95) ties with Hong Kong's as the highest in the world. Singapore has strong indicators in all Economic Performance categories, including average annual growth in 1990–94 (8.3 percent), annual growth of exports in 1990–94 (12.3 percent), and per capita GDP growth in 1985–94 (6 percent). In Competitiveness Singapore ranks first in the world at 94, with strong scores on all indicators.

Social Development and the Environment. Social development in Singapore is comparable to levels in OECD countries. Life expectancy is high at seventy-five years. Singapore scores 96 on Health, the highest among the Asian NICs. Singapore receives a lower score of 80 on Edu-

cation. Primary education is universal, and the literacy rate and secondary enrollment ratio are slightly below the levels in OECD countries.

As the most densely populated country in the world, Singapore's environmental problems are caused by congestion, urbanization, and industrial development. The city's rapid growth has brought congestion, air and noise pollution, and waste disposal problems. The proximity of residential areas to industrial operations exacerbates the effects of industrial pollution. Singapore scores 49 on Environment, in line with the average for Asia and for the Asian NICs.

Democracy and Freedom. The government of Singapore is technically freely elected, although the ruling People's Action Party has maintained supremacy through a series of media regulations, electoral law advantages, discriminatory use of security measures, and intimidation of opposition figures. Presidential candidates are required to have held one of several senior public offices or to have run a company with paid-up capital of over $62.5 million, resulting in a pool of only 400 citizens eligible to run for president in a country of 3 million people. The judiciary is subject to executive pressures. The media are strongly controlled. The majority of TV channels and radio stations are state run, while the circulation of major international publications is restricted because of their critical reporting of the government. Public assemblies of more than five people require government authorization. Singapore scores 23 on Democracy and Freedom, the lowest among the Asian NICs.

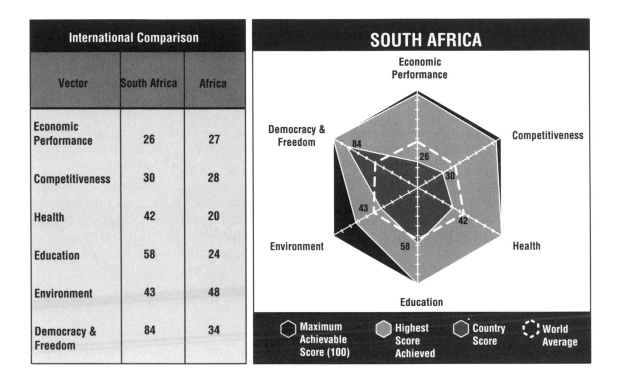

International Comparison		
Vector	South Africa	Africa
Economic Performance	26	27
Competitiveness	30	28
Health	42	20
Education	58	24
Environment	43	48
Democracy & Freedom	84	34

SOUTH AFRICA

Economic
Performance

Competitiveness

Health

Education

Environment

Democracy &
Freedom

Maximum Achievable Score (100) Highest Score Achieved Country Score World Average

SOUTH AFRICA

Economic Development. South Africa is one of the most prosperous countries in sub-Saharan Africa, with a per capita GDP of over U.S. $3,000 in 1994. It enjoys many economic assets, including abundant minerals and natural resources, a modern industrial sector, an advanced infrastructure, and well-developed capital markets. In the past the government maintained substantial control over the economy. The government has recently undertaken a number of economic liberalization measures such as tariff reform and the liberalization of foreign exchange controls. The country has also strongly benefited from the relaxation of eco-

nomic and trade sanctions imposed upon South Africa during the apartheid years.

In the economic performance area, South Africa receives a very low score of 26 due to a declining GDP per capita between 1985 and 1994, negative GDP growth, and slow investment and export growth in the early 1990s. On Competitiveness South Africa receives a low score of 30. Its weakest Competitiveness indicators are its level of foreign direct investment, persistently high government deficits, double-digit inflation rates, and a poor sovereign risk rating.

Social Development and the Environment. South Africa has some of sub-Saharan Africa's best social indicators. However, poverty is widespread in this racially polarized society, and the disparity between the incomes of the white and black populations is very wide. These conditions are reflected in the country's social indicators, which are less favorable than those of other countries at similar levels of development. The social service infrastructure is poor in the rural areas and shantytowns. Rapid growth in the number of HIV infections is a serious health problem. An estimated 18 percent of the population is illiterate. Although primary enrollment is nearly universal, only 71 percent of children complete at least grade five. Tertiary education enrollment levels are low. South Africa receives 42 in Health and 58 in Education.

South Africa's environment and natural resources are threatened by land-use and economic development policies. In the eastern regions, where coal-fired power stations are located, stagnant air masses allow pollution to build to extremely high levels, causing severe acid rain. As demand increases, water supply and quality are becoming concerns. South Africa receives a score of 43 on Environment, below the average for Africa.

Democracy and Freedom. South Africans from all racial backgrounds are now eligible to choose their government. After decades of apartheid and denial of political rights for its nonwhite citizens, democratic process and institutions are taking hold in the country. A new constitution drafted in 1996 guarantees human rights and equality under the law for all citizens. The judicial power closely guards the constitutionality of all laws and decrees. However, South Africa will suffer the effects of apartheid for years, with vast income disparities between whites and others translating into far different standards of living. South Africa scores 84 on Democracy and Freedom, among the highest in Africa.

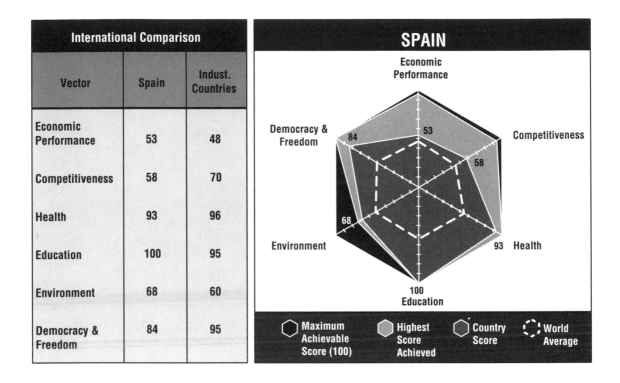

International Comparison		
Vector	Spain	Indust. Countries
Economic Performance	53	48
Competitiveness	58	70
Health	93	96
Education	100	95
Environment	68	60
Democracy & Freedom	84	95

SPAIN

Economic Performance · Competitiveness · Health · Education · Environment · Democracy & Freedom

- Maximum Achievable Score (100)
- Highest Score Achieved
- Country Score
- World Average

SPAIN

Economic Development. Spain joined the European Union in 1986, consequently exposing the country's economy to increased competition that resulted in an increase in overall economic efficiency. However, in 1992 Spain fell into a deep recession from which it still has not recovered. Between 1990 and 1994, GDP growth was sluggish at 0.7 percent a year, and gross domestic investment declined at over 5 percent a year. By mid-1997, Spain's unemployment rate was 22 percent, the highest in the European Union.

On Economic Performance Spain receives a score of 53, higher than the industrialized country average. Its score is boosted by rapid export growth and a healthy level of foreign exchange reserves. On Competitiveness Spain receives a score of 58, much lower than the industrialized country average of 70. Its Competitiveness score is hurt by a persistent government deficit (averaging 4 percent of GDP), a low ratio of exports to GDP, and less developed infrastructure relative to other western European countries.

Social Development and the Environment. Social indicators in Spain are in line with the levels in other industrialized countries. The Spanish education system is similar to that in the rest of western Europe. Primary education, which covers ages six through twelve, is compulsory and free of charge. Compulsory secondary education spans four years until age sixteen. State schools are free up to the university level. Private primary and secondary schools meeting certain conditions may receive government funding. Tertiary enrollment in Spain is high at 44 percent. Spain receives a perfect score of 100 on Education. On Health Spain scores 93, which is below the industrialized country average. Its Health score is hurt by a low prevalence of contraceptive use among women (59 percent) relative to the level in the rest of western Europe.

Spain's major cities suffer from high levels of air pollution. Poor sewage and water treatment facilities as well as offshore oil and gas production have contributed to the pollution in

the Mediterranean. Spain still lags behind many of its European neighbors in its wastewater treatment facilities. Spain scores 68 on Environment, higher than the average for industrialized countries.

Democracy and Freedom. Spain has regular elections in which citizens elect their government. The fundamental freedoms of speech, association, and collective bargaining are constitutionally guaranteed. The Spanish media are free, although the state-controlled TV station is often charged with progovernment bias. As of 1978 Roman Catholicism is no longer the official state religion. There are complaints of discrimination against minorities, particularly immigrants. There are no antidiscrimination laws. Spain receives a score of 84 on Democracy and Freedom, lower than the industrialized country average of 95.

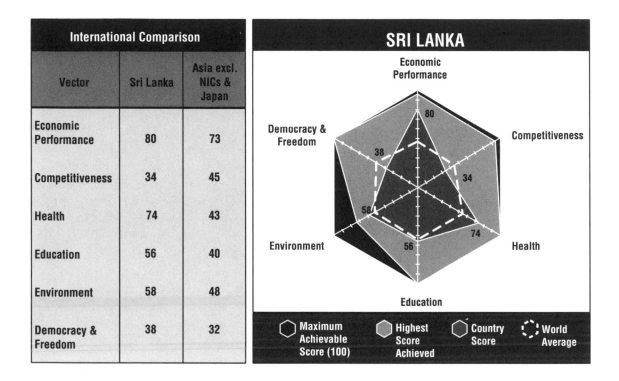

International Comparison		
Vector	Sri Lanka	Asia excl. NICs & Japan
Economic Performance	80	73
Competitiveness	34	45
Health	74	43
Education	56	40
Environment	58	48
Democracy & Freedom	38	32

SRI LANKA

Economic Development. With a per capita GDP of U.S. $690 in 1995, Sri Lanka ranks among the low-income developing nations. Sri Lanka's per capita GDP growth of 3 percent a year since 1960, which is below the potential afforded by its strong natural resource endowments, can be attributed to a long history of ethnic conflict, political unrest, and inconsistent economic policies. In 1995 widespread violence broke out between government forces and Tamil separatists, exacting a heavy toll on the economy. Rising defense expenditures and interest on the public debt have resulted in fiscal imbalances as well an underfunding of pub-

lic investment and inadequate maintenance of facilities. The high interest rates induced by the large fiscal deficit have also crowded out private investment, reducing economic growth and employment opportunities.

Sri Lanka receives a high score of 80 on Economic Performance as a result of very strong indicators that include per capita GDP growth, gross investment growth, export growth, and a healthy level of foreign exchange reserves until the end of 1994. On Competitiveness Sri Lanka scores much lower at 34, well below the Asian average, because of a large and persistent government deficit averaging 7 percent over 1991–94, high inflation rate of 11 percent in 1984–94, and poor infrastructure compared with that in the rest of Asia.

Social Development and the Environment. The Sri Lankan government's solid commitment to improving social conditions is demonstrated in the country's very impressive social indicators, which match those of higher-income economies. Life expectancy at birth is now seventy-two years, and infant and child mortality rates are very low for a country at Sri Lanka's income level. The illiteracy rate is under 10 percent, and primary education is nearly universal. Primary completion rates are high. Sri Lanka has also made significant progress in reducing poverty, although 22 percent of households are still below the poverty line. Sri Lanka scores 74 on Health, the highest score in Asia after the NICs. On Education a score of 56 keeps Sri Lanka above the Asia average.

Industrial discharge and improper sewage disposal have caused severe water pollution problems in Sri Lanka. More than two-thirds of the population has no access to safe water. Other environmental problems in the country include deforestation, coastal pollution and degradation, and wildlife destruction. Sri Lanka scores 58 on Environment, higher than the Asian average of 49, mainly as a result of low levels of greenhouse gas emissions.

Democracy and Freedom. Sri Lankans are able to choose their government through democratic means. However, the country continues to be ravaged by a long civil conflict waged by the Tamil minority. The war has created approximately 700,000 refugees, of which only 19,000 were eligible to vote in the 1994 parliamentary elections. Both the army and the Tamil guerrilla forces are responsible for massive human rights violations against unarmed civilians. A state of emergency remains in effect in Colombo, the capital, allowing the government to detain suspects indefinitely without trial. Citizens enjoy freedom of assembly and religion. Among the most serious problems affecting the country are violence against women and child prostitution. Sri Lanka scores 38 on Democracy and Freedom, higher than the regional average of 32.

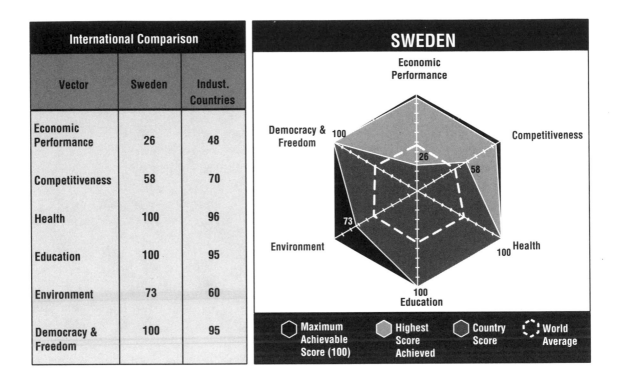

International Comparison		
Vector	Sweden	Indust. Countries
Economic Performance	26	48
Competitiveness	58	70
Health	100	96
Education	100	95
Environment	73	60
Democracy & Freedom	100	95

SWEDEN

Economic Performance

Democracy & Freedom 100

Competitiveness

26

58

73

Environment

100 Health

100 Education

○ Maximum Achievable Score (100)   ○ Highest Score Achieved   ○ Country Score   ⬡ World Average

SWEDEN

Economic Development. Sweden has achieved a very high standard of living, with a per capita GNP of U.S. $23,530 in 1994. The country has a system of high-tech capitalism combined with extensive welfare benefits. Sweden's assets include modern infrastructure, an excellent communications system, and a highly skilled work force. Timber, hydropower, and iron ore constitute the natural resource base of the economy. Until recently, Sweden had the highest marginal personal income tax rate in the world, at 98 percent. The top marginal rate was recently reduced to 50 percent—still high by world standards. In the early 1990s the econ-omy fell into deep recession, and GDP declined 1 percent annually from 1990 to 1994.

Sweden's Economic Performance score of 26 is the lowest for an industrialized country. Its score is hurt by stagnated per capita income since 1985 and sluggish growth in gross domestic investment and exports. On Competitiveness Sweden scores 58, one of the lowest among industrialized countries. Most of its indicators are close to the world average but below the industrialized country average. Sweden is strong in the concentration of scientists, engineers, and technicians in the population, foreign exchange freedom, and quality and breadth of infrastructure. Its Competitiveness score is hurt by a large and persistent fiscal deficit, which averaged 11 percent of GDP in 1991–94.

Social Development and the Environment. The combination of very high income, a generous welfare system, and comprehensive public health benefits has earned Sweden the best social indicators in the world. Life expectancy at birth is seventy-eight years, and illiteracy is practically nonexistent. Sweden receives perfect scores of 100 in both the education and the health vectors.

Free, compulsory education spans nine years starting at age seven. About 98 percent of students attend secondary school thereafter. Participation in tertiary education is very high at about 40 percent. Public expenditures for education amount to 5.4 percent of the country's GDP, a figure comparable to that of other European countries.

Health care has long been regarded as an important part of the Swedish welfare system. Equal access to health care is regarded as a fundamental right, and Sweden developed a health care delivery system with district physicians more than 300 years ago. Total expenditures on health care in Sweden account for almost 9 percent of GDP, the fourth highest among industrialized nations and above the OECD average.

The Swedish seeks to conserve its environment through an ambitious environmental program. It has already reduced its source of acid rain significantly. Currently over 80 percent of the nation's sulphur in acid deposition comes from nearby countries, particularly Poland and Germany. Sweden's wastewater treatment facilities are advanced and extensive, serving over 90 percent of its population. Sulfur dioxide emissions are now among the lowest in Europe. Sweden scores 73 on Environment, one of the highest scores in the world.

Democracy and Freedom. Swedish citizens are free to choose their government through democratic means. Citizens vote every three years in national elections. All fundamental freedoms and rights are guaranteed and enforced. A recent national debate has centered on questions regarding freedom of expression and incitement to racism and racial violence. A new constitution changed the role of the king, whose functions are now ceremonial. Sweden grants the Lappic minority significant power over its own educational and cultural matters. Parliament is composed of largely the same number of men and women. Sweden receives a perfect score of 100 on Democracy and Freedom.

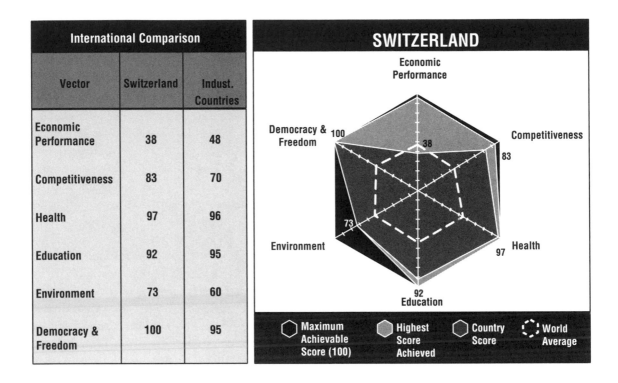

International Comparison		
Vector	Switzerland	Indust. Countries
Economic Performance	38	48
Competitiveness	83	70
Health	97	96
Education	92	95
Environment	73	60
Democracy & Freedom	100	95

SWITZERLAND

- Maximum Achievable Score (100)
- Highest Score Achieved
- Country Score
- World Average

SWITZERLAND

Economic Development. Switzerland's economic performance has been characterized by high per capita income, low inflation, low unemployment, and relatively slow economic growth over 1991–95. Switzerland has several industries that are considered world class in quality, including banking, watch manufacturing, pharmaceuticals, chemicals, chocolate manufacturing, and tourism. The traditional neutrality of the country has made it a favorite site for international conventions and the negotiation of peace accords and international agreements. It is the seat of the World Trade Organization and other United Nations agencies.

In recent years Switzerland has registered only modest economic growth. On Economic Performance it earns a score of only 38. The country has experienced slow output growth, a decline in investment growth, and slow growth in exports. The only Economic Performance indicator on which it scores well is the ratio of M2 to GDP, owing to its deep and well-developed capital markets. On Competitiveness Switzerland has a very high overall score of 83. The score is boosted by a high national saving rate, an excellent sovereign bond rating, low inflation, freedom of foreign exchange, and the quality and breadth of infrastructure.

Switzerland

Social Development and the Environment. Switzerland's social indicators reflect its status as an advanced, high-income country. Publicly funded compulsory education spans nine years starting from the age of six. An unusual characteristic of the Swiss educational system is the diversity of languages that can be used as the medium of instruction. Public expenditures for education amount to 5.4 percent of the country's GDP, a figure in line with other western European countries. Switzerland scores 92 on Education, below the industrialized country average, as a result of slightly lower enrollment levels at the secondary and tertiary levels.

Under Switzerland's constitution, public health is the general responsibility of the cantons, while heath insurance is a federal responsibility. Health insurance is optional, with nearly 99 percent of the population receiving coverage. Switzerland's Health indicators are excellent, and it scores 97 in the health vector.

Vehicular emissions are the main source of air pollution in Switzerland. To combat the problem, the country has established much stricter emissions standards than required by the European Community. Switzerland boasts extensive municipal wastewater treatment facilities, which serve about 90 percent of the population. Switzerland scores 73 on Environment, tied with Sweden as the highest score worldwide.

Democracy and Freedom. Swiss citizens can change their government democratically. Citizens have the power to call for federal plebiscites and initiate constitutional amendments, and they frequently use it. Fundamental freedoms are guaranteed and respected. The judiciary is free and independent. While some barriers to women's social and political advancement persist, women have had equal access to elected office under the cantonal system (designed to preserve localities' linguistic and cultural heritage) since 1990. Switzerland scores 100 in the democracy and freedom vector, higher than the industrialized country average of 95.

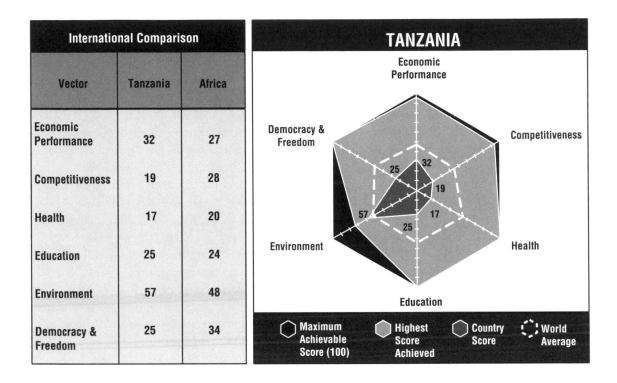

International Comparison		
Vector	Tanzania	Africa
Economic Performance	32	27
Competitiveness	19	28
Health	17	20
Education	25	24
Environment	57	48
Democracy & Freedom	25	34

TANZANIA

Economic Development. With a per capita income of U.S. $130 in 1995, Tanzania is one of the poorest countries in the world. The economy is predominantly agricultural. The main crops are coffee, cotton, tea, cashew nuts, sisal, maize, rice, wheat, cassava, and tobacco. Tanzania has a small manufacturing sector and a relatively underdeveloped mining sector. Tourism has become an increasingly important source of foreign exchange earnings.

Since 1986 the government of Tanzania has embarked on a series of economic reforms aimed at reducing state control in the economy and promoting private sector expansion.

Reform efforts have led to the elimination of restrictions on agricultural marketing and exports, the liberalization of trade and exchange regimes, and the dismantling of price controls and state monopolies. The financial sector is now open to private sector participation.

Tanzania scores 32 on Economic Performance, higher than the Africa average but below the world average. While its economy responded positively to the reforms, as shown by an annual growth rate of 4 percent over 1984–94, Tanzania's score is hurt by the fact that per capita income grew at a rate of under 1 percent during this period as a result of very rapid population growth. Tanzania receives a low Competitiveness score of 19. It is particularly weak in such indicators as inflation rate, saving rate, foreign exchange freedom, and infrastructure.

Social Development and the Environment. Low per capita income, slow output growth, and rapid population expansion have hurt Tanzania's social performance. Poverty is widespread. Life expectancy is low at fifty-one years, and the fertility rate is high at 5.8 children per woman. Tanzania has some of the worst child mortality and health indicators in the world as well as one of the highest rates of HIV infection. Tanzania receives only 17 in Health, lower than the Africa average.

Primary school enrollment is at 70 percent, while secondary enrollment is very low at 5 percent. The government has made poverty reduction its development priority and seeks to address it by improving the quality of and access to basic education as well as overall service delivery. Tanzania's Education score, 25, is in line with the regional average.

Forested areas cover half the country. However, accelerating deforestation threatens to wipe out all of its forests in the next one hundred years. The expansion of agriculture into arid and semiarid regions is causing desertification and soil degradation. Destructive fishing methods, especially the use of dynamite, are diminishing the country's marine resources, including coral reefs. Tanzania scores 57 on Environment, compared with the Africa average of 48.

Democracy and Freedom. Citizens of Tanzania are able to participate in elections to choose their government, but these have been marred by irregularities. The ruling party has unfairly used its power over state media and government resources to gain popular support. Since the establishment of a multiparty system in 1992, the media have become significantly freer and the judiciary has grown more independent. Fundamental freedoms, such as the constitutionally guaranteed freedom of assembly, are often restricted. Workers' rights to organize, enter trade unions of their choice, and strike are restricted. Tanzania receives a score of 25 on Democracy and Freedom, lower than the Africa average of 34.

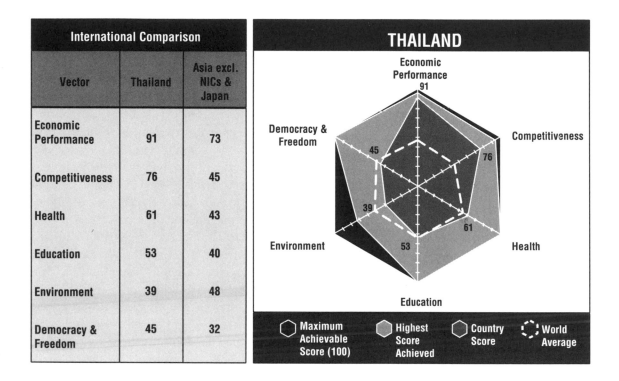

International Comparison		
Vector	Thailand	Asia excl. NICs & Japan
Economic Performance	91	73
Competitiveness	76	45
Health	61	43
Education	53	40
Environment	39	48
Democracy & Freedom	45	32

THAILAND

Economic Performance 91

Democracy & Freedom 45

Competitiveness 76

Environment 39

Health 61

Education 53

Maximum Achievable Score (100) · Highest Score Achieved · Country Score · World Average

THAILAND

Economic Development. Thailand, with its rapid economic expansion over the past three decades, has often been regarded as one of the upcoming Asian NICs. Real per capita income growth has been positive and has averaged almost 4 percent every year since 1960. During this period Thailand's economy has been transformed from traditional, heavily dependent on agriculture and natural resources, to diverse, with competitive export sectors, especially in manufactured products. The performance of the Thai economy has been particularly impressive since the mid-1980s following reforms undertaken in the early 1980s. Between 1987 and 1990, real GDP growth was among the highest in the world, averaging almost 12 percent a year. Despite the recession in the country's main export markets in industrial countries and its own domestic political uncertainties, Thailand's economy continued to expand at an 8 percent rate over 1991–94.

Thailand receives a high Economic Performance score of 91, which ranks it fourth in Asia and in the world. It scores 76 on Competitiveness, the fourth highest in Asia, after Hong Kong, Malaysia and Singapore. Its strong Competitiveness indicators include a high saving rate, a high export to GDP ratio, government surpluses, low inflation, and a relatively free foreign exchange environment.

Social Development and the Environment. Social indicators in Thailand have improved significantly as rapid rises in per capita income have expanded employment opportunities and reduced the incidence of poverty. However, there is evidence that income inequality has increased since the late 1980s as a result of the disparity in wages between the tradition and nontraditional sectors. Life expectancy is now sixty-nine years. Child survival and health indicators are mostly in the middle range. A major health concern is the rapid rise in HIV infections. Overall, Thailand scores 61 on Health, higher than the Asia average. Thailand also receives an above-average score, 53, on Education, reflecting its low level of adult illiteracy and a relatively high primary school enrollment rate.

Thailand's major environmental issues are deforestation and urban environmental pollution. Its natural forest has been rapidly diminished by intense illegal logging and encroachment by farmers. In urban areas, especially in Bangkok, industrial pollution, air pollution, inadequate sewage facilities, and traffic congestion are serious problems. About one-third of Thailand's urban population has no access to safe water, more than the proportion in rural areas. Thailand scores 39 on Environment, among the lowest scores in Asia.

Democracy and Freedom. Thai citizens choose their government through elections. However, elections are often affected by such irregularities as vote buying. Government corruption is widespread and affects even the judiciary. The military has a great deal of influence over policy. The press is largely free but refrains from criticizing the military. Defaming the monarchy, advocating a communist government, and engaging in inflammatory speech are illegal. Private sector workers may join independent unions. Thailand scores 45 on Democracy and Freedom, higher than the regional average of 32.

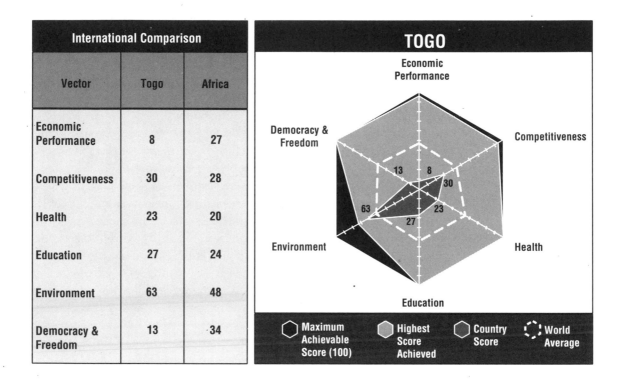

International Comparison		
Vector	Togo	Africa
Economic Performance	8	27
Competitiveness	30	28
Health	23	20
Education	27	24
Environment	63	48
Democracy & Freedom	13	34

TOGO

Economic Performance

Democracy & Freedom

Competitiveness

13   8

30

63   23

27

Environment

Health

Education

Maximum Achievable Score (100)   Highest Score Achieved   Country Score   World Average

TOGO

Economic Development. Togo, with a per capita income of U.S. $310 in 1995, is a low-income developing country. Its predominantly agricultural economy has traditionally depended on the production and export of primary commodities, primarily phosphates and cotton. In the 1980s, bolstered by the success of a stabilization and adjustment program in liberalizing its economy and improving efficiency, Togo's economy was one of the fastest growing in western Africa despite an unfavorable external environment. However, the economy stalled in 1991 amid a protracted period of political instability and a nine-month strike. As a result

of improvements in political and security conditions as well as increased competitiveness brought by the CFA franc devaluation, brisk growth returned in 1994.

Togo receives a very low Economic Performance score of 8 because of poor growth indicators between 1990 and 1994. National output, gross domestic investment, and exports all declined during this period. Togo scores higher on Competitiveness at 30, just above the Africa average. Its score is boosted by a low inflation rate and a moderate ratio of exports to GDP but is hurt by low saving and low levels of foreign direct investment.

Togo

Social Development and the Environment. Togo's social indicators are average for sub-Saharan Africa. The economic crisis in the early 1990s significantly increased the incidence of poverty, particularly in the urban areas. The majority of the poor are subsistence farmers. Mortality and child health and survival indicators are poor. The fertility rate is high at 6.4 children per woman. Rapid population growth is straining Togo's already poor social service infrastructure. Female-headed households are among the most vulnerable to poverty because of their relatively restricted access to land, credit, and education. Close to half of the adult population is illiterate, and the rate of illiteracy among female adults is much higher. Primary school enrollment exceeds 100 percent for the age group because of high repeat rates, while secondary and tertiary enrollment rates are low. Togo scores 23 on Health and 27 on Education, both of which are just higher than the regional averages.

Togo suffers from problems of deforestation, soil degradation, and erosion. Natural forests have been cleared for grazing, and traditional slash-and-burn farming exacerbates ero-sion. Close to one-third of the population does not have access to safe drinking water. Togo scores 63 in the environment vector, a relatively high score in Africa, as a result of low levels of greenhouse gas emissions associated with minimal industrial activity.

Democracy and Freedom. In theory citizens of Togo are able to elect their government. However, electoral fraud is pervasive. President Gnassingbe Eyadema wields almost unrestrained power. The opposition won the 1994 legislative election despite voting irregularities but has little real power. Legal procedures are generally respected, although the police and armed forces operate without restraint against opponents of the government. Journalists and editors of independent newspapers are often harassed by security forces. Freedom of religion is respected, but the right of assembly is ignored. Discrimination on the basis of ethnicity is widespread, with most power concentrated on a few ethnic groups from the north. Togo receives a score of 13 in the democracy and freedom vector, below the regional average of 34.

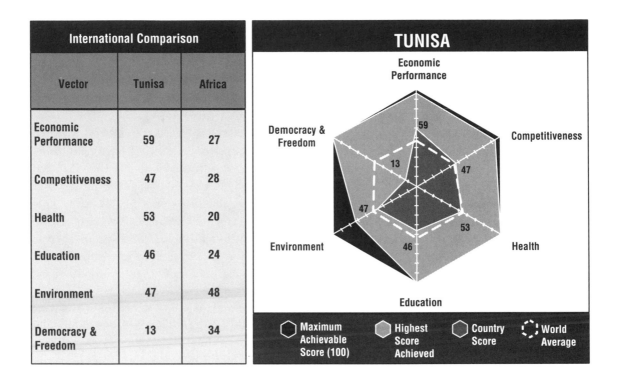

International Comparison		
Vector	Tunisia	Africa
Economic Performance	59	27
Competitiveness	47	28
Health	53	20
Education	46	24
Environment	47	48
Democracy & Freedom	13	34

TUNISA

Economic Performance

Democracy & Freedom — 59 — Competitiveness

13 — 47

47 — 53

Environment — 46 — Health

Education

- Maximum Achievable Score (100)
- Highest Score Achieved
- Country Score
- World Average

TUNISIA

Economic Development. In the mid-1980s Tunisia abandoned its three-decade-old economic strategy of relying on large public enterprises and strict state control in favor of a market-based system. The government's new strategy has focused on maintaining a stable macroeconomic environment, reducing price distortions, and liberalizing the trade and investment regimes. Tunisia's economy has become more dynamic and diversified since the introduction of reforms, and its economic performance has been impressive. Tunisia is now embarking on closer economic ties with Europe through trade. The free-trade agreement signed with the European Union in 1995 commits the government to deepen its trade reforms.

Tunisia's score of 59 on Economic Performance ranks fourth in Africa. Its score is earned by a high GDP growth rate (4.5 percent) between 1990 and 1994 and a steady rise in per capita GDP between 1985 and 1994. Tunisia scores 47 on Competitiveness, just above the world average and much higher than the Africa average. The country is strong in saving, ratio of exports to GDP, and level of foreign direct investment.

Social Development and the Environment. Tunisia has some of the best social indicators in

Africa. Improvement of social conditions has always been a priority for the Tunisian government. Expenditures have been maintained at 5.0–6.0 percent of GDP for education and 2.2 percent for health, even in periods of the most severe budget cutbacks during stabilization. Life expectancy at birth is now sixty-eight years. Access to health care is almost universal—currently 90 percent of the population lives within an hour's walking distance of a health facility. Tunisia's Health score (53) is the second highest in Africa. The government has made nine years of education compulsory, and net primary enrollment rates reach almost 100 percent. Tunisia scores 46 on Education, much higher than the average in Africa.

A large portion of Tunisia's land area is threatened by erosion, mainly as a result of overgrazing and population pressure, which lead to indiscriminate expansion into marginal lands. Water is a scarce commodity, its supply often threatened by recurring drought. As in many other countries in the region, treatment of toxic wastes is almost nonexistent, causing public health and environmental problems. Tunisia scores 47 on Environment, in line with the average in Africa.

Democracy and Freedom. Tunisians cannot freely elect their government. Most opposition candidates were restricted from participating in the 1992 elections. The government's repression of dissent is increasingly taking the form of restrictions on political activity. The state controls the media and closely monitors all broadcasts. Satellite dishes are heavily taxed. Anti-defamation rules are used to restrict criticisms of the government. The executive controls the judiciary. Islam is the official religion, but other religions, except for Baha'i, are allowed as long as they do not proselytize. Tunisia has only one labor federation, which is under tight government control. Tunisia scores 13 on Democracy and Freedom, well below the average of 34 for Africa.

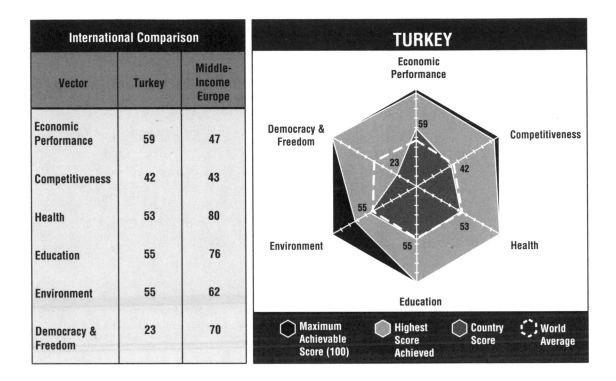

International Comparison		
Vector	Turkey	Middle-Income Europe
Economic Performance	59	47
Competitiveness	42	43
Health	53	80
Education	55	76
Environment	55	62
Democracy & Freedom	23	70

TURKEY

Economic Development. Turkey, with a per capita income of U.S. $2,670 in 1995, is a middle-income country. Economic reforms launched in the early 1980s initially brought about a period of steady growth, as national income increased at an annual rate of 6 percent throughout the 1980s. However, in recent years inadequate fiscal management and expansionary monetary policies have led to an erratic economic performance characterized by growth spurts and stagnation as the government has periodically attempted to control inflation and external imbalances. Per capita income increased at a slow rate of 1.4 percent between 1985 and 1994.

Turkey receives a score of 59 on Economic Performance, much higher than the average among middle-income European countries. On Competitiveness Turkey scores lower at 42, hurt by a persistent government deficit, high inflation rates averaging 66 percent from 1984 to 1994, and a poor sovereign risk rating. Its stronger indicators are foreign exchange freedom and a high saving rate of 23 percent.

Social Development and the Environment. The government's recent financial difficulties have taken a toll on Turkey's social performance. Income disparities are significant and could be worsening. High inflation and real interest rates

have limited employment growth. Turkey's health indicators are poor compared with those for countries at similar income levels. The infant mortality rate is high, at 62 per 1,000 live births, as is the maternal mortality rate, at 180 per 100,000 live births. Immunization rates are relatively low. About 18 percent of all adults are illiterate, and the rate of illiteracy among female adults is much higher. While primary enrollment is almost universal, less than two-thirds of the relevant age group attends secondary school. The average number of years of schooling for females is only half that for males. Quality of and access to basic education are serious problems. Turkey receives 53 in Health and 55 in Education, both of which are much lower than the average for middle-income Europe.

Industrial and urban development has brought problems of air and water pollution to Turkey. In major urban centers such as Istanbul, high levels of greenhouse gases have been detected. Deforestation is also an increasing problem, with more forests being converted to farmland and grazing land. Turkey receives a score of 55 on Environment, the lowest score in middle-income Europe.

Democracy and Freedom. Turkey's government is freely elected. Violations of human rights, however, are widespread. The government has been fighting against Kurdish separatists in the southeastern part of the country since 1984. Insurgents and sympathizers have been subject to killing and detention without trial, and torture and other abuses are common. The judiciary is independent. During the 1990s restrictions on the media eased, but the government still tightly regulates media coverage and the police routinely detain journalists who are critical of the government. Demonstrations are often dispersed. Non-Muslim minorities are closely watched by the government. Turkey scores 23 on Democracy and Freedom, the lowest score in middle-income Europe.

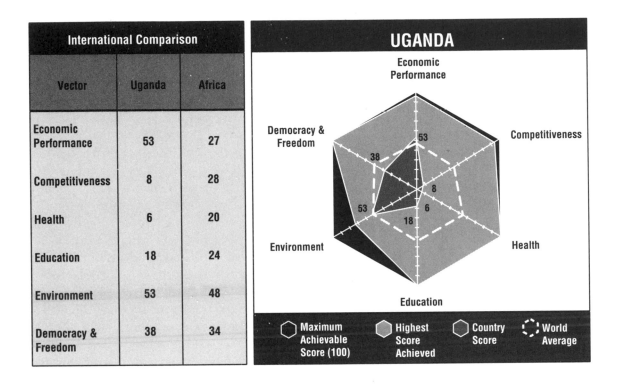

International Comparison		
Vector	**Uganda**	**Africa**
Economic Performance	53	27
Competitiveness	8	28
Health	6	20
Education	18	24
Environment	53	48
Democracy & Freedom	38	34

UGANDA

Maximum Achievable Score (100) Highest Score Achieved Country Score World Average

UGANDA

Economic Development. Uganda has substantial natural resources, including fertile soils, regular rainfall, and sizable deposits of cobalt and copper. The economy is primarily agricultural, with coffee as the principal export crop. During the 1960s Uganda had one of the most promising economies in sub-Saharan Africa. However, for over a decade beginning in 1972, the economy was devastated by political turmoil, civil war, and economic mismanagement. The nation's real GDP per capita declined by almost 40 percent between 1971 and 1986. Uganda now ranks among the world's poorest countries, with a per capita income of U.S. $240 in 1995.

Since 1986 the government has implemented a major stabilization and economic restructuring program. The combination of a more favorable policy environment, rising foreign investment, and a coffee boom has led to substantial economic growth in the 1990s.

On Economic Performance Uganda receives a relatively high score of 53, second in sub-Saharan Africa (after Botswana). Its score is earned by a GDP growth rate of 5.6 percent in 1990–94 and a per capita income growth rate of 2.3 percent between 1985 and 1994. Uganda's Competitiveness score is much lower at 8, as a result of its high inflation rate (which

averaged 75 percent in the 1984–94 period), a low saving rate, a low ratio of exports to GDP, lack of foreign exchange freedom, and poor infrastructure.

Social Development and the Environment. Over a decade of economic decline has kept Uganda's social indicators near the bottom of the world scores. Life expectancy at birth is a low forty-two years, mainly as a result of very high infant and child mortality rates. Population is growing at an unsustainable pace; the fertility rate is seven children per woman. Uganda also has one of the world's highest rates of HIV infection. Overall, Uganda scores 6 on Health, among the lowest in Africa. An estimated 38 percent of the adult population is illiterate. Two-thirds of the relevant age group attends primary school, and just over half completes grade five. Uganda scores 18 on Education, below the Africa average of 24.

Blessed with abundant fertile soil and natural water resources, Uganda is a biologically rich country and a net absorber of carbon dioxide. Its major environmental concerns are wet-land protection and forest and wildlife management. Overall access to safe water is limited. Uganda scores 53 in the environment vector, higher than the Africa average of 48.

Democracy and Freedom. Citizens of Uganda are not able to elect their government democratically. President Yoweri Museveni, who took power in a 1986 coup, wields enormous power. Elections for a constitutional assembly, judged by foreign observers to be clean, took place in 1994. Under the new constitution, elections are to be held for legislative and executive posts, but political parties are banned and candidates run as individuals. While citizens and media exercise freedom of speech, sedition laws are often used to harass journalists. Freedom of assembly is respected. Political party meetings, which are banned, have gone on undisturbed. The army has often disregarded civilian courts, but the judicial system is gaining strength and independence. Ethnic tensions are a threat to long-term peace. Uganda scores 38 on Democracy and Freedom, just above the Africa average.

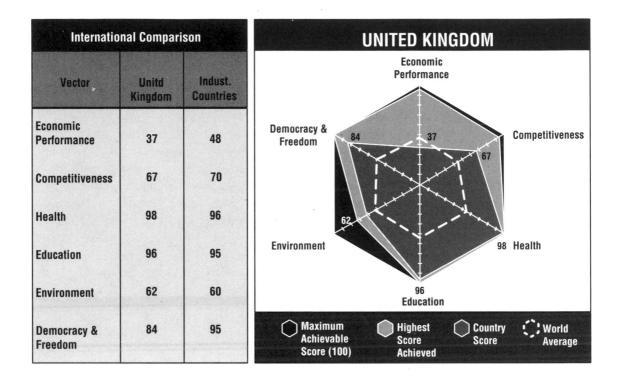

International Comparison		
Vector	Unitd Kingdom	Indust. Countries
Economic Performance	37	48
Competitiveness	67	70
Health	98	96
Education	96	95
Environment	62	60
Democracy & Freedom	84	95

UNITED KINGDOM

Economic Performance · Competitiveness · Health · Education · Environment · Democracy & Freedom

- Maximum Achievable Score (100)
- Highest Score Achieved
- Country Score
- World Average

UNITED KINGDOM

Economic Development. The United Kingdom is one of the world's great trading powers and financial centers. The economy is essentially capitalistic, with a mixture of general social welfare programs and government ownership. In the 1980s the government of Margaret Thatcher transformed the policy framework toward a strong free-market system through privatization and deregulation. The country is energy rich, with extensive reserves of coal, natural gas, and oil. The U.K. economy fell into recession in 1990 after eight years of strong economic expansion.

The United Kingdom's overall Economic Performance score is 37. It receives low scores in economic growth, growth in domestic investment, and exports of goods and nonfactor services based on its performance in 1990–94. On Competitiveness it scores a much higher 67. The country is relatively strong in level of foreign investment, sovereign bond rating, foreign exchange freedom, infrastructure, and the concentration of scientists, engineers, and technicians in its population.

Social Development and the Environment. The combination of high living standards and a system of generous social benefits gives the United Kingdom some of the best social indicators in

GLOBAL Benchmarks

the world. Education in the United Kingdom, which is dominated by the public system, is compulsory from ages five through sixteen. Secondary and tertiary enrollment rates are both very high. About 24 percent of the work force has advanced professional, management, academic, or vocational training. State funding for education represented 5.2 percent of GDP in 1992. A comprehensive and generous public health system is accessible to citizens and residents at no cost. The United Kingdom scores 96 on Education and 98 on Health, both of which are higher than the averages for industrialized countries.

Environmental conditions in the United Kingdom have improved significantly from the early days of industrial revolution. However, the country still suffers from air pollution, mainly from power stations and motor vehicles, and water pollution. It is a major source of pollution of the North Sea, and its industrial emissions have been carried into neighboring countries. The United Kingdom accounts for 9–12 percent of the sulfur deposited in Norway. The United Kingdom scores 62 on Environment, just above the average for industrialized countries.

Democracy and Freedom. U.K. citizens freely elect their government. The country's democratic system functions without a written constitution or bill of rights, relying instead on unwritten norms. Some critics point out that, as a result, the United Kingdom has been able to pass laws restricting basic freedoms. Most fundamental freedoms are respected, including freedom of religion, the press, expression, and movement. The press is subject to strong libel regulations. Labor groups are powerful and active. The United Kingdom scores 84 on Democracy and Freedom.

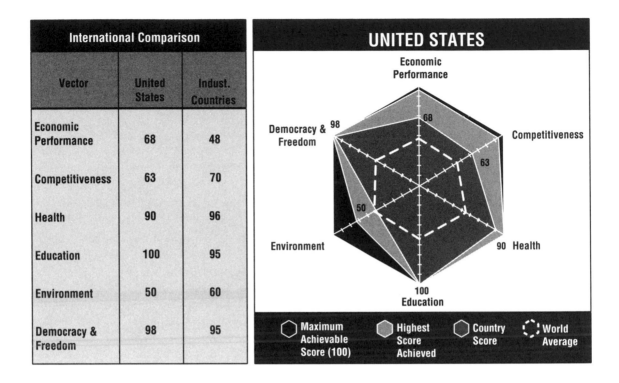

International Comparison		
Vector	United States	Indust. Countries
Economic Performance	68	48
Competitiveness	63	70
Health	90	96
Education	100	95
Environment	50	60
Democracy & Freedom	98	95

UNITED STATES

Economic Performance · Competitiveness · Health · Education · Environment · Democracy & Freedom

Maximum Achievable Score (100) · Highest Score Achieved · Country Score · World Average

UNITED STATES

Economic Development. The United States has the largest, most diverse, and most technologically advanced economy in the world and one of the highest per capita incomes as measured by purchasing-power parity. In 1996 the U.S. economy enjoyed its fifth consecutive year of economic growth—one of the longest periods of expansion in U.S. postwar history. The expansion has featured consistent growth with only moderate wage and price increases and a steady reduction in unemployment to less than 5 percent of the work force. In recent years the fiscal deficit has decreased significantly as a result of rising revenues.

On Economic Performance the United States scores 68, the highest among industrialized countries. The country is strong in a number of indicators, including economic growth, gross domestic investment, exports, and ration of M2 to GDP. On Competitiveness the United States receives a score of 63, below the industrialized country average. While the United States is strong on such Competitiveness indicators as a sovereign bond rating, concentration of scientists and engineers, foreign exchange freedom, and infrastructure, its score is hurt by a low ratio of exports to GDP and a persistent and moderately high government deficit.

United States

Social Development and the Environment. In the United States education is the responsibility of individual states and communities. However, the federal government provides funding to states and school districts and financial aid to students to support their participation in higher education. Compulsory, free education spans ten years beginning at age six. The public sector predominates at the elementary and secondary levels of education. The structure of higher education in the United States is diverse, with nearly 1,600 public institutions and almost 2,000 private institutions offering a wide range of programs. The country has the highest rate of enrollment worldwide at the tertiary level. The United States scores a perfect 100 on Education.

The United States spends more on health care services than any other country does—on average, more than twice as much per person as other OECD countries. Health expenditures are financed by a complex mixture of public payers (federal, state, and local governments) as well as private insurance and individual payments. The country relies primarily on employers to provide voluntary health insurance coverage to their employees and dependents. Government programs are confined to the elderly, the disabled, and the poor. However, high health care spending does not yield a perfect Health score for the United States. It scores only 90, below the industrialized country average, as a result of a higher infant mortality rate, a relatively high rate of HIV infection, and lower immunization rates and contraceptive prevalence than in other OECD countries.

As a major industrialized country, the United States emits a vast amount of pollutants. The nation is the largest single emitter of greenhouse gases, accounting for over 20 percent of global carbon dioxide emissions from burning fossil fuels. U.S. emissions carry over to neighboring Canada, contributing to acid rain that falls on parts of the United States and Canada. The United States scores 50 on Environment, below the industrialized country average.

Democracy and Freedom. Citizens of the United States elect their government in free elections. However, only about 50 percent of eligible voters turn out for presidential elections, and fewer for nonpresidential ones. Fundamental freedoms are generally guaranteed and respected. Hateful expression has been outlawed in several states and localities. University and media efforts to ban allegedly racist and sexist language and to conform to "politically correct" views may constrain academic and press freedoms. The judiciary is independent but severely overburdened with civil and criminal cases. The United States scores 98 on Democracy and Freedom.

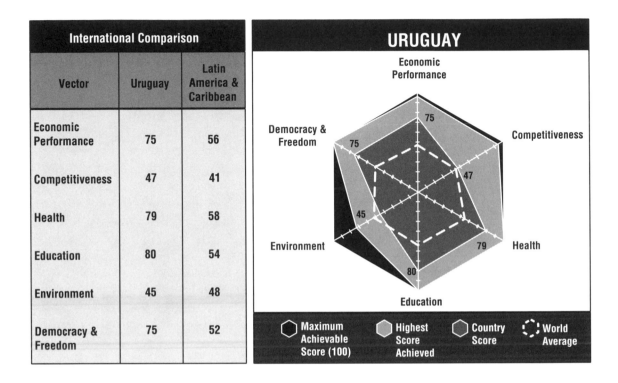

International Comparison		
Vector	Uruguay	Latin America & Caribbean
Economic Performance	75	56
Competitiveness	47	41
Health	79	58
Education	80	54
Environment	45	48
Democracy & Freedom	75	52

URUGUAY (chart)

Economic Performance — 75
Competitiveness — 47
Health — 79
Education — 80
Environment — 45
Democracy & Freedom — 75

○ Maximum Achievable Score (100) ○ Highest Score Achieved ○ Country Score ⟨⟩ World Average

URUGUAY

Economic Development. With a per capita GDP of U.S. $5,100 in 1995, Uruguay has one of the highest incomes of the countries in Latin America. However, economic growth has been sluggish since the mid-1950s, with annual GDP growth averaging just over 1 percent. The country's economic strategy has been based on import substitution and extensive social benefits, financed by heavy taxes on the working population. In recent years the government has initiated comprehensive structural reforms to reorient the economy toward market incentives and private sector participation. While progress is uneven, reform efforts contributed to a healthy GDP growth rate of 4.4 percent and investment growth of 12 percent over the 1990–94 period. Exports expanded at a 8 percent annual rate in the same period. Accelerated growth earns Uruguay an Economic Performance score of 75, ranking it fourth in Latin America and the Caribbean.

Uruguay scores much lower on Competitiveness, at 47, but still higher than the regional average. Its score is hurt particularly by a high average inflation rate of 74 percent between 1984 and 1994 and a relatively low ratio of exports to GDP.

Social Development and the Environment.

Uruguay's social indicators are among the best in Latin America, reflecting the country's tradition of and commitment to extensive social service. The poverty rate in Uruguay is the lowest in Latin America, and income distribution compares favorably with that of many developed countries. Life expectancy is high at seventy-three years. Maternal and child health and mortality indicators are much better than in the rest of Latin America. The population is mostly urban (90 percent) and literate. Primary education is practically universal, and secondary and tertiary education enrollment rates are high. Uruguay's Health score of 79 is the second highest, after Cuba, in Latin America and the Caribbean. Its equally high Education score (80) is second only to Argentina in the region.

The major environmental problems in Uruguay are the clearing and destruction of natural forests and the inadequate treatment of industrial pollutants in urban and industrial areas. More than 15 percent of the population does not have access to safe water. Emissions of greenhouse gases are very high on a per capita basis, reaching the levels found in industrialized countries. Uruguay scores 45 in the environment vector, just below the average for Latin America and the Caribbean.

Democracy and Freedom. Uruguayans elect their government through democratic means. Political apathy is increasing, however, as factionalism has caused gridlock in policymaking. All fundamental rights are constitutionally guaranteed and respected. The judicial system is independent but backlogged as a result of mounting crime. The press is independent and free. The labor force is very well organized, and unions play an important role in the country's politics. Uruguay receives a score of 75 on Democracy and Freedom, much higher than the average of 52 for Latin America and the Caribbean.

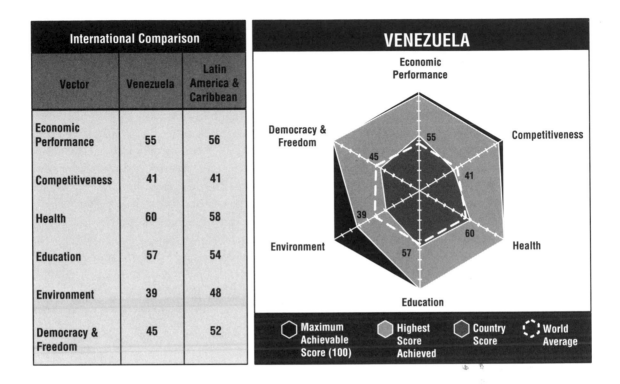

International Comparison		
Vector	Venezuela	Latin America & Caribbean
Economic Performance	55	56
Competitiveness	41	41
Health	60	58
Education	57	54
Environment	39	48
Democracy & Freedom	45	52

VENEZUELA

Economic Development. Venezuela's per capita income of U.S. $3,020 in 1995 is close to the average for Latin America and the Caribbean. The country is rich in natural resources, including petroleum. Petroleum has accounted for the majority of the country's export earnings, tying Venezuela's economic fortune to the international oil prices.

Two decades of economic mismanagement led to a pattern of erratic economic growth. The country fell into a deep recession after the boost received by the 1973–74 oil price hike, and by 1985 per capita GNP was 20 percent below its 1972 level. The government that took office in 1989 introduced a comprehensive reform program to restructure and jump-start the economy, with uneven results. Since early 1994 the country has been struggling with the mounting problem of bank failures. In 1994 alone the government spent 13 percent of GDP to rescue failing banks.

Both Venezuela's Economic Performance score (55) and its Competitiveness score (41) are in line with regional averages. Its Economic Performance indicators are mostly in the average range. Foreign exchange reserves are strong, averaging nine months of import coverage. On Competitiveness Venezuela earns points for its high saving rate but loses points for a high annual inflation rate of 36 percent from 1984 to 1994 and a poor sovereign bond rating.

Social Development and the Environment. Social indicators for Venezuela are mostly close to or just above the average in the region. Life expectancy—seventy-one years at birth—is relatively high for a country at its income level. However, over a decade of slow economic growth has taken a toll on social conditions. There is evidence that the incidence of poverty has increased, particularly in the urban areas. In addition, social indicators have not improved as rapidly as in many middle-income developing countries. While primary education is almost universal, secondary enrollment is low at 35 percent. Venezuela scores 60 on Health and 57 on Education.

Deforestation is the most serious environmental problem in Venezuela. During the 1980s, its forested area diminished at a rate of 1,000 square miles per year. Urban and industrial wastes cause considerable pollution along the Caribbean coast. Sewage treatment and industrial pollution controls are both inadequate. The contamination of drinking water is also a serious problem. Venezuela scores 39 on Environment, well below the regional average of 48.

Democracy and Freedom. Venezuelans elect their government officials through democratic means. Corruption, much of it related to the growing drug trade in the country, has undermined national institutions. Coup attempts in the early 1990s reflected a growing lack of confidence in the country's leadership structure. Most fundamental rights are constitutionally guaranteed and protected. However, security forces often use excessive force in repressing popular protests and labor strikes. Corruption has seriously eroded confidence in the judicial system, which is slow and subject to intimidation. Venezuela receives a score of 45 on Democracy and Freedom, lower than the regional average of 52.

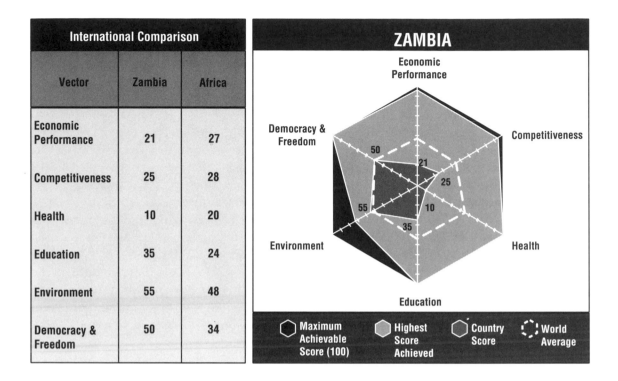

International Comparison		
Vector	Zambia	Africa
Economic Performance	21	27
Competitiveness	25	28
Health	10	20
Education	35	24
Environment	55	48
Democracy & Freedom	50	34

ZAMBIA

Economic Performance · Competitiveness · Democracy & Freedom · Environment · Health · Education

Maximum Achievable Score (100) · Highest Score Achieved · Country Score · World Average

ZAMBIA

Economic Development. Zambia's economy has been on the decline since the mid-1970s, as its foreign debt rose and world copper prices fell. Copper and cobalt account for nearly 85 percent of Zambia's total exports. Dependence on a single commodity and excessive government intervention have constrained the economy's ability to diversify and adjust to the sustained decline in the world copper prices since 1975. Per capita income in Zambia was halved between 1974 and 1994. In 1995 its per capita GNP of U.S. $370 was below the average in sub-Saharan Africa. A structural adjustment program undertaken in 1990 by the Zambian government to arrest the economic decline has involved trade policy and exchange rate reforms, deregulation, and stabilization policies to improve the macroeconomic environment.

Zambia's Economic Performance score of 21 and Competitiveness score of 25 are both below the regional averages. Its scores are hurt by poor growth rates and a generally unfavorable macroeconomic environment from the mid-1980s through 1994. Growth rates were mostly negative, the government deficit was alarmingly high (averaging 11 percent of GDP), and inflation rates were high, as prices on average nearly doubled every year from 1984 to 1994. The only bright spot was the brisk export growth recorded during the 1990–94 period.

Social Development and the Environment. Social indicators, already poor in Zambia, have worsened in recent years due to overall economic decline. Poverty is pervasive, and hunger is reported to be the worst problem facing the poor. Life expectancy is low at forty-seven years, partly because of an infant mortality rate that exceeds 10 percent of all live births. Zambia also has one of the world's highest rates of adult HIV infection. Over one-fifth of the adult population is illiterate. School enrollment rates are above the average for sub-Saharan Africa. Zambia's Health score of 10 is half of the average in Africa, while its Education score of 35 is higher than the regional average of 24.

Zambia has less severe environmental problems than many parts of Africa. Nonetheless, urbanization has caused the rapid destruction of many indigenous woodlands. Overgrazing and overstocking have contributed to land degradation and reduced production. Poaching of ivory and rhino horn continues to be a serious problem. Zambia receives a score of 55 on Environment, higher than the average in Africa.

Democracy and Freedom. In 1991 Zambians elected their government freely for the first time. Democratic institutions are still weak, as the ruling Movement for Multiparty Democracy controls the political scene and faces with a weak opposition. Citizens participate freely in religious and other types of organizations with no government interference. The press is subject to much pressure, including physical assault, surveillance, restriction of printing facilities, and libel actions when government corruption is reported. Abuses of inmates in prisons and police brutality are widely reported. The courts are independent but strained by backlogged cases. Constitutional rights regarding labor are respected, and Zambia's labor unions are among the strongest in Africa. Zambia receives a score of 50 on Democracy and Freedom, higher than the regional average of 34.

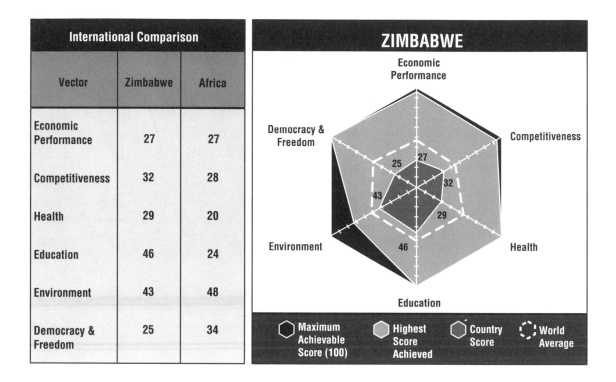

International Comparison		
Vector	Zimbabwe	Africa
Economic Performance	27	27
Competitiveness	32	28
Health	29	20
Education	46	24
Environment	43	48
Democracy & Freedom	25	34

ZIMBABWE

Economic Performance

Democracy & Freedom — 25 27 — Competitiveness

43 32

29

Environment — 46 — Health

Education

⬡ Maximum Achievable Score (100)   ⬡ Highest Score Achieved   ⬡ Country Score   ⬡ World Average

ZIMBABWE

Economic Development. When it became independent in 1980, Zimbabwe's manufacturing sector was the most developed in sub-Saharan Africa, providing more than 25 percent of GDP. Despite the country's diverse economy, output growth did not keep up with population expansion, and unemployment rose in the 1990s. Since 1991 the government has adopted a series of structural reforms to steer the economy toward a market-oriented system. However, public enterprise reform has been slow, and fiscal deficits have not been contained. Continued, large public sector borrowing and several severe droughts in 1992 and 1995 have compounded the slow adjustment to structural reforms. On average GDP per capita fell by about 2 percent a year from 1991 to 1995.

Zimbabwe's Economic Performance score of 27 is the average for Africa. Its score is hurt by slow real growth in output and investment and declining per capita income. On Competitiveness Zimbabwe's score of 32 is slightly above the average for Africa. It is strong in the ratio of exports to GDP and the relative reliability of electricity supply. The weakest indicators are a chronic government deficit and a relatively high annual inflation rate from 1984 to 1994.

Zimbabwe

Social Development and the Environment. Despite drought and a low rate of economic growth, Zimbabwe's achievements in the social sector are impressive. Food relief and supplementary feeding programs have prevented a rise in malnutrition. Child survival and health indicators are better than average for Africa. One of Zimbabwe's most pressing public health problem is its rate of HIV infection, the world's highest. An estimated 5 percent of babies born in 1994 were HIV positive. Zimbabwe scores 29 on Health, higher than the regional average of 20. It scores 46 on Education, much higher than the Africa average, reflecting a relatively low adult illiteracy rate as well as one of sub-Saharan Africa's highest school enrollment rates.

To promote sustainable development and project a growing tourism sector, Zimbabwe has established one of the most ambitious and effective conservation programs in Africa. Currently 7 percent of the country's total land area is protected, including many game reserves. Major environmental issues are deforestation and land degradation. Industrialization has been linked to increasing pollution in both urban and rural areas. Only one-third of the population has access to safe drinking water. Zimbabwe scores 43 in the environment vector, just below the average for Africa.

Democracy and Freedom. Despite regular elections, citizens of Zimbabwe cannot change their government through democratic methods. The African National Union–Patriotic Front (ZANU-PF), Zimbabwe's dominant party, controls the electoral process, receives government subsidies, and monopolizes the state media. Such authoritarianism is pushing Zimbabwe closer to a one-party system. Of the 150 seats in parliament, only 3 are held by the opposition. The press practices a considerable amount of self-censorship. The judicial system is independent but continues to be subverted by constitutional amendments passed by the ZANU-PF-controlled legislature. Women face significant discrimination, and domestic violence is a common problem. Zimbabwe scores 25 on Democracy and Freedom, below the Africa average of 34.

Appendix A

SUMMARY OF VECTOR SCORES

	TABLE A.1					
	Vector[a]					
Country	Economic Performance	Competitiveness Foundations	Health	Education	Environment	Democracy and Freedom
Argentina	67	48	71	84	36	59
Australia	62	66	96	96	56	98
Austria	51	76	96	100	66	98
Bahrain	31	22	68	72	65	0
Bangladesh	66	22	26	11	66	50
Belgium	43	66	93	97	70	100
Benin	46	40	14	10	48	75
Bhutan	69	38	9	5	43	0
Bolivia	62	39	31	48	34	59
Botswana	75	59	47	48	30	73
Brazil	42	28	55	49	60	56
Burkina Faso	12	32	8	6	57	38
Burundi	4	22	2	17	49	0
Cambodia	n.a.	0	10	21	42	0

	Vector[a]					
Country	**Economic Performance**	**Competitiveness Foundations**	**Health**	**Education**	**Environment**	**Democracy and Freedom**
Cameroon	4	42	24	24	45	11
Canada	42	68	96	100	56	98
Cape Verde	40	0	43	39	34	88
Central African Republic	18	37	9	15	40	50
Chile	88	67	76	71	70	73
China	88	55	73	54	52	0
Colombia	69	49	71	55	53	50
Congo (Zaire)	0	0	1	17	51	0
Costa Rica	84	60	78	65	59	86
Côte d'Ivoire	10	56	12	15	60	13
Cuba	n.a.	5	87	74	49	0
Cyprus	90	26	92	77	71	100
Denmark	43	78	98	100	51	100
Djibouti	n.a.	0	7	4	53	13
Dominican Republic	61	46	60	49	41	50
Ecuador	61	50	60	50	42	63
Egypt	30	50	43	59	72	25
El Salvador	79	39	44	39	38	50

TABLE A.1 CONTINUED

	Vector[a]					
Country	Economic Performance	Competitiveness Foundations	Health	Education	Environment	Democracy and Freedom
Ethiopia	12	14	1	5	49	38
Fiji	65	34	72	68	46	50
Finland	36	62	100	100	55	100
France	44	70	97	95	68	86
Germany	30	73	94	92	61	86
Ghana	44	35	25	36	61	48
Greece	57	37	90	94	61	73
Guatemala	58	40	39	16	59	34
Guyana	25	3	50	73	45	75
Haiti	2	16	18	4	48	25
Honduras	48	51	48	36	51	48
Hong Kong	95	80	95	81	53	53
Hungary	24	50	83	72	67	88
Iceland	56	60	97	75	53	100
India	62	32	37	36	69	48
Indonesia	85	67	41	49	37	0
Iran	47	37	49	55	44	0
Iraq	n.a.	0	32	37	39	0
Ireland	67	86	92	96	40	100

	Vector[a]					
TABLE A.1 CONTINUED						
Country	**Economic Performance**	**Competitiveness Foundations**	**Health**	**Education**	**Environment**	**Democracy and Freedom**
Israel	90	53	95	83	60	73
Italy	44	54	92	88	70	86
Jamaica	57	47	75	64	57	63
Japan	57	79	97	91	64	86
Jordan	57	46	60	67	71	50
Kenya	16	37	27	37	41	0
Korea, Republic of	87	74	78	96	44	75
Kuwait	74	71	78	53	44	25
Lebanon	n.a.	0	50	75	57	13
Madagascar	11	23	21	6	36	63
Malawi	6	20	13	27	65	63
Malaysia	96	83	68	57	34	36
Mali	36	37	5	10	46	64
Mauritania	32	32	18	17	31	0
Mauritius	75	54	71	61	63	88
Mexico	47	32	59	57	52	45
Morocco	37	52	39	25	70	25
Mozambique	77	22	3	4	52	50
Netherlands	42	91	100	96	56	100

TABLE A.1 CONTINUED

Country	Vector[a]					
	Economic Performance	Competitiveness Foundations	Health	Education	Environment	Democracy and Freedom
New Zealand	54	80	91	95	50	100
Nicaragua	30	24	48	35	46	45
Norway	60	81	99	100	48	100
Pakistan	66	33	24	4	43	34
Panama	59	73	74	64	52	63
Papua New Guinea	56	57	21	27	47	63
Paraguay	50	60	47	53	23	50
Peru	59	43	50	65	48	34
Philippines	52	51	49	72	54	56
Poland	39	54	86	89	58	86
Portugal	58	51	90	79	71	98
Romania	14	49	79	65	60	50
Rwanda	6	22	14	24	58	0
Saudi Arabia	38	80	55	51	35	0
Senegal	10	40	15	13	45	38
Sierra Leone	20	27	3	0	37	0
Singapore	95	94	96	80	49	23
South Africa	26	30	42	58	43	84
Spain	53	58	93	100	68	84

TABLE A.1 CONTINUED

Country	Vector[a]					
	Economic Performance	Competitiveness Foundations	Health	Education	Environment	Democracy and Freedom
Sri Lanka	80	34	74	56	58	38
Sudan	0	0	26	16	34	0
Swaziland	20	0	17	49	34	13
Sweden	26	58	100	100	73	100
Switzerland	38	83	97	92	73	100
Syria	0	59	47	58	41	0
Tanzania	32	19	17	25	57	25
Thailand	91	76	61	53	39	45
Togo	8	30	23	27	63	13
Tunisia	59	47	53	46	47	13
Turkey	59	42	53	55	55	23
Uganda	53	8	6	18	53	38
United Arab Emirates	25	86	79	69	40	13
United Kingdom	37	67	98	96	62	84
United States	68	63	90	100	50	98
Uruguay	75	47	79	80	45	75
Venezuela	55	41	60	57	39	45
Zambia	21	25	10	35	55	50
Zimbabwe	27	32	29	46	43	25

GLOBAL Benchmarks

TABLE A.1 CONTINUED

Country	Vector[a]					
	Economic Performance	Competitiveness Foundations	Health	Education	Environment	Democracy and Freedom
Countries scored	103	108	108	108	108	108
Maximum	96	94	100	100	73	100
Minimum	0	0	1	0	23	0
Average	47	45	55	54	52	50
Median	48	46	54	55	51	50

SOURCE: Calculations by SRI International. See chapter 4 and appendixes C and D.

n.a. Not available.

a. Maximum score = 100.

WEIGHTED VECTOR SCORES

	Indicator							
Country	GDP growth, 1990–94	Per capita GNP growth, 1985-94	GNP per capita, 1994	Growth of gross domestic investment, 1990–94	Growth of exports, 1990–94	M2 as percent of GDP, 1994	Gross international reserves, 1994	Total weighted score[a]
Argentina	16	10	12	20	5	0	4	67
Australia	12	10	16	5	15	2	2	62
Austria	8	10	16	5	5	4	3	51
Bahrain	0	0	31	0	0	0	0	31
Bangladesh	12	10	4	15	20	1	4	66
Belgium	4	16	17	0	5	0	1	43
Benin	12	0	4	20	5	1	4	46
Bhutan	0	59	10	0	0	0	0	69
Bolivia	12	10	4	15	15	2	4	62
Botswana	21	39	14	0	0	1	0	75
Brazil	8	0	8	5	16	0	4	42
Burkina Faso	8	0	0	0	0	0	4	12

TABLE B.1 WEIGHTED SCORES FOR ECONOMIC PERFORMANCE INDICATORS

TABLE B.1 CONTINUED

Country	Indicator							
	GDP growth, 1990–94	Per capita GNP growth, 1985-94	GNP per capita, 1994	Growth of gross domestic investment, 1990–94	Growth of exports, 1990–94	M2 as percent of GDP, 1994	Gross international reserves, 1994	Total weighted score[a]
Burundi	0	0	0	0	0	0	4	4
Cambodia	n.a.	n.a.	n.a.	n.a.	n.a.	n.a.	n.a.	n.a.
Cameroon	0	0	4	0	0	0	0	4
Canada	4	5	16	0	15	2	0	42
Cape Verde	0	30	10	0	0	0	0	40
Central African Republic	0	0	4	0	10	0	4	18
Chile	16	20	12	20	15	1	4	88
China	16	20	4	20	20	4	4	88
Colombia	12	15	8	20	10	0	4	69
Congo (Zaire)	0	0	0	0	0	0	0	0
Costa Rica	14	18	0	24	24	1	2	84
Côte d'Ivoire	0	0	4	5	0	1	0	10
Cuba	n.a.	n.a.	n.a.	n.a.	n.a.	n.a.	n.a.	n.a.
Cyprus	0	59	31	0	0	0	0	90
Denmark	8	10	16	0	5	3	1	43
Djibouti	n.a.	n.a.	n.a.	n.a.	n.a.	n.a.	n.a.	n.a.
Dominican Republic	12	15	8	15	10	1	0	61

	Indicator							
TABLE B.1 CONTINUED								
Country	GDP growth, 1990–94	Per capita GNP growth, 1985-94	GNP per capita, 1994	Growth of gross domestic investment, 1990–94	Growth of exports, 1990–94	M2 as percent of GDP, 1994	Gross inter-national reserves, 1994	Total weighted score[a]
Ecuador	12	5	8	16	16	0	4	61
Egypt	4	10	8	0	0	4	4	30
El Salvador	16	15	4	20	20	1	3	79
Ethiopia	0	0	0	0	0	4	8	12
Fiji	0	44	20	0	0	0	0	65
Finland	0	0	16	0	15	2	3	36
France	4	10	16	0	10	3	1	44
Germany	5	0	20	0	0	3	2	30
Ghana	12	10	4	0	15	0	3	44
Greece	4	10	12	5	20	2	4	57
Guatemala	12	5	8	20	10	1	2	58
Guyana	0	15	10	0	0	0	0	25
Haiti	0	0	0	0	0	2	0	2
Honduras	12	5	4	20	5	1	1	48
Hong Kong	15	27	0	27	27	0	0	95
Hungary	0	0	8	10	0	2	4	24
Iceland	0	15	41	0	0	0	0	56

Country	GDP growth, 1990–94	Per capita GNP growth, 1985-94	GNP per capita, 1994	Growth of gross domestic investment, 1990–94	Growth of exports, 1990–94	M2 as percent of GDP, 1994	Gross inter-national reserves, 1994	Total weighted score[a]
India	12	15	4	5	20	2	4	62
Indonesia	17	21	8	16	21	0	3	85
Iran	19	0	0	0	26	1	0	47
Iraq	n.a.	n.a.	n.a.	n.a.	n.a.	n.a.	n.a.	n.a.
Ireland	12	20	12	0	20	2	1	67
Israel	16	15	16	20	20	1	2	90
Italy	4	10	17	0	10	0	2	44
Jamaica	12	20	8	15	0	1	1	57
Japan	4	20	16	0	10	4	3	57
Jordan	16	0	8	15	10	4	4	57
Kenya	4	0	4	0	5	1	2	16
Korea, Republic of	16	20	12	15	20	2	2	87
Kuwait	0	26	37	0	0	5	5	74
Lebanon	n.a.	n.a.	n.a.	n.a.	n.a.	n.a.	n.a.	n.a.
Madagascar	0	0	0	0	10	1	0	11
Malawi	0	0	0	0	5	1	0	6
Malaysia	16	20	12	20	20	4	4	96

Country	TABLE B.1 CONTINUED Indicator							
	GDP growth, 1990–94	Per capita GNP growth, 1985–94	GNP per capita, 1994	Growth of gross domestic investment, 1990–94	Growth of exports, 1990–94	M2 as percent of GDP, 1994	Gross inter-national reserves, 1994	Total weighted score[a]
Mali	8	5	0	15	5	0	3	36
Mauritania	12	5	4	10	0	1	0	32
Mauritius	12	20	12	15	10	3	3	75
Mexico	8	5	8	15	10	1	0	47
Morocco	8	10	8	0	5	2	4	37
Mozambique	17	22	0	22	16	0	0	77
Netherlands	4	10	16	0	5	4	3	42
New Zealand	8	5	16	10	10	3	2	54
Nicaragua	4	0	4	10	10	1	1	30
Norway	12	10	16	0	15	3	4	60
Pakistan	12	10	4	15	20	2	3	66
Panama	17	0	8	21	10	3	0	59
Papua New Guinea	16	15	4	0	20	1	0	56
Paraguay	8	5	8	5	20	1	3	50
Peru	12	0	8	20	15	0	4	59
Philippines	8	10	4	10	15	2	3	52
Poland	8	5	8	0	15	1	2	39

	TABLE B.1 CONTINUED							
	Indicator							
Country	GDP growth, 1990–94	Per capita GNP growth, 1985-94	GNP per capita, 1994	Growth of gross domestic investment, 1990–94	Growth of exports, 1990–94	M2 as percent of GDP, 1994	Gross international reserves, 1994	Total weighted score[a]
Portugal	4	20	12	10	5	3	4	58
Romania	0	0	10	0	0	0	4	14
Rwanda	0	0	0	0	5	0	1	6
Saudi Arabia	13	0	20	0	0	2	2	38
Senegal	0	0	4	0	5	0	1	10
Sierra Leone	4	0	0	5	10	0	0	20
Singapore	17	21	17	16	21	4	0	95
South Africa	0	0	8	10	5	2	1	26
Spain	4	15	12	0	15	3	4	53
Sri Lanka	12	15	8	20	20	1	4	80
Sudan	0	0	0	0	0	0	0	0
Swaziland	0	0	20	0	0	0	0	20
Sweden	0	0	16	0	5	2	3	26
Switzerland	4	5	16	0	5	4	4	38
Syria	0	0	0	0	0	0	0	0
Tanzania	21	10	0	0	0	1	0	32
Thailand	16	20	8	20	20	3	4	91

Country	TABLE B.1 CONTINUED — Indicator							
	GDP growth, 1990–94	Per capita GNP growth, 1985–94	GNP per capita, 1994	Growth of gross domestic investment, 1990–94	Growth of exports, 1990–94	M2 as percent of GDP, 1994	Gross international reserves, 1994	Total weighted score[a]
Togo	0	0	4	0	0	1	3	8
Tunisia	12	15	8	10	10	2	2	59
Turkey	12	10	8	10	15	1	3	59
Uganda	12	16	4	10	10	0	0	53
United Arab Emirates	0	25	0	0	0	0	0	25
United Kingdom	4	10	17	0	5	0	1	37
United States	8	10	16	15	15	3	1	68
Uruguay	12	15	8	20	15	1	4	75
Venezuela	12	5	8	15	10	1	4	55
Zambia	0	0	0	0	21	0	0	21
Zimbabwe	4	0	4	5	10	1	3	27

SOURCE: Authors' calculations. For descriptions of indicators and weighting system, see chapter 4 and appendixes C and D.

n.a. Not available.

a. Maximum total weighted score = 100.

TABLE B.2 WEIGHTED SCORES FOR COMPETITIVENESS FOUNDATIONS INDICATORS

Country	Gross domestic saving, 1994	Openness of economy, 1994	Foreign direct investment, 1993	Budget surplus or deficit, latest three years available	S&P long-term sovereign bond rating, 1997	Inflation, 1984–94	Scientists and engineers per million persons, latest available	Technicians per million persons, latest available	Foreign exchange freedom, 1995	Production of electricity, latest available	Electrical power system loss, latest available	Telephone main lines per 1,000 persons, latest available	Road density (km/ million persons), latest available	Total weighted score[a]
Argentina	8	0	8	12	2	0	1	1	12	1	1	1	1	48
Australia	8	3	6	8	6	12	2	2	12	2	2	2	2	66
Austria	16	9	4	4	8	12	2	2	12	2	2	2	2	76
Bahrain	0	0	0	22	0	0	0	0	0	0	0	0	0	22
Bangladesh	5	4	2	0	0	11	0	0	0	0	0	0	0	22
Belgium	12	12	5	0	6	12	2	2	12	2	2	2	2	66
Benin	5	7	0	0	0	20	1	1	0	0	2	0	0	40
Bhutan	0	0	0	38	0	0	0	0	0	0	0	0	0	38
Bolivia	4	3	8	12	0	0	1	1	9	0	1	1	0	39
Botswana	13	13	6	18	0	4	0	0	3	1	0	1	1	59
Brazil	12	0	2	8	2	23	1	1	0	1	1	1	1	28
Burkina Faso	6	4	0	0	0		0	0	0	0	0	0	1	32
Burundi	0	4	2	0	0	16	0	0	0	0	0	0	0	22
Cambodia	0	0	0	0	0	0	0	0	0	0	0	0	0	0

Indicator

Cameroon	8	6	0	8	0	17	0	0	0	0	2	0	0	42
Canada	9	7	0	9	6	13	2	2	13	2	2	2	2	68
Cape Verde	0	0	0	0	0	0	0	0	0	0	0	0	0	0
Central African Republic	5	8	2	0	0	21	0	0	0	0	0	0	0	37
Chile	16	6	6	16	4	4	1	1	9	1	1	1	1	67
China	16	6	8	8	4	8	1	1	0	1	2	0	0	55
Colombia	8	3	6	16	4	0	0	0	9	1	1	1	0	49
Congo (Zaire)	0	0	0	0	0	0	0	0	0	0	0	0	0	0
Costa Rica	13	10	8	13	0	4	1	0	10	0	2	1	1	60
Côte d'Ivoire	16	11	5	0	0	21	0	0	0	0	0	0	0	56
Cuba	0	0	0	0	0	0	3	3	0	0	0	0	0	5
Cyprus	0	0	0	12	12	0	1	1	0	0	0	0	0	26
Denmark	12	9	4	8	6	16	2	2	12	2	2	2	2	78
Djibouti	0	0	0	0	0	0	0	0	0	0	0	0	0	0
Dominican Rep.	9	6	6	18	2	0	0	0	3	0	0	1	0	46
Ecuador	12	6	4	16	0	4	1	1	9	1	0	1	0	50
Egypt	4	6	6	12	4	4	1	1	9	1	1	1	1	50
El Salvador	4	3	2	13	2	0	0	1	9	0	0	1	0	39
Ethiopia	5	4	2	0	0	0	0	0	0	0	2	0	0	14

TABLE B.2 CONTINUED

Country	Gross domestic saving, 1994	Openness of economy, 1994	Foreign direct investment, 1993	Budget surplus or deficit, latest three years available	S&P long-term sovereign bond rating, 1997	Inflation, 1984–94	Indicator Scientists and engineers per million persons, latest available	Tech-nicians per million persons, latest available	Foreign exchange freedom, 1995	Production of electricity, latest available	Electrical power system loss, latest available	Telephone main lines per 1,000 persons, latest available	Road density (km/ million persons), latest available	Total weighted score[a]
Fiji	0	0	0	26	0	0	0	0	8	0	0	0	0	34
Finland	8	9	4	0	6	12	2	2	12	2	2	2	2	62
France	8	6	4	4	8	16	2	2	12	2	2	2	2	70
Germany	16	7	0	16	9	0	2	2	15	2	2	2	0	73
Ghana	4	6	4	13	0	0	0	0	6	0	2	0	0	35
Greece	4	6	0	0	4	4	2	1	9	2	2	2	2	37
Guatemala	4	3	6	12	0	4	0	1	9	0	1	1	0	40
Guyana	0	0	0	0	0	0	1	2	0	0	0	0	0	3
Haiti	0	0	0	0	0	7	0	0	9	0	0	0	0	16
Honduras	11	12	10	0	0	6	0	0	12	2	1	1	0	51
Hong Kong	24	17	0	0	5	12	0	0	17	2	1	2	0	80
Hungary	8	6	8	12	4	4	2	2	0	2	1	1	2	50
Iceland	0	0	0	24	8	0	3	3	23	0	0	0	0	60
India	12	3	2	0	2	8	1	1	3	0	0	0	1	32

Indonesia	16	6	6	16	4	8	1	0	9	0	1	0	0	67
Iran	16	6	0	12	0	0	0	0	0	1	1	1	0	37
Iraq	0	0	0	0	0	0	0	0	0	0	0	0	0	0
Ireland	16	12	2	12	6	16	2	2	12	2	2	2	2	86
Israel	9	10	0	9	4	4	2	2	7	2	2	2	1	53
Italy	8	6	4	0	6	8	2	2	12	2	2	2	2	54
Jamaica	10	14	9	0	0	0	0	0	11	1	0	1	1	47
Japan	16	0	0	16	8	16	2	2	12	2	2	2	2	79
Jordan	4	9	0	16	2	8	1	0	3	1	1	1	1	46
Kenya	13	9	2	8	0	4	0	0	0	0	1	0	0	37
Korea, Republic of	16	9	2	16	6	8	2	1	9	1	2	2	1	74
Kuwait	33	28	0	0	0	0	2	1	0	2	2	2	0	71
Lebanon	0	0	0	0	0	0	0	0	0	0	0	0	0	0
Madagascar	4	6	4	4	0	4	0	1	0	0	0	0	0	23
Malawi	0	6	0	9	0	4	0	0	0	0	0	0	0	20
Malaysia	16	12	8	16	4	12	0	1	9	1	2	1	0	83
Mali	6	8	2	0	0	17	0	0	4	0	0	0	0	37
Mauritania	6	12	2	0	0	11	0	0	0	0	0	0	1	32
Mauritius	13	12	4	13	0	8	1	1	0	0	0	1	1	54

TABLE B.2 CONTINUED

Country	Gross domestic saving, 1994	Openness of economy, 1994	Foreign direct investment, 1993	Budget surplus or deficit, latest three years available	S&P long-term sovereign bond rating, 1997	Inflation, 1984–94	Indicator — Scientists and engineers per million persons, latest available	Technicians per million persons, latest available	Foreign exchange freedom, 1995	Production of electricity, latest available	Electrical power system loss, latest available	Telephone main lines per 1,000 persons, latest available	Road density (km/ million persons), latest available	Total weighted score[a]
Mexico	8	3	6	0	2	0	0	0	9	1	1	1	1	32
Morocco	8	6	6	13	0	13	0	0	3	0	2	1	0	52
Mozambique	5	8	9	0	0	0	0	0	0	0	0	0	0	22
Netherlands	12	12	8	12	8	16	2	2	12	2	2	2	2	91
New Zealand	13	10	0	13	6	13	2	2	13	2	2	2	2	80
Nicaragua	0	6	8	8	0	0	1	1	0	0	0	1	0	24
Norway	16	9	4	8	8	12	2	2	12	2	2	2	2	81
Pakistan	8	3	4	0	2	8	0	1	6	0	1	0	1	33
Panama	13	9	0	17	2	17	0	0	12	1	0	1	1	73
Papua New Guinea	18	13	8	4	0	13	0	0	0	0	0	0	0	57
Paraguay	9	10	8	16	0	0	0	0	10	2	2	1	0	60
Peru	8	3	4	12	2	0	1	0	9	1	1	1	0	43
Philippines	8	9	6	12	2	4	0	0	9	0	1	0	0	51
Poland	8	6	6	12	4	0	2	2	9	2	1	1	2	54

Portugal	8	6	6	4	6	4	1	1	9	2	1	2	2	51
Romania	12	6	4	12	2	0	2	2	6	1	1	1	1	49
Rwanda	0	0	2	4	0	13	0	0	3	0	0	0	0	22
Saudi Arabia	30	15	0	0	0	30	0	0	0	2	2	1	1	80
Senegal	5	11	0	0	0	20	1	1	0	0	2	0	1	40
Sierra Leone	4	3	8	4	0	0	0	0	6	0	0	0	0	27
Singapore	18	13	0	18	8	13	2	2	13	2	2	2	1	94
South Africa	8	6	0	0	2	4	1	1	3	2	2	1	1	30
Spain	9	3	8	9	6	9	2	2	13	2	2	2	2	58
Sri Lanka	8	9	0	0	0	4	1	1	3	0	1	0	1	34
Sudan	0	0	0	0	0	0	0	0	0	0	0	0	0	0
Swaziland	0	0	0	0	0	0	0	0	0	0	0	0	0	0
Sweden	8	9	2	0	6	12	2	2	9	2	2	2	2	58
Switzerland	21	11	2	0	9	16	0	0	15	2	2	2	2	83
Syria	0	0	0	51	0	0	0	0	8	0	0	0	0	59
Tanzania	5	8	5	0	0	0	0	0	0	0	1	0	0	19
Thailand	16	9	6	16	4	12	1	1	9	1	1	1	1	76
Togo	6	8	0	0	0	17	0	0	0	0	0	0	0	30
Tunisia	12	9	6	4	0	8	1	1	3	1	2	1	1	47

TABLE B.2 CONTINUED

Country	Indicator													
	Gross domestic saving, 1994	Openness of economy, 1994	Foreign direct investment, 1993	Budget surplus or deficit, latest three years available	S&P long-term sovereign bond rating, 1997	Inflation, 1984–94	Scientists and engineers per million persons, latest available	Technicians per million persons, latest available	Foreign exchange freedom, 1995	Production of electricity, latest available	Electrical power system loss, latest available	Telephone main lines per 1,000 persons, latest available	Road density (km/ million persons), latest available	Total weighted score[a]
Turkey	12	6	4	4	2	0	1	0	9	1	1	1	2	42
Uganda	6	0	2	0	0	0	0	0	0	0	0	0	0	8
United Arab Emirates	30	20	0	30	0	0	0	0	0	2	2	2	1	86
United Kingdom	8	6	6	4	8	12	2	2	12	2	2	2	2	67
United States	8	0	4	8	8	12	2	0	12	2	2	2	2	63
Uruguay	8	3	4	13	2	0	0	0	12	1	1	1	1	47
Venezuela	12	6	4	8	2	0	1	0	3	2	1	1	2	41
Zambia	4	9	6	0	0	0	0	0	3	1	1	0	1	25
Zimbabwe	8	9	4	0	0	4	0	0	3	1	2	1	1	32

SOURCE: Authors' calculations. For descriptions of indicators and weighting system, see chapter 4 and appendixes C and D.

a. Maximum total weighted score = 100.

TABLE B.3 WEIGHTED SCORES FOR HEALTH INDICATORS

Country	Life expectancy at birth, 1994	Contra-ceptive prevalence, latest available	Fertility rate, 1994	Births attended by trained health professionals, latest available	Maternal mortality rate, 1993	Infant mortality rate, 1994	Under-five mortality rate, 1994	One-year-old children immunized against measles, latest available	One-year-old children immunized against tuberculosis, latest available	Natural rate of population increase, latest available	HIV prevalence, 1995	Total weighted score[a]
Argentina	15	3	3	9	6	12	12	2	2	4	3	71
Australia	21	4	4	12	12	16	16	2	0	6	3	96
Austria	25	3	4	0	14	19	19	1	0	9	3	96
Bahrain	20	0	1	0	11	15	15	0	0	2	3	68
Bangladesh	5	2	1	0	0	4	4	2	2	2	4	26
Belgium	21	4	4	12	12	16	12	1	0	8	3	93
Benin	0	0	0	3	0	4	4	1	1	0	1	14
Bhutan	0	0	0	0	0	0	0	1	2	2	4	9
Bolivia	5	2	1	3	3	4	4	1	2	2	4	31
Botswana	10	1	1	9	6	8	8	2	2	2	0	47
Brazil	10	3	3	12	6	4	8	1	2	4	2	55
Burkina Faso	0	0	0	3	0	0	0	0	1	0	0	8
Burundi	0	0	0	0	0	0	0	0	1	0	1	2
Cambodia	5	0	0	3	0	0	0	1	1	0	1	10

TABLE B.3 CONTINUED

Country	Life expectancy at birth, 1994	Contraceptive prevalence, latest available	Fertility rate, 1994	Births attended by trained health professionals, latest available	Maternal mortality rate, 1993	Infant mortality rate, 1994	Under-five mortality rate, 1994	One-year-old children immunized against measles, latest available	One-year-old children immunized against tuberculosis, latest available	Natural rate of population increase, latest available	HIV prevalence, 1995	Total weighted score[a]
Cameroon	5	1	0	6	3	4	4	0	0	0	1	24
Canada	21	3	4	12	12	16	16	2	0	6	3	96
Cape Verde	17	0	1	0	0	13	6	0	0	5	0	43
Central African Republic	0	0	0	3	3	0	0	0	1	2	0	9
Chile	15	2	3	12	9	12	12	2	2	4	3	76
China	15	4	4	12	9	8	8	2	2	6	4	73
Colombia	18	3	3	10	0	14	14	2	2	2	3	71
Congo (Zaire)	0	0	0	0	0	0	0	0	0	0	1	1
Costa Rica	20	3	3	12	9	12	12	2	2	2	2	78
Côte d'Ivoire	5	0	0	3	0	4	0	0	0	0	0	12
Cuba	21	3	4	9	9	16	12	0	2	6	4	87
Cyprus	27	0	4	0	15	20	15	0	0	7	3	92
Denmark	21	4	4	12	12	16	16	1	0	8	3	98

Indicator

Djibouti	0	0	0	0	4	0	0	0	0	2	1	7
Dominican Republic	15	2	3	12	6	8	8	2	1	2	2	60
Ecuador	15	2	3	9	6	8	8	2	2	2	3	60
Egypt	10	2	1	3	6	4	8	2	2	2	4	43
El Salvador	10	2	1	6	3	8	8	1	1	2	2	44
Ethiopia	0	0	0	0	0	0	0	0	0	0	1	1
Fiji	20	0	3	0	11	15	15	0	0	2	4	72
Finland	20	4	4	12	12	16	16	2	2	8	4	100
France	20	4	4	12	12	16	16	1	1	8	3	97
Germany	21	3	2	12	12	16	16	1	0	8	3	94
Ghana	5	1	0	6	3	4	4	0	1	0	1	25
Greece	21	0	2	12	12	17	13	1	0	8	4	90
Guatemala	10	1	0	6	6	8	4	1	1	0	3	39
Guyana	16	0	3	0	0	12	12	0	0	5	1	50
Haiti	5	1	1	0	0	4	4	0	0	2	1	18
Honduras	10	2	1	9	6	8	8	2	2	0	1	48
Hong Kong	20	4	2	12	12	16	16	1	2	6	4	95
Hungary	15	3	4	12	9	12	12	2	2	8	4	83
Iceland	27	0	4	0	15	20	20	0	0	7	3	97

GLOBAL Benchmarks

TABLE B.3 CONTINUED

Country	Life expectancy at birth, 1994	Contraceptive prevalence, latest available	Fertility rate, 1994	Births attended by trained health professionals, latest available	Maternal mortality rate, 1993	Infant mortality rate, 1994	Under-five mortality rate, 1994	One-year-old children immunized against measles, latest available	One-year-old children immunized against tuberculosis, latest available	Natural rate of population increase, latest available	HIV prevalence, 1995	Total weighted score[b]
India	10	2	1	3	3	4	4	2	2	4	3	37
Indonesia	10	2	3	3	3	4	4	2	2	4	4	41
Iran	10	2	1	6	6	8	8	2	2	0	4	49
Iraq	10	1	0	3	3	4	8	2	1	0	4	32
Ireland	26	0	4	0	14	20	20	1	0	7	0	92
Israel	22	0	3	13	13	17	17	2	0	4	4	95
Italy	25	4	2	0	14	19	19	0	0	9	0	92
Jamaica	20	3	4	9	6	12	12	1	2	4	2	75
Japan	20	3	4	12	12	16	16	1	2	8	4	97
Jordan	15	1	0	9	6	8	12	2	0	2	4	60
Kenya	5	1	0	6	3	4	4	1	2	2	0	27
Korea, Republic of	15	4	4	9	6	12	16	2	1	6	4	78
Kuwait	21	1	3	12	9	12	12	2	0	2	3	78

Lebanon	15	2	3	3	3	8	8	1	0	2	4	50
Madagascar	5	1	0	6	0	0	0	1	1	0	4	21
Malawi	0	0	0	6	0	0	0	2	2	0	0	13
Malaysia	15	2	1	9	1	12	12	1	2	2	3	68
Mali	0	0	0	3	0	0	0	0	1	0	1	5
Mauritania	5	0	0	3	0	4	0	1	2	2	2	18
Mauritius	15	3	4	9	6	12	12	2	1	1	4	71
Mexico	15	2	3	9	6	8	8	0	2	2	3	59
Morocco	10	2	1	3	3	4	8	1	2	2	4	39
Mozambique	0	0	0	0	0	0	0	2	1	1	0	3
Netherlands	21	4	4	12	12	16	16	1	0	0	4	100
New Zealand	20	3	4	12	9	16	16	1	0	6	4	91
Nicaragua	10	2	1	9	6	4	4	2	1	2	4	48
Norway	25	4	4	0	14	19	19	1	0	9	4	99
Pakistan	5	0	0	3	3	12	4	1	1	0	4	24
Panama	15	2	3	12	9	4	12	0	2	4	2	74
Papua New Guinea	5	0	1	0	0	4	4	2	2	2	3	21
Paraguay	10	2	1	6	6	8	8	1	2	0	3	47
Peru	10	2	3	6	6	8	8	1	2	2	3	50

GLOBAL Benchmarks

TABLE B.3 CONTINUED

Country	Life expectancy at birth, 1994	Contraceptive prevalence, latest available	Fertility rate, 1994	Births attended by trained health professionals, latest available	Maternal mortality rate, 1993	Infant mortality rate, 1994	Under-five mortality rate, 1994	One-year-old children immunized against measles, latest available	One-year-old children immunized against tuberculosis, latest available	Natural rate of population increase, latest available	HIV prevalence, 1995	Total weighted score[a]
Philippines	10	1	1	6	6	8	8	2	1	2	4	49
Poland	15	3	4	12	12	12	12	2	2	8	4	86
Portugal	20	3	4	9	12	16	12	2	2	8	3	90
Romania	15	2	4	12	6	12	12	2	2	8	4	79
Rwanda	0	1	0	0	0	5	5	0	0	2	0	14
Saudi Arabia	16	0	0	9	6	8	8	2	2	0	4	55
Senegal	0	0	0	3	0	4	4	0	1	2	1	15
Sierra Leone	0	0	0	0	0	0	0	0	0	2	1	3
Singapore	20	3	4	12	12	16	16	2	2	6	4	96
South Africa	12	2	1	0	7	5	9	1	2	2	1	42
Spain	21	2	2	12	12	16	16	2	0	8	2	93
Sri Lanka	15	3	4	12	6	12	12	1	1	4	4	74
Sudan	5	0	0	6	3	4	4	1	1	0	2	26
Swaziland	7	0	0	0	4	0	5	0	0	0	1	17

Indicator

Sweden	21	4	4	12	12	16	16	2	0	8	4	100
Switzerland	21	3	4	12	12	16	16	1	0	8	3	97
Syria	10	2	0	6	6	8	8	1	2	0	4	47
Tanzania	5	1	0	6	3	0	0	1	1	0	0	17
Thailand	15	3	4	9	6	8	8	2	2	4	1	61
Togo	5	0	0	6	3	4	4	1	1	0	0	23
Tunisia	10	2	3	6	6	8	8	2	1	4	4	53
Turkey	10	3	3	9	6	8	4	1	1	4	4	53
Uganda	0	0	0	3	0	0	0	1	2	0	0	6
United Arab Emirates	21	0	1	12	9	13	13	2	2	4	3	79
United Kingdom	21	3	4	12	12	16	16	2	0	8	4	98
United States	21	3	4	12	12	16	12	1	0	6	2	90
Uruguay	16	0	4	12	9	13	13	1	2	6	3	79
Venezuela	15	2	3	6	6	8	12	2	2	2	3	60
Zambia	0	0	0	6	0	0	0	2	2	0	0	10
Zimbabwe	5	2	1	6	3	4	4	1	1	2	0	29

SOURCE: Authors' calculations. For descriptions of indicators and weighting system, see chapter 4 and appendixes C and D.

TABLE B.4 WEIGHTED SCORES FOR EDUCATION INDICATORS

| Country | Adult illiteracy, 1995[a] | Enrollment ratio, latest available | | | Primary school-children reaching grade 5, latest available | Repeaters, latest available | | Total weighted score[b] |
		Primary	Secondary	Tertiary		Primary	Secondary	
Argentina	36	21	11	16	0	0	0	84
Australia	27	17	13	17	22	0	0	96
Austria	27	17	17	17	22	0	0	100
Bahrain	16	20	20	10	0	3	3	72
Bangladesh	0	8	0	0	0	3	0	11
Belgium	25	17	17	17	21	1	0	97
Benin	0	4	0	0	5	1	0	10
Bhutan	0	0	0	0	0	1	3	5
Bolivia	12	12	4	8	5	4	3	48
Botswana	6	16	8	0	10	4	4	48
Brazil	13	17	4	4	10	1	0	49
Burkina Faso	0	0	0	0	5	1	0	6
Burundi	0	4	0	0	10	1	2	17
Cambodia	0	21	0	0	0	0	0	21
Cameroon	6	8	4	0	5	0	1	24
Canada	27	17	17	17	22	0	0	100
Cape Verde	12	16	4	0	5	1	1	39

TABLE B.4 CONTINUED

Country	Adult illiteracy, 1995[a]	Enrollment ratio, latest available			Primary school-children reaching grade 5, latest available	Repeaters, latest available		Total weighted score[b]
		Primary	Secondary	Tertiary		Primary	Secondary	
Central African Republic	6	4	0	0	5	0	0	15
Chile	20	17	9	9	16	0	0	71
China	12	16	8	0	10	4	4	54
Colombia	18	16	8	4	5	3	1	55
Congo (Zaire)	6	4	0	0	5	1	0	17
Costa Rica	18	16	4	12	10	3	2	65
Côte d'Ivoire	0	4	0	0	10	0	1	15
Cuba	24	16	8	4	15	4	3	74
Cyprus	0	30	30	8	0	5	5	77
Denmark	27	17	17	17	22	0	0	100
Djibouti	0	0	0	0	0	2	2	4
Dominican Republic	17	21	5	5	0	1	0	49
Ecuador	13	17	8	4	5	3	0	50
Egypt	6	12	12	4	21	3	0	59
El Salvador	12	8	4	4	5	3	3	39
Ethiopia	0	0	0	0	0	3	2	5

		TABLE B.4 CONTINUED						
Country	Adult illiteracy, 1995[a]	Enrollment ratio, latest available			Primary school-children reaching grade 5, latest available	Repeaters, latest available		Total weighted score[b]
		Primary	Secondary	Tertiary		Primary	Secondary	
Fiji	18	16	8	4	15	4	3	68
Finland	25	17	17	17	21	4	0	100
France	25	17	17	17	16	4	0	95
Germany	25	12	17	12	21	4	0	92
Ghana	6	8	4	0	10	4	4	36
Greece	0	17	22	22	29	4	0	94
Guatemala	6	8	0	0	0	1	0	16
Guyana	25	17	8	0	21	0	2	73
Haiti	0	0	0	0	0	2	2	4
Honduras	12	16	4	0	0	2	2	36
Hong Kong	19	17	12	8	21	4	0	81
Hungary	0	17	17	6	29	4	0	72
Iceland	0	25	33	17	0	0	0	75
India	6	17	4	0	5	4	0	36
Indonesia	12	16	4	0	10	3	4	49
Iran	12	16	8	4	10	3	2	55
Iraq	6	12	4	4	10	1	0	37

TABLE B.4 CONTINUED

Country	Adult illiteracy, 1995[a]	Enrollment ratio, latest available			Primary school-children reaching grade 5, latest available	Repeaters, latest available		Total weighted score[b]
		Primary	Secondary	Tertiary		Primary	Secondary	
Ireland	25	17	17	12	21	4	0	96
Israel	0	17	17	17	31	0	0	83
Italy	25	12	12	12	21	4	0	88
Jamaica	12	16	8	0	20	4	4	64
Japan	27	17	17	9	22	0	0	91
Jordan	12	12	8	8	20	4	3	67
Kenya	13	13	0	0	11	0	0	37
Korea, Republic of	25	12	17	17	21	0	4	96
Kuwait	12	4	8	8	15	4	2	53
Lebanon	27	21	16	11	0	0	0	75
Madagascar	0	5	0	0	0	0	1	6
Malawi	6	16	0	0	0	1	4	27
Malaysia	13	13	9	0	22	0	0	57
Mali	0	0	0	0	10	0	0	10
Mauritania	0	4	0	0	10	1	2	17
Mauritius	12	16	8	0	20	3	2	61
Mexico	12	16	8	4	10	3	4	57

		Enrollment ratio, latest available			Primary school-children reaching grade 5, latest available	Repeaters, latest available		
Country	Adult illiteracy, 1995[a]	Primary	Secondary	Tertiary		Primary	Secondary	Total weighted score[b]
Morocco	0	8	4	0	10	2	1	25
Mozambique	0	4	0	0	0	0	0	4
Netherlands	27	13	17	17	22	0	0	96
New Zealand	25	17	17	17	16	4	0	95
Nicaragua	6	16	4	0	5	1	3	35
Norway	27	17	17	17	22	0	0	100
Pakistan	0	4	0	0	0	0	0	4
Panama	18	16	8	8	10	2	2	64
Papua New Guinea	13	9	0	0	5	0	0	27
Paraguay	19	17	4	0	10	3	0	53
Peru	16	20	10	15	0	2	2	65
Philippines	18	16	12	8	10	4	4	72
Poland	0	22	22	11	29	4	0	89
Portugal	0	22	17	17	22	2	0	79
Romania	0	17	17	6	22	4	0	65
Rwanda	6	8	0	0	5	2	3	24
Saudi Arabia	6	8	8	4	20	3	2	51

TABLE B.4 CONTINUED

TABLE B.4 CONTINUED

Country	Adult illiteracy, 1995[a]	Enrollment ratio, latest available			Primary school-children reaching grade 5, latest available	Repeaters, latest available		Total weighted score[b]
		Primary	Secondary	Tertiary		Primary	Secondary	
Senegal	0	0	0	0	10	1	2	13
Sierra Leone	0	0	0	0	0	0	0	0
Singapore	20	17	9	13	22	0	0	80
South Africa	13	17	12	4	10	2	0	58
Spain	0	22	22	22	29	4	0	100
Sri Lanka	12	16	8	0	15	3	2	56
Sudan	0	0	0	0	16	0	0	16
Swaziland	12	16	8	0	10	1	2	49
Sweden	27	17	17	17	22	0	0	100
Switzerland	25	17	12	12	21	4	0	92
Syria	0	21	5	5	21	3	2	58
Tanzania	6	4	0	0	10	4	0	25
Thailand	19	8	4	8	10	3	0	53
Togo	6	16	0	0	5	0	0	27
Tunisia	6	16	8	4	10	1	1	46
Turkey	12	12	8	4	15	3	1	55
Uganda	6	4	0	0	5	2	0	18

TABLE B.4 CONTINUED

Country	Adult illiteracy, 1995[a]	Enrollment ratio, latest available			Primary school-children reaching grade 5, latest available	Repeaters, latest available		Total weighted score[b]
		Primary	Secondary	Tertiary		Primary	Secondary	
United Arab Emirates	12	16	12	4	20	3	2	69
United Kingdom	27	17	13	17	22	0	0	96
United States	27	17	17	17	22	0	0	100
Uruguay	25	17	12	8	16	2	0	80
Venezuela	18	12	4	8	10	2	3	57
Zambia	13	8	0	0	10	4	0	35
Zimbabwe	13	17	4	0	11	0	0	46

SOURCE: Authors' calculations. For descriptions of indicators and weighting system, see chapter 4 and appendixes C and D.

a. Percentage of population over age 15.

b. Total weighted score = 100.

GLOBAL Benchmarks

TABLE B.5 WEIGHTED SCORES FOR ENVIRONMENTAL INDICATORS

Country	Access to safe water, 1993	Emissions CO₂, 1992	Emissions Other greenhouse gases (tons), 1991	Environ- mental NGOs registered, 1996	Participation in global environ- mental conventions, 1993	Urban center solid wastes, 1993	Change in forest and woodland, 1983–93	Total weighted score[a]
Argentina	7	5	n.a.	12	9	1	2	36
Australia	28	n.a.	n.a.	12	12	n.a.	4	56
Austria	30	5	10	9	9	n.a.	2	66
Bahrain	60	n.a.	n.a.	4	n.a.	1	n.a.	65
Bangladesh	14	20	10	9	9	4	n.a.	66
Belgium	30	n.a.	16	9	12	n.a.	3	70
Benin	n.a.	20	20	n.a.	6	2	n.a.	48
Bhutan	n.a.	20	15	n.a.	n.a.	4	4	43
Bolivia	n.a.	15	n.a.	9	6	2	2	34
Botswana	7	10	n.a.	6	3	2	2	30
Brazil	21	10	5	12	9	2	1	60
Burkina Faso	7	20	15	3	6	4	2	57
Burundi	n.a.	20	20	n.a.	3	4	2	49
Cambodia	n.a.	20	15	n.a.	3	4	n.a.	42
Cameroon	n.a.	20	15	n.a.	6	2	2	45
Canada	28	n.a.	n.a.	12	12	n.a.	4	56
Cape Verde	30	n.a.	n.a.	n.a.	n.a.	5	n.a.	34

TABLE B.5 CONTINUED

Country	Access to safe water, 1993	Emissions		Environ- mental NGOs registered, 1996	Participation in global environ- mental conventions, 1993	Urban center solid wastes, 1993	Change in forest and woodland, 1983–93	Total weighted score[a]
		CO_2, 1992	Other greenhouse gases (tons), 1991					
Central African Republic	n.a.	20	10	n.a.	6	2	2	40
Chile	21	10	15	9	12	1	2	70
China	15	10	5	6	12	3	n.a.	52
Colombia	21	10	5	9	6	2	n.a.	53
Congo (Zaire)	n.a.	20	20	n.a.	6	3	2	51
Costa Rica	21	10	5	12	9	2	n.a.	59
Côte d'Ivoire	14	15	20	n.a.	9	2	n.a.	60
Cuba	21	5	10	3	9	1	n.a.	49
Cyprus	60	n.a.	n.a.	9	n.a.	2	n.a.	71
Denmark	28	n.a.	5	6	12	n.a.	n.a.	51
Djibouti	22	16	5	6	3	1	n.a.	53
Dominican, Republic	7	10	15	n.a.	6	2	1	41
Ecuador	7	10	5	9	6	2	3	42
Egypt	21	10	15	12	9	3	2	72
El Salvador	n.a.	15	15	n.a.	6	2	n.a.	38
Ethiopia	n.a.	20	15	6	3	4	1	49

		Emissions			Participation in			
Country	Access to safe water, 1993	CO_2, 1992	Other greenhouse gases (tons), 1991	Environ-mental NGOs registered, 1996	global environ-mental conventions, 1993	Urban center solid wastes, 1993	Change in forest and woodland, 1983–93	Total weighted score[a]
Fiji	14	15	10	n.a.	3	2	2	46
Finland	28	n.a.	10	3	12	n.a.	2	55
France	28	5	10	9	12	1	3	68
Germany	28	n.a.	5	12	12	1	3	61
Ghana	7	15	20	12	6	1	n.a.	61
Greece	28	5	10	3	12	1	2	61
Guatemala	7	15	15	6	9	3	4	59
Guyana	14	10	10	3	3	2	3	45
Haiti	n.a.	20	20	n.a.	3	3	2	48
Honduras	14	15	15	n.a.	3	2	2	51
Hong Kong	43	7	n.a.	4	n.a.	n.a.	n.a.	53
Hungary	28	5	15	3	12	1	3	67
Iceland	28	5	5	6	6	1	2	53
India	14	15	10	12	12	3	3	69
Indonesia	n.a.	10	5	12	6	3	1	37
Iran	21	5	5	n.a.	9	2	2	44
Iraq	21	n.a.	15	n.a.	n.a.	1	2	39

TABLE B.5 CONTINUED

Country	Access to safe water, 1993	Emissions		Environ-mental NGOs registered, 1996	Participation in global environ-mental conventions, 1993	Urban center solid wastes, 1993	Change in forest and woodland, 1983–93	Total weighted score[a]
		CO_2, 1992	Other greenhouse gases (tons), 1991					
Ireland	28	n.a.	n.a.	n.a.	9	1	2	40
Israel	28	n.a.	15	6	6	1	4	60
Italy	28	5	15	6	12	1	3	70
Jamaica	14	5	20	9	6	2	1	57
Japan	30	n.a.	10	12	9	n.a.	2	64
Jordan	21	5	20	12	9	1	3	71
Kenya	n.a.	15	15	n.a.	6	3	2	41
Korea, Republic of	14	5	10	6	6	1	2	44
Kuwait	28	5	n.a.	6	3	n.a.	2	44
Lebanon	21	5	20	n.a.	6	2	3	57
Madagascar	n.a.	20	5	3	3	3	2	36
Malawi	7	20	20	6	6	4	2	65
Malaysia	14	5	5	n.a.	6	2	2	34
Mali	n.a.	20	10	6	6	3	1	46
Mauritania	7	10	5	3	3	2	1	31
Mauritius	28	10	20	n.a.	3	2	n.a.	63
Mexico	14	5	10	9	9	2	3	52

TABLE B.5 CONTINUED

Country	Access to safe water, 1993	Emissions		Environ-mental NGOs registered, 1996	Participation in global environ-mental conventions, 1993	Urban center solid wastes, 1993	Change in forest and woodland, 1983–93	Total weighted score[a]
		CO_2, 1992	Other greenhouse gases (tons), 1991					
Morocco	14	10	20	12	9	2	3	70
Mozambique	n.a.	20	20	6	3	3	n.a.	52
Netherlands	28	n.a.	n.a.	12	12	n.a.	4	56
New Zealand	21	5	n.a.	12	9	n.a.	3	50
Nicaragua	7	15	10	6	6	2	n.a.	46
Norway	28	n.a.	n.a.	6	12	n.a.	2	48
Pakistan	n.a.	15	15	n.a.	6	3	4	43
Panama	14	10	5	9	12	2	n.a.	52
Papua New Guinea	n.a.	15	20	n.a.	6	4	2	47
Paraguay	n.a.	15	n.a.	n.a.	6	2	n.a.	23
Peru	7	10	15	6	6	2	2	48
Philippines	14	15	10	3	6	2	4	54
Poland	28	n.a.	5	9	12	1	3	58
Portugal	28	5	15	6	12	1	4	71
Romania	28	5	10	3	9	2	3	60
Rwanda	7	20	20	3	3	4	1	58
Saudi Arabia	21	n.a.	n.a.	3	6	1	4	35

		Emissions			Participation in			
Country	Access to safe water, 1993	CO_2, 1992	Other greenhouse gases (tons), 1991	Environ- mental NGOs registered, 1996	global environ- mental conventions, 1993	Urban center solid wastes, 1993	Change in forest and woodland, 1983–93	Total weighted score[a]
Senegal	n.a.	15	15	3	9	2	1	45
Sierra Leone	n.a.	20	10	n.a.	3	3	1	37
Singapore	28	n.a.	15	n.a.	3	1	2	49
South Africa	n.a.	8	8	12	12	2	2	43
Spain	28	5	10	9	12	1	3	68
Sri Lanka	7	15	10	9	9	4	4	58
Sudan	n.a.	20	5	n.a.	6	3	n.a.	34
Swaziland	n.a.	15	10	n.a.	3	2	4	34
Sweden	28	5	15	9	12	1	3	73
Switzerland	28	5	15	9	12	n.a.	4	73
Syria	14	10	5	n.a.	6	2	4	41
Tanzania	7	20	15	6	6	3	n.a.	57
Thailand	14	10	n.a.	6	6	3	n.a.	39
Togo	15	21	21	n.a.	6	n.a.	n.a.	63
Tunisia	7	10	15	n.a.	9	2	4	47
Turkey	21	10	15	3	3	1	2	55
Uganda	n.a.	20	20	3	6	4	n.a.	53
United Arab Emirates	28	n.a.	n.a.	3	6	1	2	40

		Emissions			Participation in			
Country	Access to safe water, 1993	CO_2, 1992	Other greenhouse gases (tons), 1991	Environ-mental NGOs registered, 1996	global environ-mental conventions, 1993	Urban center solid wastes, 1993	Change in forest and woodland, 1983–93	Total weighted score[a]
United Kingdom	28	n.a.	5	12	12	1	4	62
United States	28	n.a.	n.a.	12	9	n.a.	1	50
Uruguay	14	10	n.a.	6	12	1	2	45
Venezuela	21	5	n.a.	6	6	1	n.a.	39
Zambia	7	15	15	9	6	2	1	55
Zimbabwe	n.a.	10	15	9	6	3	n.a.	43

TABLE B.5 CONTINUED

SOURCE: Authors' calculations. For descriptions of indicators and weighting system, see chapter 4 and appendixes C and D.

n.a. Not available.

a. Maximum total weighted score = 100.

TABLE B.6 WEIGHTED SCORES FOR DEMOCRACY AND FREEOM INDICATORS

Country	Political rights, 1996	Civil liberties, 1996	Equal protection and access to nondiscriminatory judiciary	Total weighted score[a]
Argentina	34	23	3	59
Australia	45	45	8	98
Austria	45	45	8	98
Bahrain	0	0	0	0
Bangladesh	25	25	0	50
Belgium	45	45	10	100
Benin	38	38	0	75
Bhutan	0	0	0	0
Bolivia	34	23	3	59
Botswana	34	34	5	73
Brazil	34	23	0	56
Burkina Faso	13	25	0	38
Burundi	0	0	0	0
Cambodia	0	0	0	0
Cameroon	0	11	0	11
Canada	45	45	8	98
Cape Verde	50	38	0	88
Central African Republic	25	25	0	50
Chile	34	34	5	73

TABLE B.6 CONTINUED

Country	Political rights, 1996	Civil liberties, 1996	Equal protection and access to nondiscriminatory judiciary	Total weighted score[a]
China	0	0	0	0
Colombia	25	25	0	50
Congo (Zaire)	0	0	0	0
Costa Rica	45	34	8	86
Côte d'Ivoire	0	13	0	13
Cuba	0	0	0	0
Cyprus	50	50	0	100
Denmark	45	45	10	100
Djibouti	13	0	0	13
Dominican Republic	25	25	0	50
Ecuador	38	25	0	63
Egypt	11	11	3	25
El Salvador	25	25	0	50
Ethiopia	25	13	0	38
Fiji	25	25	0	50
Finland	45	45	10	100
France	45	34	8	86
Germany	45	34	8	86
Ghana	23	23	3	48

TABLE B.6 CONTINUED

Country	Political rights, 1996	Civil liberties, 1996	Equal protection and access to nondiscriminatory judiciary	Total weighted score[a]
Greece	45	23	5	73
Guatemala	23	11	0	34
Guyana	38	38	0	75
Haiti	13	13	0	25
Honduras	23	23	3	48
Hong Kong	23	23	8	53
Hungary	50	38	0	88
Iceland	50	50	0	100
India	23	23	3	48
Indonesia	0	0	0	0
Iran	0	0	0	0
Iraq	0	0	0	0
Ireland	50	50	0	100
Israel	45	23	5	73
Italy	45	34	8	86
Jamaica	38	25	0	63
Japan	45	34	8	86
Jordan	25	25	0	50
Kenya	0	0	0	0

TABLE B.6 CONTINUED				
Country	Political rights, 1996	Civil liberties, 1996	Equal protection and access to nondiscriminatory judiciary	Total weighted score[a]
Korea, Republic of	34	34	8	75
Kuwait	13	13	0	25
Lebanon	0	13	0	13
Madagascar	38	25	0	63
Malawi	38	25	0	63
Malaysia	23	11	3	36
Mali	34	23	8	64
Mauritania	0	0	0	0
Mauritius	50	38	0	88
Mexico	23	23	0	45
Morocco	13	13	0	25
Mozambique	25	25	0	50
Netherlands	45	45	10	100
New Zealand	45	45	10	100
Nicaragua	23	23	0	45
Norway	45	45	10	100
Pakistan	23	11	0	34
Panama	38	25	0	63
Papua New Guinea	38	25	0	63

			Equal protection and access to nondiscriminatory judiciary	Total weighted score[a]
Country	Political rights, 1996	Civil liberties, 1996		
Paraguay	25	25	0	50
Peru	11	23	0	34
Philippines	34	23	0	56
Poland	45	34	8	86
Portugal	45	45	8	98
Romania	25	25	0	50
Rwanda	0	0	0	0
Saudi Arabia	0	0	0	0
Senegal	25	13	0	38
Sierra Leone	0	0	0	0
Singapore	11	11	0	23
South Africa	45	34	5	84
Spain	45	34	5	84
Sri Lanka	25	13	0	38
Sudan	0	0	0	0
Swaziland	0	13	0	13
Sweden	45	45	10	100
Switzerland	45	45	10	100
Syria	0	0	0	0

TABLE B.6 CONTINUED

	TABLE B.6 CONTINUED			
Country	Political rights, 1996	Civil liberties, 1996	Equal protection and access to nondiscriminatory judiciary	Total weighted score[a]
Tanzania	11	11	3	25
Thailand	23	23	0	45
Togo	0	13	0	13
Tunisia	0	13	0	13
Turkey	11	11	0	23
Uganda	13	25	0	38
United Arab Emirates	0	13	0	13
United Kingdom	45	34	5	84
United States	45	45	8	98
Uruguay	38	38	0	75
Venezuela	23	23	0	45
Zambia	25	25	0	50
Zimbabwe	11	11	3	25

SOURCE: Authors' calculations. For descriptions of indicators and weighting system, see chapter 4 and appendixes C and D.

a.   Maximum total weighted score = 100.

Appendix C

SCORING SYSTEM FOR VECTORS

This appendix describes the weighting system applied to the indicators in each vector.

Economic Performance Vector

Average annual GDP growth, 1990–94 (percent):

0	if	$x \leq 0$
1	if	$0 < x \leq 1.5$
2	if	$1.5 < x \leq 3$
3	if	$3 < x \leq 6$
4	if	$x > 6$

Average annual growth of gross domestic investment, 1990–94 (percent):

0	if	$x \leq 0$
1	if	$0 < x \leq 2$
2	if	$2 < x \leq 4$
3	if	$4 < x \leq 8$
4	if	$x > 8$

Average annual GNP growth per capita, 1985–94 (percent):

0	if	$x \leq 0$
1	if	$0 < x \leq 1$
2	if	$1 < x \leq 2$
3	if	$2 < x \leq 3$
4	if	$x > 3$

Average annual growth of exports, 1990–94 (percent):

0	if	$x \leq 0$
1	if	$0 < x \leq 3$
2	if	$3 < x \leq 6$
3	if	$6 < x \leq 9$
4	if	$x > 9$

Per capita GNP measured by purchasing-power parity, 1994 (current dollars):

0	if	$x \leq 1,000$
1	if	$1,000 < x \leq 3,000$
2	if	$3,000 < x \leq 8,000$
3	if	$8,000 < x \leq 15,000$
4	if	$x > 15,000$

M2 (money + quasi money), 1994 (percent of GDP):

0	if	$x \leq 20$
1	if	$20 < x \leq 40$
2	if	$40 < x \leq 60$
3	if	$60 < x \leq 80$
4	if	$x > 80$

Gross international reserves, 1994 (months of import coverage):

0   if $x \leq 1$
1   if $1 < x \leq 2$
2   if $2 < x \leq 3$
3   if $3 < x \leq 4$
4   if $x > 4$

Competitiveness Foundations Vector

Gross domestic saving, 1994 (percent of GDP):

0   if $x \leq 0$
1   if $0 < x \leq 10$
2   if $10 < x \leq 20$
3   if $20 < x \leq 25$
4   if $x > 25$

Openness of economy, 1994 (exports as a percent of GDP):

0   if $x \leq 10$
1   if $10 < x \leq 20$
2   if $20 < x \leq 30$
3   if $30 < x \leq 50$
4   if $x > 50$

Foreign direct investment, 1993 (percent of GDP):

0   if $x \leq 0$
1   if $0 < x \leq 0.25$
2   if $0.25 < x \leq 1$
3   if $1 < x \leq 2$
4   if $x > 2$

Government budget surplus or deficit, latest three years available (percent of GDP):

0   if $x \leq -6$
1   if $-6 < x \leq -4$
2   if $-4 < x \leq -2$
3   if $-2 < x \leq 0$
4   if $x > 0$

S&P's long-term sovereign bond rating, 1997:

0   if   no rating
1   if   B– to BB+
2   if   BBB– to A+
3   if   AA– to AA+
4   if   AAA– to AAA

Average annual rate of inflation, 1984–94 (percent):

0   if $x \geq 20$
1   if $10 \leq x < 20$
2   if $6 \leq x < 10$
3   if $3 \leq x < 6$
4   if $x < 3$

R&D scientists & engineers per million persons, latest available:

0   if $x \leq 100$
1   if $100 < x \leq 300$
2   if $300 < x \leq 700$
3   if $700 < x \leq 1,500$
4   if $x > 1,500$

R&D technicians per million persons, latest available:

0	if	$x \leq 50$
1	if	$50 < x \leq 100$
2	if	$100 < x \leq 500$
3	if	$500 < x \leq 1,000$
4	if	$x > 1,000$

Foreign exchange freedom, 1995 (Fraser Institute ratings, SRI calculations):

0	if	$x \leq 2$
1	if	$2 < x \leq 4$
2	if	$4 < x \leq 6$
3	if	$6 < x \leq 9$
4	if	$x > 9$

Production of electricity, latest available (kilowatt hours per person):

0	if	$x \leq 500$
1	if	$500 < x \leq 1,000$
2	if	$1,000 < x \leq 3,000$
3	if	$3,000 < x \leq 6,000$
4	if	$x > 6,000$

Electricity power loss, latest available (percent of total production output):

0	if	$x \geq 20$
1	if	$15 \leq x < 20$
2	if	$10 \leq x < 15$
3	if	$5 \leq x < 10$
4	if	$x < 5$

Telephone main lines per 1,000 persons, latest available:

0	if	$x \leq 0$
1	if	$10 < x \leq 50$
2	if	$50 < x \leq 200$
3	if	$200 < x \leq 400$
4	if	$x > 400$

Road density, latest available (kilometers per million persons):

0	if	$x \leq 500$
1	if	$500 < x \leq 2,000$
2	if	$2,000 < x \leq 5,000$
3	if	$5,000 < x \leq 10,000$
4	if	$x > 10,000$

Health Vector

Life expectancy at birth, 1994 (years):

0	if	$x \leq 50$
1	if	$50 < x \leq 60$
2	if	$60 < x \leq 68$
3	if	$68 < x \leq 73$
4	if	$x > 73$

Contraceptive prevalence, latest available, (percent of women ages fifteen to forty-nine currently using contraception):

0	if	$x \leq 15$
1	if	$15 < x \leq 40$
2	if	$40 < x \leq 60$
3	if	$60 < x \leq 75$
4	if	$x > 75$

Total fertility rate, 1994 (average number of children born to each woman in her lifetime):

0	if	$x \geq 5$
1	if	$3.5 \leq x < 5$
2	if	$x < 1.5$
3	if	$2.5 \leq x < 3.5$
4	if	$1.5 \leq x < 2.5$

Births attended by trained health professionals, latest available (percent):

0	if	$x \leq 30$
1	if	$30 < x \leq 50$
2	if	$50 < x \leq 70$
3	if	$70 < x \leq 90$
4	if	$x > 90$

Maternal mortality rate, 1993 (deaths per 100,000 live births):

0	if	$x \geq 800$
1	if	$300 \leq x < 800$
2	if	$100 \leq x < 300$
3	if	$25 \leq x < 100$
4	if	$x < 25$

Infant mortality rate, 1994 (deaths per 1,000 live births):

0	if	$x \geq 100$
1	if	$50 \leq x < 100$
2	if	$25 \leq x < 50$
3	if	$10 \leq x < 25$
4	if	$x < 10$

Under-five mortality rate, 1994 (deaths per 1,000 live births):

0	if	$x \geq 150$
1	if	$70 \leq x < 150$
2	if	$30 \leq x < 70$
3	if	$10 \leq x < 30$
4	if	$x < 10$

One-year-olds immunized against measles, latest available (percent):

0	if	$x \leq 50$
1	if	$50 < x \leq 75$
2	if	$75 < x \leq 85$
3	if	$85 < x \leq 94$
4	if	$x > 94$

One-year-olds immunized against tuberculosis, latest available (percent):

0	if	$x \leq 60$
1	if	$60 < x \leq 80$
2	if	$80 < x \leq 90$
3	if	$90 < x \leq 98$
4	if	$x > 98$

Natural rate of population increase, latest available (annual percent):

0	if	$x \geq 2.8$
1	if	$2.0 \leq x < 2.8$
2	if	$1.2 \leq x < 2.0$
3	if	$0.5 \leq x < 1.2$
4	if	$x < 0.5$

HIV prevalence among adults, 1995 (percent infected):

0	if	$x \geq 5$
1	if	$1 \leq x < 5$
2	if	$0.5 \leq x < 1$
3	if	$0.1 \leq x < 0.5$
4	if	$x < 0.1$

Education Vector

Adult illiteracy rate, 1995 (percent):

0	if	$x \geq 50$
1	if	$30 \leq x < 50$
2	if	$10 \leq x < 30$
3	if	$5 \leq x < 10$
4	if	$x < 5$

Primary-level enrollment, latest available (gross ratio):

0	if	$x \leq 60$
1	if	$60 < x \leq 75$
2	if	$75 < x \leq 90$
3	if	$90 < x \leq 99$
4	if	$x > 99$

Secondary-level enrollment, latest available (gross ratio):

0	if	$x \leq 25$
1	if	$25 < x \leq 50$
2	if	$50 < x \leq 75$
3	if	$75 < x \leq 95$
4	if	$x > 95$

Tertiary-level enrollment, latest available (gross ratio):

0	if	$x \leq 10$
1	if	$10 < x \leq 20$
2	if	$20 < x \leq 30$
3	if	$30 < x \leq 40$
4	if	$x > 40$

Primary school children reaching grade 5, latest available (percent):

0	if	$x \leq 50$
1	if	$50 < x \leq 70$
2	if	$70 < x \leq 90$
3	if	$90 < x \leq 95$
4	if	$x > 95$

Primary repeaters, latest available (percent of primary enrollment):

0	if	$x \geq 25$
1	if	$15 \leq x < 25$
2	if	$10 \leq x < 15$
3	if	$5 \leq x < 10$
4	if	$x < 5$

Secondary repeaters, latest available (percent of primary enrollment):

0	if	$x \geq 25$
1	if	$15 \leq x < 25$
2	if	$8 \leq x < 15$
3	if	$3 \leq x < 8$
4	if	$x < 3$

Environment Vector

Access to safe water, 1993 (percent of population):

0	if	$x \leq 50$
1	if	$50 < x \leq 70$
2	if	$70 < x \leq 85$
3	if	$85 < x \leq 99$
4	if	$x > 99$

CO_2 emissions, 1992 (metric tons per capita):

0	if	$x \geq 8$
1	if	$3 \leq x < 8$
2	if	$1 \leq x < 3$
3	if	$0.2 \leq x < 1$
4	if	$x < 0.2$

Other greenhouse gas emissions, 1991 (metric tons per capita):

0	if	$x \geq 70$
1	if	$40 \leq x < 70$
2	if	$30 \leq x < 40$
3	if	$15 \leq x < 30$
4	if	$x < 15$

Environmental nongovernmental organizations registered, 1996:

0	if	$x \leq 3$
1	if	$3 < x \leq 5$
2	if	$5 < x \leq 10$
3	if	$10 < x \leq 20$
4	if	$x > 20$

Participation in global environmental conventions, 1993 (of sixteen):

0	if	$x \leq 3$
1	if	$3 < x \leq 7$
2	if	$7 < x \leq 11$
3	if	$11 < x \leq 14$
4	if	$x > 14$

Urban center solid wastes, 1993 (tons per capita):

0	if	$x \geq 0.4$
1	if	$0.15 \leq x < 0.4$
2	if	$0.07 \leq x < 0.15$
3	if	$0.04 \leq x < 0.07$
4	if	$x < 0.04$

Change in forest and woodland, 1983–93 (percent):

0	if	$x \leq -5$
1	if	$-5 < x \leq -2$
2	if	$-2 < x \leq 0$
3	if	$0 < x \leq 10$
4	if	$x > 10$

Democracy and Freedom Vector

Political rights, 1996 (Freedom House ratings: 1–7, 7 being the least free):

0	if	$x \geq 6$
1	if	$5 \leq x < 6$
2	if	$3 \leq x < 5$
3	if	$2 \leq x < 3$
4	if	$x < 2$

Civil liberties, 1996 (Freedom House ratings: 1–7, 7 being the least free):

0	if	$x \geq 6$
1	if	$5 \leq x < 6$
2	if	$3 \leq x < 5$
3	if	$2 \leq x < 3$
4	if	$x < 2$

Equal protection under the law and access to a nondiscriminatory judiciary, 1995 (Fraser Institute rating: 1–10, 10 offering the most protection and access):

0	if	$x < 2$
1	if	$2 \leq x < 4$
2	if	$4 \leq x < 6$
3	if	$6 \leq x \leq 8$
4	if	$x > 8$

WEIGHTING SYSTEMS
FOR VECTORS

ECONOMIC PERFORMANCE			
Variable	Maximum base score	Weighting	Maximum weighted base score[a]
Average annual GDP growth, 1990-94	4	4	16
Average annual GNP growth per capita, 1985-94	4	5	20
Per capita GNP measured by purchasing-power parity, 1994	4	4	16
Average annual growth of gross domestic investment, 1990-94	4	5	20
Average annual growth of exports, 1990-94	4	5	20
M2 (money+ quasi money) as percent of GDP, 1994	4	1	4
Gross international reserves (months of import coverage), 1994	4	1	4
COMPETITIVENESS FOUNDATIONS			
Gross domestic savings as percent of GDP, 1994	4	4	16
Openness of economy (exports as percent of GDP), 1994	4	3	12
Foreign direct investment as percent of GDP, 1993	4	2	8
Government budget surplus or deficit as percent of GDP (latest three-year average)	4	4	16
S&P's long-term sovereign bond rating, 1997	4	2	8

COMPETITIVENESS FOUNDATIONS (CONTINUED)

Variable	Maximum base score	Weighting	Maximum weighted base score[a]
Average annual rate of inflation, 1984-94	4	4	16
R&D scientists and engineers per million population (latest available)	4	0.5	2
R&D technicians per million population (latest available)	4	0.5	2
Foreign exchange freedom (Fraser Institute Rating, 1995)	4	3	12
Infrastructure Indicators (latest available):			
Production of electricity (kwh per person)	4	0.5	2
Electricity power system loss (percent of total output)	4	0.5	2
Telephone main lines (per 1,000 persons)	4	0.5	2
Road density (km per million persons)	4	0.5	2

HEALTH

Variable	Maximum base score	Weighting	Maximum weighted base score[a]
Life expectancy at birth, 1994	4	5	20
Contraceptive prevalence (latest available)	4	1	4
Total fertility rate, 1994	4	1	4
Percent of births attended by trained health professionals (latest available)	4	3	12
Maternal mortality rate, 1993	4	3	12
Infant mortality rate, 1994	4	4	16
Under-five mortality rate, 1994	4	4	16
Percent of one-year-olds immunized against measles (latest available)	4	0.5	2

GLOBAL Benchmarks

HEALTH (CONTINUED)			
Variable	Maximum base score	Weighting	Maximum weighted base score[a]
Percent of one-year-olds immunized against tuberculosis (latest available)	4	0.5	2
Annual natural rate of population increase (latest available)	4	2	8
HIV prevalence among adults, 1995	4	1	4
EDUCATION			
Adult literacy rate, 1995	4	6	24
Primary-level enrollment (latest available)	4	4	16
Secondary-level enrollment (latest available)	4	4	16
Tertiary-level enrollment (latest available)	4	4	16
Percent of primary school children reaching grade 5 (latest available)	4	5	20
Primary repeaters as percent of primary enrollment (latest available)	4	1	4
Secondary repeaters as percent of secondary enrollment (latest available)	4	1	4
ENVIRONMENT			
Access to safe water, 1993	4	7	28
Per capita CO_2 emissions, 1992	4	5	20
Other greenhouse gas emissions per capita, 1991	4	5	20
Number of environmental NGOs registered, 1996	4	3	12

ENVIRONMENT (CONTINUED)			
Variable	Maximum base score	Weighting	Maximum weighted base score[a]
Participation in global environmental conventions, 1993	4	3	12
Urban center solid wastes per capita, 1993	4	1	4
Percent change in forest and woodland, 1983-93	4	1	4
DEMOCRACY AND FREEDOM			
Civil liberties (Freedom House, 1996)	4	11.25	45
Political rights (Freedom House, 1996)	4	11.25	45
Equal protection under the law and access to nondiscriminatory judiciary (Fraser Institute, 1995)	4	2.5	10

a. Total weighted score for each vector = 100.

GLOBAL Benchmarks

References

Asian Development Bank. 1995. *Asian Development Outlook 1995 and 1996.* Oxford University Press.

Barr, Nicholas. 1996. "People in Transition: Reforming Education and Health Care." *Finance and Development,* vol. 33 (September): 24–27.

Bengtsson, Tommy, ed. 1994. *Population, Economy and Welfare in Sweden.* Berlin: Springer- Verlag.

Binswanger, Hans P., and Pierre Landell-Mills. 1995. "The World Bank's Strategy for Reducing Poverty and Hunger: A Report to the Development Community." Environmentally Sustainable Development Studies and Monographs 4. Washington: World Bank.

Blinder, Alan S. 1993. "Free Trade." In *Fortune Encyclopedia of Economics,* 526–27. Warner Books.

Bosworth, Barry, and Alice M. Rivlin, eds. 1987. *The Swedish Economy.* Brookings.

Cho, Soon. 1994. *The Dynamics of Korean Economic Development.* Washington: Institute for International Economics.

Cole, David Chamberlin. 1980. *The Korean Economy: Issues of Development.* University of California, Institute of East Asian Studies, Center for Korean Studies.

Demery, Lionel, and others, eds. 1993. *Understanding the Social Effects of Policy Reform.* World Bank Country Study. Washington: World Bank.

Demographic and Health Surveys. Various years. Calverton, Md.: Macro International.

Economist Intelligence Unit. 1996–97. *EIU Country Reports.* London.

Friedman, Milton. 1988. "A Statistical Note on the Gastil Survey of Freedom." In *Freedom in the World,* edited by Raymond Gastil, 183–87. New York: Freedom House.

Grant, James P. 1978. *Disparity Reduction Rates in Social Indicators: A Proposal for Measuring and Targeting Progress in Meeting Basic Needs.* Washington: Overseas Development Council.

Gwartney, James, Robert Lawson, and Walter Block. 1996. *Economic Freedom of the World 1975–1995.* Vancouver: Fraser Institute.

Harvey, Charles, and Stephen R. Lewis, Jr. 1990. *Policy Choice and Development Performance in Botswana.* St. Martin's Press.

Johnson, Bryan T., and Thomas P. Sheehy. 1996. *1996 Index of Economic Freedom.* Washington: Heritage Foundation.

Hope, Kemper. 1997. *African Political Economy: Contemporary Issues in Development.* Armonk, N.Y.: M. E. Sharpe.

International Monetary Fund. 1995. *Government Finance Statistics Yearbook 1995.* Washington.

___. 1996a. *Annual Report on Exchange Arrangements and Exchange Restrictions 1996.* Washington.

___. 1996b. *International Financial Statistics Yearbook 1996.* Washington.

Kaplan, Roger, gen. ed. 1996. *Freedom in the World: Annual Survey of Political Rights and Civil Liberties, 1995–1996.* New York: Freedom House.

Kuznets, Paul W. 1994. *Korean Economic Development: An Interpretive Model.* Westport, Conn.: Praeger.

Kwon, Jene K., ed. 1990. *Korean Economic Development.* New York: Greenwood Press.

Lawrence, Robert Z. 1993. "Competitiveness." In *Fortune Encyclopedia of Economics,* 514–17. Warner Books.

Lavy, Victor, and others. 1995. "The Impact of the Quality of Health Care on Children's Nutrition and Survival in Ghana." Living Standards Measurement Series, Working Paper 106. Washington: World Bank (May).

Morris, Morris D. 1979. *Measuring the Condition of the Poor: The Physical Quality of Life Index.* Washington: Overseas Development Council.

Organization for Economic Cooperation and Development. 1994. *The Reform of Health Care Systems: A Review of Seventeen OECD Countries.* Paris.

___. 1996. *Education at a Glance: OECD Indicators.* Paris: OECD, Center for Educational Research and Innovation.

Pan American Health Organization. 1994. *Health Conditions in the Americas.* Vols. 1, 2. Scientific Publication 549. Washington.

Perrings, Charles. 1996. *Sustainable Development in Sub-Saharan Africa: The Case of Botswana.* St. Martin's Press.

Pitt, Mark. 1995. "Women's Schooling, the Selectivity of Fertility, and Child Mortality in Sub-Saharan Africa." Living Standards Measurement Series, Working Paper 119. Washington: World Bank (May).

Population Reference Bureau. 1996. *World Population Data Sheet.* Washington.

Rao, Vaman. 1984–85. "Democracy and Economic Development." *Studies in Comparative International Development,* vol. 19 (Winter): 67–81.

Reich, Robert B. 1992. *The Work of Nations.* Vintage Books.

Schnitzer, Martin. 1970. *The Economy of Sweden: A Study of the Modern Welfare State.* New York: Praeger.

SRI International. 1993. *Global Growth through Global Competition: Linking Commercial Policies, Economic Performance and USAID Assistance.* Arlington, Va.

___. 1993–97. *Commercial Policy Model and Applications.* Arlington, Va.

___. 1996. "Reaching the Full Potential of Dominicans and the Republic: An Economic Agenda." Discussion paper. Arlington, Va. (August).

Standard and Poor. 1996. *Standard & Poor's CreditWeek.* July 3.

Stedman, Stephen John. 1993. *Botswana: The Political Economy of Democratic Development.* Boulder, Colo.: Lynn Rienner.

United Nations Development Programme. 1995. *Human Development Report 1995.* New York.

___. 1996. *State of the World's Children.* New York.

United Nations Educational, Scientific, and Cultural Organization. 1996. *UNESCO Statistical Yearbook 1996.* UNESCO Publishing and Bernan Press.

Venieris, Yiannis P., and Depak K. Gupta. 1982–83. "Sociopolitical and Economic Dimensions of Development: A Cross-Section Model." *Economic Development and Cultural Change,* vol. 31 (July): 727–48.

World Bank. 1989. *Successful Development in Africa: Case Studies of Projects, Programs, and Policies.* EDI Development Policy Case Series, Analytical Case Study 1. Washington.

___. 1992. *World Development Report 1992: Development and the Environment.* Oxford University Press.

___. 1993a. *The East Asian Miracle: Economic Growth and Public Policy.* Oxford University Press.

___. 1993b. *World Development Report 1993: Investing in Health.* Oxford University Press.

___. 1994. *Adjustment in Africa: Lessons from Country Case Studies.* Washington.

___. 1995a. "The Dominican Republic Growth with Equity: An Agenda for Reform." May 15.

___. 1995b. *Trends in Developing Economies: Extracts,* vol. 3: *Sub-Saharan Africa.* Washington.

___. 1995c. *World Development Report 1995: Workers in an Integrating World.* Oxford University Press.

___. 1996a. *Social Indicators of Development.* Johns Hopkins University Press.

___. 1996b. *Trends in Developing Economies.* Washington.

___. 1996c. *World Development Report 1996: From Plan to Market.* Oxford University Press.

World Health Organization. 1996. *The World Health Report 1996: Fighting Disease, Fostering Development.* Geneva: WHO Press.

World Resources Institute. 1994. *1994 Information Please Environmental Almanac.* Houghton Mifflin.

___. 1996. *World Resources: A Guide to the Global Environment 1996–97.* Oxford University Press.

World Directory of Environmental Organizations, 5th ed. 1996. Sacramento and Claremont, Calif.: International Center for the Environment and Public Policy; and London: Earthscan Publications Ltd.; in cooperation with IUCN–The World Conservation Union and the Sierra Club.

Young, Mary Eming. 1996. *Early Child Development: Investing in the Future.* Directions in Development Series. Washington: World Bank (January).